R.W. GLESS

I0417211

Complacent
Ignorant
Apathy
{C.I.A.}
a recipe for
America's Doom

By R.W. GLESS

ISBN: 10: 151476363X
ISBN-13: 978-1514763636

Introduction

We have allowed ourselves to become enslaved. We have failed to be vigilant, and by failing to get involved and keep an eye on our elected officials, we have allowed public serpents to infest and control our government and our lives. Now they enact laws that benefit themselves and their corporate masters.

The Constitution and Bill of Rights were historic documents intended to protect freedom and the people's Right to self govern themselves. But even before the ink could dry on those historic documents, scoundrels with treasonous agendas were hard at work to enslave our Country for their personal gain.

Since the very beginning of this Country we have been gradually losing our freedom. Our Constitution is now unrecognizable because we have elected public serpents who violated the Constitution and Bill of Rights on a daily basis... and sadly, the sheeple allow those treasonous scoundrels to remain in office. We have to stop this now, or we will lose it all! Are you going to be in the Freedom camp, or the Complacent Ignorant Apathy camp? You can no longer stand aside and Say Nothing, you have to choose a side! If reality has, or it ever awakens inside you, and you realize you have been manipulated and mentally conditioned with lies and distortions... you will never, ever, be able to sleepwalk through life again, and you'll have no choice but to choose freedom or enslavement!

The facts and history chronicled in this book will hopefully educate you and wake you up to the nightmare ahead of all of us, if this out of control monster called "Government" isn't beaten back into a Government of the People, by the People and for the People once again. If we don't try and we're unable to take control and regain our freedom ... be afraid... be very afraid!

CONTENTS

Some Historic Background I

Chapter One: Thee Great American Illusion of Freedom
Chapter Two: The Laws and Rights That Were Not Granted in the Constitution. **Page 24**
Chapter Three: Laws, Rules and Actions that Cost Us Freedom. **Page 37**
Chapter Four: Public Serpents & Conflict of Interest. **Page 81**
Chapter Five: The Government Agenda. **Page 212**
Chapter Six: Destroying the Constitution with Demo-Obama-Care. **Page 226**
Chapter Seven: Jury Nullification to protect Freedom & The Too Big To Fail Conundrum. **Page 242**
Chapter Eight: The Tightening of Control with Lies! Inch by Inch it is a Synch! **Page 252**
Chapter Nine: Who is Really in command? **Page 256**
Chapter Ten: Escape from behind the American Iron Curtain? **Page 261**
Chapter Eleven: Awakening the Dumbed Down Masses. **Page 268**
Chapter Twelve: America's Food Poisoning from Corporate Greed and the Government it Owns. **Page 287**
Chapter Thirteen: Being Prepared for the Worst & Expressing Yourselves. **Page 294**
Chapter Fourteen: Defense against Abusive Law Enforcers & The Lack of Law Enforcement Protecting You From Them. **Page 300**
Chapter Fifteen: Some Quotes & Philosophies Of Our Founding Fathers. **Page: 311**
Chapter Sixteen: Can America Regain It's Freedom? **Page 326**

SOME HISTORIC BACKGROUND

I am a former elected official in California, a newspaper owner and radio talk show host. I have seen the waste and self serving attitudes of public servants, and how the government treats the citizens. Most of the people have no idea how our government works, or how it is really suppose to work. This is the reason I decided to write a book. I am going to show you some history and facts so you can get a better idea of what freedom we had and what freedom we lost, and how we can hopefully get some of it back or at least try to stop the total destruction of freedom, and keep what little freedom we have left. Sadly I have my doubts.

I was once told by a fellow politician that it is better to be the duper than the duped, and unfortunately that is exactly how many of people in the government think. The sad reality is that most elected officials only care about their popularity status, and where their elected office can take them. They go along to get along with the public servants and (serpents) even when they know what some of them are doing is just plain wrong. A lot of people in elected office think they are the Duper, but in reality they are really the Duped. Most of them are controlled and manipulated from the moment they get elected. A lot of them aren't even smart enough to realize it.

When I was a City Councilman, the City of Marysville's police chief told me that elected officials come and go, and the city staff will still be here long after I was gone. What he basically was telling me, was I wasn't going to change anything, because it really was the staff and public employees that called the shots. Well he was right, and I may not have really changed the waste and corruption I saw, but I sure gave them hell on the floor over it. I caused the political status quo grief every time I would question why we needed more enforcement or laws to further inhibit business and the citizens. One particular instance was a motion to give a micro-brewing/bar/nightclub a CDBG (Community Development Block Grant) loan to get started in business, and at the same meeting the police chief ask us to approve a DUI grant to purchase more equipment to create check-points in the City. My comment was a question to the other council members asking; if we were setting that Micro-Brewing Bar/Nightclub up for failure? Were we telling people to come and party and spend their money at the new Brewery Nightclub so we could catch them on the way out and take more money from them if they were drunk? Well, that is exactly what happened and the Nightclub went out of business and that taxpayer funded CDBG loan also was lost. I did however help out the local daily newspaper. The local daily newspaper had me on the front cover more than any other local politician in the Yuba/Sutter areas history. They relentlessly tried to paint me as a trouble maker. When my term ended and I was planning to get out of California altogether; the paper even depicted me in a cartoon with a loaded truck saying; "I'm outta here!" No other local politician had ever been elevated to cartoon character status in the opinions page… that was reserved for state and national politicians… But there I was.

Well, needless to say my outspokenness questioning their rational for ordinances and laws, coupled with my refusal to give up on my belief in the Constitution and Bill of Rights, sold a lot of local daily newspapers. Unfortunately, they relentlessly attack me, trying to make me look bad and crazy. I would call them and ask them what problem they had with me asking questions, and one answer I got was I should be a team player…"Team Player? Even if what I am voting on is wrong?" I said, "I don't think so!" I was even told that California has its own Constitution that comes first. The editor at the time finally told me; when I start buying ink by the barrels I could write whatever I liked, but until that time, they would do the reporting the way they saw it. Well two could play that game I said, and I started my own newspaper in 1997 called The Nor-Cal Paper. It was a small weekly political paper that informed the citizens and told the real truth about was going on in our local and state government. We took to task those elected official that in some cases blatantly violated laws or used their position of power for personal gain.

A local Mayor was investigated and indicted by the Yuba County Grand Jury because of the paper trail of illegal real estate activity in a Redevelopment Zone he was involved in. The Nor-Cal Paper was the only media that was willing to investigate the numerous complaints by citizens and even a standing City Councilman. People in Office and City Staff knew about the violations and would say nothing. The Police Chief even knew about it and did nothing because his daughter lived at the property that the Mayor was indicted over. In California it is not legal for a Standing Elected Official to purchase property in a Redevelopment Zone, and especially illegal to purchase property for the purpose of developing it for profit. Why? Well public officials are the ones who dole out the Redevelopment Grants and Loans and also make the rules and laws governing those zones. So it is like inside trading in the stock market. But this Mayor/Developer by trade, thought he could get away with it since he was the cities fair-haired boy, no one was going to say a thing. Well that didn't happen.

We uncovered documents, of a lot line adjustment that was signed by the former owner 6 months after her death. Now how in the world do you explain that? There was also testimony from tenants that stated the Mayor told them he bought the property with a friend and planned of developing it when he would come to collect the rent. Of course the Mayor wasn't so stupid as to put the property in his name, no he put it in his partners name thinking it would put him in the clear. He probably would have gotten away with it, if he hadn't bragged about buying the property in front of another City Councilman who then told me about it. The worst part was there were a lot of City Officials that knew this was going on and said nothing! This eventually caused the mayor to resign in a deal cut with the district attorney.

There was also a councilman who resigned because of evidence uncovered by The Nor-Cal paper against him of Abuse of Power. The local daily newspaper would never have reported or even investigated any of this news if the Grand Jury had not ruled for the mayor to be indicted. Only after the Grand Jury report came out basically indicting the mayor did the local daily newspaper report it. If it would have been me doing something illegal, I would have been crucified, but the Mayor was the City's and local daily newspaper's fair-haired boy. There was one reporter at the local daily that knew what I was telling the citizens was true, and years later he said as much in one of his opinion columns when he mentioned me in a story about a school board member that was being censured for pointing out facts that the other school board members didn't want the general public to know, but it was too little too late. Most of the people back in the 90s and early 2000s still believed the media and whatever the hustlers in office said for the most part. Now people are waking up and realizing most of the media have their own political spin or agenda, and report the news by omission or half-truths and sometimes bold faced lies planted by the government. Well this is ancient history… or at least back as far as the 90s and early 2000s anyway. This is just some background about me and my awakening into the politics of this country, which is the reason for this book.

Sadly many local newspapers never report the real abuse of power committed by corrupt elected officials, because they rely on the Legal Ads from the city and county and also the courts because they are a "Legally Adjudicated" newspaper by the local court. That means they are legally recognized as a newspaper by the government and they are the only newspapers that can legally accept "Legal Notices". So they don't want to upset the powers that be, especially since newspapers aren't read like they used to be and Legal Ads are a big part of their revenue. Anymore, I like many of you, get most of my news on line, like most internet savvy people do, and thank God, I don't have to read the spin you see in newspapers unless I decide to see what they are up to. I think most of you have also noticed that a lot of newspapers and media create the news by omission and down right lies. Especially if they are supporting a political point of view or politician and don't want negative news to get out to the voters... or when they spin the truth when they are trying to discredit a politician that they don't want in office. Consequently the local Yuba-Sutter daily newspaper eventually went bankrupt and was sold to another news group who isn't any better at reporting the real truth in my opinion.

The City of Marysville is like so many other cities in California and across the nation that are getting close to the same fate "bankruptcy". Yet people across the nation still tend to believe the lies of the deceptive politicians and those media outlets, both with their own agendas, and they keep electing people who tell them what they want to hear and make grandiose promises. Then once those con-artists are elected they don't do what they promised and make things worse.

It has been over 20 years since I first stepped into the political arena as an elected official. I tried to tell people the truth about what is really going on in our government, and I soon found out that most people don't want to hear it. They just want to hear the warm and fuzzy positive things that most of the politicians contrive... Unfortunately when people refuse to see or hear the negative detrimental things, and the lies, there can never be a positive outcome or any truth for that matter... only a dreamy illusion in their mind that everything is coming up roses. If we keep looking through those rose colored glasses, and refuse to see the dark true reality, things will eventually come crashing down and will turn into our darkest nightmare. Then it will be too late to do anything about it… hell, it maybe too late already.

It is amazing to me that people don't seem to care about any of the blatant corruption, crimes, un-constitutional acts and out of control spending that is going on in our government. Most people just seem to ignore it and put up with it. I can't understand why people are so complacent and apathetic? Maybe it's because they feel helpless and don't know what to do? Or maybe they just don't care about their freedom or the financial stability of our Country? So they keep allowing our elected leaders to spend way too much on salaries, Cadillac pensions and health insurance plans for public employees that normally only CEO executives of multi-million dollar corporations have. Because of this, there are many Cities on the edge of bankruptcy, and their States are following close behind if the elected leaders voted into office don't start conserving the Taxpayers money.

The lies most of our politicians spew, such as, giving up our freedom for security because it's better for America, is a lie that will hurt our freedom! Everything isn't going to be "just fine", if we give up our freedom for security! Sadly the dumbed down masses tend to believe it and love it when they hear their new God Government tell them; "Don't worry, everything will be fine, I'll take good care of you. We are here to help you." This is why this once much freer Nation is headed for total enslavement. Shoot fire…it's almost there now! So I pose this question to you: When do you think it is time to talk about resisting tyranny? After they load you up in a cattle car headed for a FEMA concentration camp? Or is now the time to say enough is enough and fight the tyrants before they totally enslave us and we can't say or do anything about it?

Complacent: adjective

1. Pleased, especially with oneself or one's merits, advantages, situation, etc., often without awareness of some potential danger or defect; self-satisfied: *The voters are too complacent to change the tyrannical government.*

Ignorant: adjective

1. Lacking in knowledge or training; unlearned: an ignorant man.

2. Lacking knowledge or information as to a particular subject or fact: *ignorant of political manipulation.*

3. Uninformed; unaware.

4. due to or showing lack of knowledge or training: makes an ignorant statement.

Apathy: noun, plural apathies.

1. Absence or suppression of passion, emotion, or excitement: *The people didn't care their freedom was being taken. They just stood aside with a blank look on their faces.*

2. lack of interest in or concern for things that others find moving or exciting.

Also, apatheia, apathia [ap-uh-thee-uh] (Show IPA). Stoicism. freedom from emotion of any kind.

I want to dedicate this to all of you who remember the freedom we once had and are willing to fight to get it back!

The events and quotes are from documented facts and statements recorded down in time so they are as factual as anyone can get today or as factual as those who recorded history wanted people to believe. Because as many of you know; to the victor goes the spoils and how history is to be written. This book is filled with facts and figures that many of you don't know. – R.W. Gless

Chapter One
Thee Great American Illusion of Freedom

There was never total freedom in America from its conception. There was only an idea written down in the Bill of Rights that granted free men inalienable rights, yet the chains of bondage were alive and well. Men, woman, and children of all races and colors were in servitude for a plethora of different reasons, and it was only going to get worse.

Our Founding Fathers never intended Public Service to become a permanent get rich job at the taxpayer's expense. And they definitely and defiantly never wanted to see government control every aspect of our lives, or they wouldn't have fought a war with England to gain freedom! It was never intended that we should have to give up our freedom for the illusion of security. Thank God not everyone wants to hear those lies, and refuses to allow the liars to take anymore freedom from them. Thank God many of you want to regain your freedom we've lost, and thank God some of you are waking up and joining the crusade to be free again.

I know that those of you who are starting to wake-up are seeing the same things I see. It is looking like our freedom and security will soon come to an end if this Country doesn't get back to its intended limited republic form of government. One of our founding fathers had foreseen this 226 years ago. At the close of the Constitutional Convention on September 17, 1787, as Benjamin Franklin left the hall in Philadelphia, he was asked, "What kind of government have you given us, Dr. Franklin?" He replied: "A republic, if you can keep it." From what I can deduce by his statement, he foresaw a less than tolerable outcome for this country.

In the beginning of this country things were much more free than today. The people didn't have to worry about the dictates of a king or about paying half of everything they had to a controlling government. They didn't have to worry about over regulation of everything they owned and everything they did. Times may have been harder, but it was also a much simpler time, the people were able to adapt to survive and become self-sufficient. You either lived or died by your own toil and cunning, no one gave you a free ride. Today Americans resemble ants in a nest and bees in a hive, swarming around the government catering to their every need, like bees and ants swarm around their queen. I often wonder what our founding fathers would think if they could see how most of our Constitution has become null and void and how draconian our government has become. I am sure that the founders wouldn't be too happy with how it has all turned out. Some of them might not be too surprised, but they definitely wouldn't be happy.

The beginning of the Revolutionary War wasn't a total rebellion of all the people, most of the people living in the colonies were subservient to the King of England and liked it. What has not been taught in school is that only about 35% of the population was directly involved in fighting the King and his Red Coats. About 15% of them were comprised of wealthy colonists that were unhappy with what they saw as excessive taxation, that was arbitrary, and they were really the ones who started the rebellion. The Taxes back then were a lot like taxes we see today, but nowhere near to the excess we see today. Of the other 65% about half were Loyalists and the other half were what I like to call "Complacent" and "Apathetic", they would change suit to whatever side fit them at the time, a lot like Americans are today.

Most people today think the founding fathers and all of the patriots fought because they were being oppressed and over taxed by England, and for the most part they would be right; people also wanted control of their own lives and realized they did not need the British or any other government to survive. What a lot of people don't know is that a majority of those who fought against the British were actually mercenaries who expected to be paid, and were promised payment by the Continental Congress which was mostly made up of unhappy wealthy colonists. Now the problem was, where was the money going to come from? The Articles of Confederation did not allow the newly formed government to tax. So the only idea they could come up with was one that was as old as warfare itself, Plunder. Plunder was what the buccaneers and privateers would take from the British, and for their service a percentage of the plunder they took was given to them and they were also given safe haven in ports controlled by the colonial army. The Privateers were very helpful when we needed ships and supplies, but later some of them went rogue which became very problematic. Privateers work for a side or government and fly that government's flag, but some really started to like the plunder and decided to attack all ships and they later became pirates.

The British on the other side also used privateers, loyalist and slaves. In 1775 at the start of what the Royal Governor Lord Dunmore of Virginia, saw as a rebellion brewing, issued a proclamation that promised freedom to servants and slaves of all color who were able to bear arms and join the Loyalist Regiments. The Regiment most talked about was his Loyalist Ethiopian Regiment. About 800 black slaves joined and they helped beat the Virginia militia at the Battle of Kemp's Landing. They also fought in the Battle of Great Bridge on the Elizabeth River, wearing the motto "Liberty to Slaves", which they lost. Black colonial slaves were often the first to come forward to volunteer and a total of 12,000 African Americans served with the British from 1775 to 1783. What most of you were never taught in school was there was also white slaves and among them were the number of Irish slaves that is never taught. The Irish slave trade began when James II sold 30,000 Irish prisoners as slaves to the New World. His Proclamation of 1625 required Irish political prisoners be sent overseas and sold to English settlers in the New World and West Indies. Over 300,000 Irish were sold as slaves. The black slaves were late comers that fitted into a white slave trade that was well established. Anyway, the British proclamation to free all slaves who would join them, forced the Patriot rebels to also offer freedom to those who would serve in the Continental Army, but sadly many of the promises were reneged upon by both sides.

The British also had the largest fleet in the world at the time, and getting supplies from allies like France and Spain at the start of the war was a problem. France finally allied with American Colonies February 6, 1778 when Benjamin Franklin went to France and signed the Treaty of Amity and Commerce and the Treaty of Alliance. The Treaty of Amity and Commerce recognized the U.S. as an independent nation and promoted trade between France and America. The second agreement, the Treaty of Alliance, made the fledgling United States and France allies against Great Britain in the Revolutionary War. France decided to back the U.S. in its military efforts until the U.S. had full independence from Great Britain. After that, the treaty required France and the U.S. to work together on any peace agreement. Without the help from France the U.S. could not have won the Revolutionary War. The Dutch, Spanish and South India Kingdom of Mysore ruled by the Wodeyar family also helped us during the war. They saw this as a way to weaken England, but not quite as openly as France did. Even with all the help we had, the war raged on and the Revolution was in jeopardy. Many of the troops demanded payment and were about to turn and march in on the Continental Congress. General George Washington was not about to let that happen, he stopped the troops from turning by executing their leaders and then told them that whoever spoke of treason again would meet the same fate. This was the beginning of intimidation by force and threat of death long before this country had won its independence.

After America finally won the war it needed to make good on the promise it made to pay those who help them defeat the British. The newly formed government had no money and needed to raise some fast before what they fought so hard for fell apart. The USA was deeply in debt, 79 million was owed in total. 54 million was owed by the Continental Congress and 25 million was owed by the states. The newly elected Secretary of Treasury Alexander Hamilton was a staunch Federalist and wanted to create a system that would give power to the Federal Government to control the States and place the government debt on the citizens. They needed a new set of laws to do that, so the Constitution was created and ratified replacing the Articles of Confederation that did not give the government power to tax the people. In 1789 the new Federal Government was created at the behest of Alexander Hamilton following the ratification of the United States Constitution. There was only one way they could come up with the money fast and that was Taxes! This was the very thing they opposed that the British had done, yet they were about to embark on the same path that would one day pale in comparison.

A National Democracy or a Republic?

From the beginning there were those who wanted a democracy which would have doomed America and our freedom much quicker, but the virtues of a Republican form of government prevailed and it was never totally accepted by the Federalists who believed in a stronger government controlled Democracy.

The Federalists pushed for a national bank, tariffs, and good relations with Britain and came up with the Jay Treaty that was negotiated in 1794. Hamilton also developed the concept of implied powers, and successfully argued that his interpretation was in the United States Constitution. Their political opponents, the newly formed Republicans, led by Thomas Jefferson and James Madison, denounced most of the Federalist policies, especially the National bank and implied powers, which gave the Federal Government a wider range of powers and they vehemently attacked the Jay Treaty as a sell-out of republican values to the British monarchy… Which is exactly what it was.

Most people aren't aware that there were independents, like Franklin and Washington (though Washington leaned Federalist), Jefferson, and Madison (who helped write the Federalist Papers), who weren't part of a political party in the beginning. There were the Federalists, like Hamilton and Adams which believed in strong government powers but they really were more of a philosophy than a political party at that time. Luckily, they saw the down-side to a Democratic Democracy and the rest is history.

John Adams who was a Federalist had said; *"Remember, democracy never lasts long. It soon wastes, exhausts, and murders itself. There never was a democracy yet that did not commit suicide."*

Article 4, Section 4 of the United States Constitution shall guarantee to every state in this union a republican form of government, and shall protect each of them against invasion; and on application of the legislature, or of the executive (when the legislature cannot be convened) against domestic violence. This meant all States would have the same form of government and the Federal Government would protect them against invasion and attack. But Article 4, Section 4 was shredded when the north and federal government invaded the south in 1860.

James Madison, who has been called the Father of the Constitution had this to say; *"Hence it is that such democracies have ever been spectacles of turbulence and contention; have ever been found incompatible with personal security or the rights of property; and have in general been as short in their lives as they have been violent in their deaths... A republic, by which I mean a government in which the scheme of representation takes place, opens a different prospect and promises the cure for which we are seeking."*

The Whiskey Tax Rebellion

The Whiskey tax began in 1791, during the Presidency of George Washington. Farmers who used their leftover grain and corn to make whiskey to exchange for goods were forced to pay a new tax. The tax was a part of Treasury Secretary Alexander Hamilton's program to increase the Federal government's power, to fund the war debt by taxing the citizens of states which had failed to pay.

Whiskey Tax was not a popular tax at all, and the distillers resisted, many of whom were war veterans that had fought in the

Revolutionary war, and were against taxation without local representation and affirmation. Of course the Federal Government maintained the taxes were legal under the taxation powers of Congress. But those against the Whiskey Tax saw this as a major betrayal of what they had fought for by the newly created government.

Protest arose and the people violently refused to pay. They used intimidation and threats of another revolution to prevent federal officials from collecting the tax. Resistance came to a head in July 1794, when a U.S. marshal arrived in western Pennsylvania to serve writs to whiskey distillers who had not paid the excise tax. The people were furious, and more than 500 armed men attacked the fortified home of tax inspector General John Neville.

President Washington responded by sending peace commissioners to western Pennsylvania to negotiate with the rebels, while at the same time he called on state governors to send a militia army to enforce the excise tax which was later called a luxury tax. 13,000 militiamen were sent by the

governors of Virginia, Maryland, New Jersey, and Pennsylvania, to put down the rebellion. President Washington rode at the head of the army to suppress those who would not comply and pay the tax. The stage was set for the new American Taxation that would bring down freedom by Federal government enforcement of any tax or law the Federal government deemed legal.

The Whiskey Rebellion also demonstrated to the people that the new national government had the willingness and ability to suppress violent resistance to its laws. The whiskey excise tax always remained difficult to collect. However the event contributed to the quick formation of another political party in the United States, a process that was already underway, but the oppression of the people by the Federalists made those against this oppression move much more quickly. So the newly created Republican Party, which was more like the Conservative Constitutionalist Libertarians of today, was formed by Thomas Jefferson, which opposed Hamilton's Federalist Party because the Federalist policies called for a national bank, tariffs, and they especially opposed any good relations with Britain. This was something Jefferson and Madison strongly disagreed with... After all we just fought a bloody war with the British and they despised the Constitution. The Republicans also believed that Policitical Parties were divisive and harmful to republicanism, but to combat the Federalists and contrary to their beliefs, Jefferson's Republican Party was formed anyway.

Basically Constitutionalists and Libertarians feel the same way, that the 2 party system does more harm than good. All Elections should be non-partisan and people should be allowed to vote in all of the elections both primary and general.

The whiskey tax was repealed in 1802 after Thomas Jefferson's newly named Democratic-Republican Party won the election against Federalist John Adams, who was the only Federalist ever elected. The Federalist Party started to fall apart after Adams was elected in the late 1700s when many of the

Federalists joined the Democratic-Republicans, which no doubt was changed to attract them. So the Federalist came to an end in the early 1800s after Jefferson was President.

For a short time the Republicans ended some of the unpopular taxation, but freedom from taxation was short lived because it was later replaced with another luxury tax. This type of tax was called direct tax, because it was a recurring tax paid directly by the taxpayer to the government based on the value of an item. The issue of direct tax as opposed to indirect tax shaped the evolution of the Federal tax policy.

When Thomas Jefferson was elected President in 1802 direct tax was abolished and for the next 10 years there was no internal revenue tax other than excise tax

The reason why the Whiskey Tax did not cause more revolt was a combination of the people being tired of war and some just decided to move outside the boundaries of the US influence and continued to make whiskey. What we do not hear in school is that most of the larger distillers were in favor of the tax, because it put those who couldn't afford it out of business thus stopping much of the competition. Later those larger distillers would band together and work with the government to make only those licensed with the federal government allowed to make whiskey.

Shortly after the demise of the Federalist in the early 1800s came the demise of the Democratic-Republicans. Many of the Federalists had joined the Democratic-Republicans, which was originally just called the Republicans. In 1824 the Democratic-Republican Party dissolved and split into two factions, the Democrats and the Whigs which was inevitable since many of the same disputes arose that did between the Federalist and the Republicans. The Democratic Party was led by the Seventh President of the United States Andrew Jackson and the Eighth President of the United States Martin Van Buren. The Whigs was led by Henry Clay of Kentucky. Both of these parties proclaimed their stand for American Republicanism, but the

Democratic Party kept the platform of the Democratic-Republican Party as its own.

The Democratic Party became the majority party, and basically the only party in the United States until shortly before the Civil War. In the 1850's the party split again and those in opposition to slavery left the Democratic Party and helped with the reformation of the Republican Party. The Whig party was pretty much dead and many of the former Whigs finally got assimilated into either the Democrat or Republican Party. In 1910 the Democratic Party regained control of Congress in Washington D.C. and their platform changed once again. They started supporting new progressive ideals and laws, and a more liberal form of government. The Republicans became more conservative and were against the liberal ideals that people like Karl Marx preached in the 1800's. But Marx's philosophy was catching on in America, Europe and especially in Russia where Vladimir Lenin was busy forming what would become the Bolshevik Party a year later in 1911. So the Political Parties basically switched polarity 3 times before becoming what we have today.

Property Tax

In 1796 came the property tax, and all but Delaware imposed a tax on owning property. Delaware only taxed the sale of property, but the road to serfdom was under way. Property Tax was another British Tax that many fought against during the Revolutionary War, and now the new American Government was doing the same to the Citizens. The Citizens didn't mind it quite as much since it was staying in America and not going to the King. They were worried however because the King could take property from subjects whenever he wanted. So many did speak out against this tax but were told the 5th Amendment protected them against the government taking their property without just cause and compensation.

Text of the 5th Amendment Passed on December 15th 1791

"No person shall be held to answer for a capital, or otherwise infamous crime, unless on a presentment or indictment of a Grand Jury, except in cases arising in the land or naval forces, or in the Militia, when in actual service in time of War or public danger; nor shall any person be subject for the same offence to be twice put in jeopardy of life or limb; nor shall be compelled in any criminal case to be a witness against himself, nor be deprived of life, liberty, or property, without due process of law; nor shall private property be taken for public use, without just compensation."

They were also told it was necessary because the State had to document the ownership of the land and record who owned what land so there was no dispute over ownership, and that required paying someone to do that. This gave property value, and gave proof of ownership to who ever had the deed. So then a Value could be placed on that property and compensation would be paid for that property and the government could recognize the property and who the owner(s) were.

This type of record keeping has been done for thousands of years as a way of keeping track of land parcels and the owners. Otherwise anyone could claim they own something and try and sell it to someone else without really owning anything. This also gives the rightful owners help from the government or rulers when someone tries to take property without compensation. So it is helpful to people who worked hard to create a home, farm, ranch or business, put a value on that property and be able to protect it by showing title with a legally recognized Deed.

Unfortunately this once beneficial record keeping practice and acknowledgement of property ownership has been distorted into all out theft by the government of today, and this happened because the citizens allowed it to become an excuse for the better good of society, i.e. "Eminent Domain" and Failing to pay Property Tax.

Taking something from one person and giving it to another you deem more worthy, is exactly what the King of England had done to the colonists, and exactly what dictators and the communist and social fascist do to their citizens.

Thomas Jefferson wrote regarding the "General Welfare" clause: *"To take from one, because it is thought his own industry and that of his father has acquired too much, in order to spare to others who (or whose fathers) have not exercised equal industry and skill, is to violate arbitrarily the first principle of association, to guarantee to everyone a free exercise of his industry and the fruits acquired by it."*

In short if you worked hard to obtain your own property and built a home, farm, ranch and or any business or industry etc, you should not have to share it with anyone; especially lazy people who do not want to work and expect something for nothing!

As America grew there were states and territories that had no property tax and families could live on that land all their lives and then pass it on to their children without the fear of the government taking it from them for failure to pay a tax for something they had worked so hard to create. Today all states have property tax, so anymore you really do not own anything; you just rent it from the government. If you fail to pay the government for your property, they can take it from you just as the King of England and his Governors had done to the colonists.

13

The Right of Ownership is no Right at all in America today. It is a privilege granted by the Government as long as you can afford to pay them rent for it.

Income Tax

From 1791 to 1802, the United States government was supported by internal taxes on carriages/wagons, distilled spirits, refined sugar, tobacco and snuff, property sold at auction, corporate bonds, and slaves, which were considered a luxury tax on the wealthy. But as the government grew so did its need for more revenue and as the new war with the British approached new taxes were proposed that all Americans would have to pay.

The War of 1812 added sales tax on gold, silverware, jewelry, and watches. The whiskey tax which had come to an end 10 years prior was replaced with other luxury taxes.

In 1817, Congress did away with all internal tariff tax, which relied on tariffs of imported goods from one state to another to provide money for running the government. To raise money for the War of 1812, Congress imposed additional excise tax, raised certain customs duties, and raised money by issuing Treasury notes. For the next 44 years the Federal Government collected no internal revenue. Instead the Government received most of its revenue from high customs duties and excise or luxury tax and through the sale of public land.

But the taxation of gold, silver, and jewelry along with the indirect tax on cotton and other farm products grown in the south was creating a rift in the country that years later would come to a boil. Not all States were going to take the excess of taxation lying down and a rebellion was starting to grow in the States who wanted a return to the Articles of Confederation and out of the United States which they felt had gotten way too controlling.

Southerners felt that the Federal government was passing laws and taxes that favored the wealthy industrialists in the north, such as the import tax that treated them unfairly. Many of the Southern plantation owners were Democrats that relied on slave labor for economic success to produce an affordable crop. Their crops were sold to cotton mills in England, and the ships would return with cheap manufactured goods from Europe.

Unfortunately for the Southern States by the early 1800s Northern factories were producing many of the same goods, but at a higher price. So the Northern politicians passed heavy taxes on imported goods from Europe that made the goods so expensive that it was cheaper for the Southerners to buy the more expensive goods from the North. These taxes angered the Southerners because it was obvious to just about everyone what the North and the Federal Government was up to: Revenue Generation Taxation (RGT). They believed that individual states had the right to "nullify", or overturn any law the Federal government passed, which Under the Constitution they should have had. They also believed that individual states had the right to leave the United States and form their own independent country.

But those wealthy industrialists in the North and the Country's newly elected President Abraham Lincoln believed that the concepts of "nullification and state's rights" would make the United States weaker and them poorer, so they were against these ideas and set out to rewrite or to re-interpret the Constitution's 8th and 10th Amendments. In 1860 it all boiled over and the Civil War started and more of our Constitution was shredded when the North defied many of the Rights given the States and the People.

In 1862 in order to support the Civil War effort that the Union

15

was not necessarily winning at the time, the Northern Congress and Abraham Lincoln enacted the nation's first income tax law on those in the Union. It was a forerunner of our income tax today, based on the principles of progressive taxation by withholding income at the source; taking it out of our pay check. This way the government could make sure they got paid. During the Civil War, a person earning from $600 to $10,000 per year paid tax at the rate of only 3%, which wasn't bad compared to today. Those with incomes of more than $10,000 paid tax at a higher rate. Then in 1862 sales and excise tax were added back into law, the very same tax that was abolished by President Jefferson 60 years before in 1802.

Also added to the list of seizure tax was the "inheritance" tax that made its debut in 1862, robbing many families of their homes and property that were unable to pay the tax after a parent or husband had died. On July 1, 1862 the Congress also passed new excise luxury tax on such items as playing cards, gunpowder, feathers, telegrams, iron, leather, pianos, yachts, billiard tables, drugs and patent medicines, and 'whiskey' once again! Even legal documents were taxed. License fees were collected from people for almost all professions, business and trades. In 1866 the internal revenue collections reached their highest point in the nation's 90-year history with more than $310 million dollars being collected and taken from the American Citizens. This was a record until 1911, so it seems that President Abe Lincoln wasn't quite the great American hero portrayed in history, but a Progressive and the greatest taxing President the Country had ever seen at the time; as well as some of the other crimes he committed against the Constitution and Freedom.

The Tax Act of 1862 also established the office of Commissioner of Internal Revenue Services, IRS. The Commissioner was given the power to assess, levy, and collect taxes, and the right to enforce the tax laws through "seizure of property" and income through prosecution. A Right Never Granted to the Federal Government in the Constitution and another deception and lie the American People begrudgingly accepted under the guise it was for the betterment of the Country. This was a way to steal personal property and income without compensation as laid out in the 5th Amendment. The Constitution gives the Congress the power to impose and collect taxes to pay the debts of the government and provide for the common defense and general welfare of the United States, but is subject to the following rules pertaining only to the two classes of taxation permitted, and they are;

1. DIRECT TAXES, which are subject to the rule of apportionment among the states of the Union.
2. INDIRECT TAXES, imposts, duties and excises, subject to the rule of uniformity.

Article 1, Section 2, Clause 3 of the Constitution

"Representatives and direct Taxes shall be apportioned among the several States which may be included within this Union, according to their respective Numbers, which shall be determined by adding to the whole Number of free Persons, including those bound to Service for a Term of Years, and excluding Indians not taxed, three fifths of all other Persons. The actual Enumeration shall be made within three Years after the first Meeting of the Congress of the United States, and within every subsequent Term of ten Years, in such Manner as they shall by Law direct. The Number of Representatives shall not exceed one for every thirty Thousand, but each State shall have at Least one Representative; and until such enumeration shall be made, the State of New Hampshire shall be entitled to choose three, Massachusetts eight, Rhode-Island and Providence Plantations one, Connecticut five, New-York six, New Jersey four, Pennsylvania eight, Delaware one, Maryland six, Virginia ten, North Carolina five, South Carolina five, and Georgia

three."

Luckily for those who wanted freedom back in the early years of America there was still a lot of wild country that was not under the government's control. But even in those days many went west to escape the regulations and taxation, because they could not afford to own a place of their own in America. But as the people went west the American government saw some of their possible tax generation escaping and started to incorporate territories that did not belong to them.

The Constitution did not allow the government either one of the two classifications to tax CITIZENS or PERMANENT RESIDENT ALIENS of the United States of America arbitrarily as the new Health-care tax law does. Some groups are exempt while others are forced by threat of fines and imprisonment or death if they refuse to obey.

No where in the Constitution does it give the government the right to force a citizen to buy a product from a private party.

The brief mention of "Direct taxes" in the first sentence of Article 1, Section 2, Clause 3 of the Constitution makes it impossible for the government to use a tax system like the one we have today. It required taxes to be charged by each state's population, rather than by each citizens individual income. In a 5-4 vote, Pollock vs. Farmers Loan Trust Co, the U.S. Supreme Court ruled in 1895 that the income tax is a direct tax. Chief Justice Melville Fuller, writing for the majority, first showed a surprisingly keen awareness of economic concept of incidence: *"Ordinarily, all taxes paid primarily by persons who can shift the burden upon someone else, or who are under no legal compulsion to pay them, are considered indirect taxes; but a tax upon property holders in respect of their estates, whether real or personal, or of the income yielded by such estates, and the payment of which cannot be avoided, are direct taxes."*

He went even further and analyzed the writings of the Framers, the tax writings of Adam Smith, the ratification debates in the states, and observations by early justices and members of Congress. From this he concluded that it was well understood that "all taxes on real estate or personal property or the rents or income there of were regarded as direct taxes."

Since direct taxes must be apportioned by state population under the Constitution, the 1894 law was void. While admitting that such a method of imposing income taxes would be considered unfair by many, its purpose was "to restrain the exercise of the power of direct taxation to extraordinary emergencies, and to prevent an attack upon accumulated property by mere force of numbers." So those in power under the presidencies of republicans Theodore Roosevelt (1901-1909); William H. Taft (1909-1913 and democrat Woodrow Wilson (1913-1921) did what other presidents did to get what they wanted, and that was to cut out the part of our Constitution they didn't like. Since our President appoints the Supreme Court Justice and the House and Senate approve those Supreme Court Justice, they try to appoint people who think like they do to make us believe that they are interpreting the Constitution Legally. But this was nothing more than an illusion and the 16th Amendment was finally past in 1913 to get rid of those pesky Constitutional requirements, making it possible for the government to create the modern income tax system we now have. Individual income tax was never legal under the Constitution, but people were once again threatened and lied to and told by those in power that it was legal, so they begrudgingly paid. There were still Constitutionalists on the Supreme Court 94 years ago who would later rule against the 16th Amendment, but unfortunately it was ignored just like our supposed representatives do today if they don't like a law or ruling.

Sadly the populace of the United States was never able to directly vote on this, nor did the required three-forths of the States sign off on this, and it was a proven fact. Because of that one citizen Bill Benson would challenge it almost 90 years later. The federal government rests its authority to collect income tax on the 16th Amendment to the U.S. Constitution, the federal income tax amendment, which was suppose to have been ratified in 1913 after several years of deceptive wrangling to get it to pass.

The 16th Amendment to the Constitution of the United States of America: *"The Congress shall have power to lay and collect taxes on incomes, from whatever source derived, without apportionment among the several States, and without regard to any census or enumeration."*

After an extensive year long nationwide research project in 1984, William J. Benson discovered that the 16th Amendment was not ratified by the legally required three fourths of the states and that Secretary of State Philander Knox had fraudulently declared ratification. It was a shocking revelation that reached deep into the core of our American system of government. Even the court system was in on this sham to force citizens to give more to the government. The Government was so annoyed at Bill Benson for exposing this deception that on January 10, 2008, the Federal District Court in Chicago issued a permanent injunction against Bill Benson on the grounds that by offering information demonstrating that the 16th Amendment was not legally ratified by the States, he was promoting an abusive tax shelter. The Court then refused to look at the government-certified documentary evidence, deciding instead that the facts necessary to prove his statements true were "irrelevant." So the American court system has clearly become in league with the politicians and public serpents that make a living from the public dole, and they no longer protect our Rights under the Constitution. Now the government courts routinely accuse citizens of either lying or deeming their arguments as irrelevant and then prohibit them from presenting a defense in court!

If you talk to tax attorneys or other so called tax professionals they will tell you that the 16th Amendment allowed the income tax to be collected as a direct tax without apportionment among the 50 States. This is total BS, and it is the major problem with today's tax collection efforts. Everyone is lied to, and will comply! The IRS believes that the income tax can now be collected as a direct tax without apportionment. It is totally unconstitutional to collect a direct tax in the 50 states without apportionment. So we are the victims of mass brainwashing by the government. But people are waking up and that's why you'll be hearing more politicians talking about a flat tax or a federal sales tax or excise tax, to get around 100 years of Unconstitutional taxation.

So what is Apportion and "Apportionment?"

Black's Law Dictionary says; *Apportion:* "To divide and distribute proportionally." Apportionment: "The process by which legislative seats are distributed among units entitled to representation. The U.S. Constitution provides for a census every ten years, on the basis of which Congress apportions representatives according to population; but each state must have at least one representative."

This gives the people a voice through an elected representative who represents a certain number of citizens in each state.

U. S. CONSTITUTION: *Article 1, Section 2, Clause 3:*

"Representatives and direct taxes shall be apportioned among the states which may be included within this Union, according to their respective numbers..." Article 1, Section 9, Clause 4:"No capitation, or other direct tax, shall be laid, unless in proportion to the census or enumeration herein before directed to be taken."

Direct taxes must be apportioned among the states, not among the people. The 16th Amendment did not change that! The income tax is an excise tax on corporate profit, and always has been therefore it does not need to be apportioned. Before the 16th Amendment, an individual's income was NOT taxable, either with apportionment or without. Eliminating apportionment, among the states, would still require the tax to be imposed on the states, not on the people. This has been a contention for many people over the last century and conflicting rulings have been made by the courts over the years.

In 1920, the Supreme Court said: Eisner vs. Macomber 252 U.S. 189 at 205 (1920). "The Sixteenth Amendment must be construed in connection with the taxing clauses of the original Constitution and the effect attributed to them before the Amendment was adopted."

There it is as Ruled by the Supreme Court! The 16th Amendment had to leave the income tax as an indirect excise tax and should be enforced as such and collected from the states. It is a tax on corporate incomes not requiring the tax to be apportioned on individual citizens! This is not an opinion, but a Supreme Court ruling. An important point to remember is that the Supreme Court rulings must be followed by all lesser courts in this country. They cannot be overruled by lower courts or government officials unless we allow them to get away with it!

The intent of the Founders was to keep the government the servant and to prevent it from becoming the master we have allowed it to become. The People should have a say in their own destiny and were originally meant to through representatives who echoed their concerns. But now most only echo self interest and financial gain and sadly the people allow them to continue their crimes against the Constitution and the people they are supposed to represent.

These Taxes that were the foundation our government used to build its empire are in direct contrast to what our Founding Fathers had in mind. So it does seem that Benjamin Franklin had foreseen what the government he helped to create would become as he left the hall in Philadelphia on September 17, 1787, and was asked: "What kind of government have you given us, Dr. Franklin?" And He replied: "A republic, if you can keep it."

In my opinion Franklin, Jefferson, Mason and Madison were the smartest of the group, and I think they saw the danger that Federalists like Hamilton and John Adams could create if not put in check. That is why the Checks and Balances were in the Constitution so no one group could change the rules to affect another group detrimentally. Unfortunately many of those checks and balances have been removed or are totally ignored today and we have a government totally out of control, detrimentally affecting everyone. Many of the founding Fathers were partly responsible for the problem we have today. Founders like John Adams who tried to quietly stack the Courts with 39 new Federalist Justices who would side with him on legal opinion just months before Thomas Jefferson was to take over as President in 1802... That deception infuriated Jefferson, and the divide between the political parties was well underway.

Chapter Two
The Laws and Rights That Were Not Granted in the Constitution

There have always been those who want to control, and with that control comes the need for more control. This is pretty much the reason why this country has changed into something it was never intended to become. Most laws were intended to protect, not just one individual, but to protect all individuals. Unfortunately those who wanted power and control perverted laws to suit their own agendas.

Quaker and Puritan laws were some of the first laws used in early American history. Many of the laws directly came out of the Bible, and if broken, had harsh punishment. Most were meant to humiliate the law breaker, like being put in the block, or being chained to a tree where kids would throw crap and tease and torment the law breaker. Harsher punishments were also given like servitude, (enslavement) for a period of time or until the enslaved could pay to be freed. Laws were arbitrary in the colonial period prior to the American Revolution, and no distinctive American legal system really existed. Criminal codes, punishments, and courts varied from colony to colony. But in the mid-1700s a national legal set of laws was underway to create a more unified American legal system. The Revolution sped up that process, and the victory over Britain brought independence and a new justice system that provided both protection and rights for American citizens. The first several decades following the Revolution were pretty much an experimental time for criminal justice. Those early court decisions and legislations formed the foundation for the criminal justice system we have now. They had to recognize Rights given each citizen under the State laws and the Constitution first. States wrote up Declarations Of

Citizen's Rights, and one of those became the template for the U.S. Constitution.

Virginia's 1776 declaration of rights was the model for the U.S. Bill of Rights, and much of it was added to the U.S. Constitution in 1791, which gave citizens specified Rights. The Virginia Declaration of Rights is a document drafted in 1776 by George Mason to proclaim the inherent rights of men, including the right to rebel against "inadequate" government. Something Abraham Lincoln would later declare treason.

The following is the complete text of the Virginia Declaration of Rights and why George Mason is considered the Father of the Bill of Rights. James Madison is known as the Father of the Constitution, but he and Jefferson consulted George Mason while drafting the US Constitution as their mentor on matters of political theory.

"A DECLARATION OF RIGHTS made by the representatives of the good people of Virginia, assembled in full and free convention which rights do pertain to them and their posterity, as the basis and foundation of government.

Section 1. That all men are by nature equally free and independent and have certain inherent rights, of which, when they enter into a state of society, they cannot, by any compact, deprive or divest their posterity; namely, the enjoyment of life and liberty, with the means of acquiring and possessing property, and pursuing and obtaining happiness and safety.

Section 2. That all power is vested in, and consequently derived from, the people; that magistrates are their trustees and servants and at all times amenable to them.

Section 3. That government is, or ought to be, instituted for the common benefit, protection, and security of the people, nation, or community; of all the various modes and forms of government, that is best which is capable of producing the greatest degree of happiness and safety and is most effectually secured against the danger of maladministration. And that, when any government shall be found inadequate or contrary to these purposes, a majority of the community has an indubitable, inalienable, and indefeasible right to reform, alter, or abolish it, in such manner as shall be judged most conducive to the public weal.

Section 4. That no man, or set of men, is entitled to exclusive or separate emoluments or privileges from the community, but in consideration of public services; which, nor being descendible, neither ought the offices of magistrate, legislator, or judge to be hereditary.

Section 5. That the legislative and executive powers of the state should be separate and distinct from the judiciary; and that the members of the two first may be restrained from oppression, by feeling and participating the burdens of the people, they should, at fixed periods, be reduced to a private station, return into that body from which they were originally taken, and the vacancies be supplied by frequent, certain, and regular elections, in which all, or any part, of the former members, to be again eligible, or ineligible, as the laws shall direct.

Section 6. That elections of members to serve as representatives of the people, in assembly ought to be free; and that all men, having sufficient evidence of permanent common interest with, and attachment to, the community, have the right of suffrage and cannot be taxed or deprived of their property for public uses without their own consent or that of their representatives so elected, nor bound by any law to which they have not, in like manner, assented for the public good.

Section 7. That all power of suspending laws, or the execution of laws, by any authority, without consent of the representatives of the people, is injurious to their rights and ought not to be exercised.

Section 8. That in all capital or criminal prosecutions a man has a right to demand the cause and nature of his accusation, to be confronted with the accusers and witnesses, to call for evidence in his favor, and to a speedy trial by an impartial jury of twelve men of his vicinage, without whose unanimous consent he cannot be found guilty; nor can he be compelled to give evidence against himself; that no man be deprived of his liberty except by the law of the land or the judgment of his peers.

Section 9. That excessive bail ought not to be required, nor excessive fines imposed, nor cruel and unusual punishments inflicted.

Section 10. That general warrants, whereby an officer or messenger may be commanded to search suspected places without evidence of a fact committed, or to seize any person or persons not named, or whose offense is not particularly described and supported by evidence, are grievous and oppressive and ought not to be granted.

Section 11. That in controversies respecting property, and in suits between man and man, the ancient trial by jury is preferable to any other and ought to be held sacred.

Section 12. That the freedom of the press is one of the great bulwarks of liberty, and can never be restrained but by despotic governments.

Section 13. That a well-regulated militia, composed of the body of the people, trained to arms, is the proper, natural, and safe defense of a free state; that standing armies, in time of peace, should be avoided as dangerous to liberty; and that in all cases the military should be under strict subordination to, and governed by, the civil power.

Section 14. That the people have a right to uniform government; and, therefore, that no government separate from or independent of the government of Virginia ought to be erected or established within the limits thereof.

Section 15. That no free government, or the blessings of liberty, can be preserved to any people but by a firm adherence to justice, moderation, temperance, frugality, and virtue and by frequent recurrence to fundamental principles.

Section 16. That religion, or the duty which we owe to our Creator, and the manner of discharging it, can be directed only by reason and conviction, not by force or violence; and therefore all men are equally entitled to the free exercise of religion, according to the dictates of conscience; and that it is the mutual duty of all to practice Christian forbearance, love, and charity toward each other. Written by George Mason, and adopted by the Virginia Constitutional Convention on June 12, 1776."

As you can see by this document, Christian Laws were the foundation of early American laws. But as the country grew so did the laws, many of which were created to address who could own what and where, and laws against vice were created to combat sinful behavior. But as the country grew, and more laws were created, so did the need to control. Laws were also created that had nothing to do with protecting the people, but to protect the government's control over the people.

Women's Rights

Women's Rights varied from State to State and married women were considered property of their husbands in many of the States. Single women on the other hand had many of the Rights given to males. In every state, the legal status of free women depended upon their marital status. Unmarried women, including widows, were called "femes soles," or "women alone." They had the legal right to live where they pleased and to support themselves in any occupation that did not require a license or a college degree restricted to males. Single women could enter into contracts, buy and sell real estate, or accumulate personal property, which was called "personality". It consisted of everything from cash, stocks and bonds, livestock, and in the South, slaves. Most of the Northern States abolished slavery after the Revolutionary War. As long as they remained unmarried, they could sue and be sued, write wills, serve as guardians, and act as executors of estates. These rights were a continuation of the colonial legal tradition. But the revolutionary emphasis on equality brought some important changes in women's inheritance rights. State lawmakers everywhere abolished primogeniture and the tradition of double shares of a parent's estate, inheritance customs that favored the eldest son. Instead, equal inheritance for all children became the rule which was a big gain for daughters.

Women were not allowed to vote or hold office until 1920 when the 19th Amendment was passed. Women were also not allowed by law to tend a bar right up to the mid 1970s. One such law was passed in Michigan in 1945 making it illegal for a woman, with the exception of the wife or daughter of the saloon keeper, to mix drinks behind the bar. Valentine Goesaert and three other women from Michigan challenged the statute as unconstitutional, taking their case all the way to the Supreme Court. Writing the majority opinion in Goesaert v. Cleary in 1948 was, Associate Justice of the Supreme Court Felix Frankfurter (1939-1962) who seemed downright amused that anyone would think the "equal-protection" clause of the 14th

Amendment would apply to women and cocktails. Despite the centuries of old tradition of "sprightly and ribald" alewives, Frankfurter wrote, "Michigan could, beyond question, forbid all women from working behind a bar." Frankfurter was a progressive that was also a stickler for respecting the prerogative of state legislature and courts, and he even gave a wink and a nudge to indicate that he knew exactly what the law was all about. The Court, he wrote; "cannot give ear to the suggestion that the real impulse behind this legislation was an unchivalrous desire of male bartenders to try to monopolize the calling."

Michigan dropped the law in 1955, but other states had similar restrictions on the books. In 1971 California still officially barred women from "pouring whiskey." The court case that finally overturned that state law involved a topless bar called Sail'er Inn, which wanted to move some dancers behind the bar to mix drinks.

Craig v. Boren, 429 U.S. 190 (1976), was the first case in which a majority of the United States Supreme Court determined that statutory or administrative sex classifications had to be subjected to an intermediate standard of judicial review.

Voting Laws

The Right to vote was not allowed for all citizens until restrictions were lifted about 40 years ago. In many places people had to prove they were intelligent enough in politics to be able to vote. It was later deemed discriminatory and was abolished. When you come to think of it maybe that might have been a big mistake because people should really know what is going on in politics before they vote; all too often people just go in blindly without a clue as to what or who they are voting on or for. I liken it to allowing a person to drive a car or fly a plane without ever learning how. This may sound a bit harsh; but when we allow a dictator to get elected just because he or she is a certain color or gender that we may like. Or they just might be mister or miss popular at the time, and we really do not even know who they are, or what they really believe in or stand for, we could be in for some big trouble which has been the fall of many a nation. If we the voters do not start to read, learn and understand our Constitution; and we do not also start to realize that this document was put in place for us to keep our freedom, and we keep electing people whose main goal is to shred it... Then our country is doomed for disaster, and is destined to fail as history has seen before!

Here are some of the Voting Laws from 1776 to Today

1776-1787: Declaration of Independence ("All men are created equal"), Articles of Confederation, U.S. Constitution leave voting rights to state jurisdiction. "Suffrage" = (Right to vote) is limited to white male property owners.

1776-1807: New Jersey women, age 21 and over, can vote if they fulfill residency and property requirements. In 1807 the New Jersey legislature rescinds women's suffrage.

1776: Free black men can vote in New Jersey, Pennsylvania and Connecticut.

1792-1838: The Constitutions of Connecticut, Delaware, Kentucky, Maryland, New Jersey, North Carolina, Tennessee, and Virginia, were changed ending the black male voting Right and exclude blacks from voting but expand white male suffrage.

1848: The Treaty of Guadalupe-Hidalgo ends the Mexican-American War and guarantees U.S. citizenship to Mexicans living in the newly acquired territories of Arizona, California, Colorado, New Mexico, Nevada and Texas. English language requirements limit their access to voting rights.

1860: Five states (Maine, New Hampshire, Vermont, Rhode Island, and Massachusetts) allow free black men to vote.

1867: Kansas holds the first referendum on women's suffrage in the U.S. The measure fails.

1869: Wyoming Territorial legislature grants full voting rights to women. Wyoming was not yet a State.

1870: Utah Territorial legislature grants full voting rights to women. Utah was not yet a State.

1870: Passage of the 15th Amendment prohibits states from denying citizens the vote based on "race, color, or previous condition of servitude," but many Blacks, Asians, and Hispanics remain disfranchised in the South by poll taxes and literacy tests.

1882: The Chinese Exclusion Act bars people of Chinese ancestry from becoming American citizens.

1883: Washington Territorial legislature grants full voting rights to women. Washington was not yet a State.

1884: The U.S. Supreme Court rules, in Elk vs. Wilkins, that Native Americans are not citizens as defined by the 14th Amendment.

1887: Passage of the Dawes Act grants citizenship to Native Americans who give up their tribal affiliations. U.S. Congress rescinds women's suffrage in Utah. The Territorial Supreme Court rescinds women's suffrage in Washington Territory.

1888: Act of 1888 grants citizenship to Indian women who marry white men. Washington Territorial legislature grants women the right to vote but the Territory's Supreme Court quickly rescinds that right, for the second time.

1889: Washington state referendum defeats women's suffrage.

1890: Wyoming enters the Union as the first state granting full women's suffrage (Right to Vote) in State Elections. Also in 1890 on a National level; The Indian Naturalization Act grants citizenship to American Indians whose applications are approved (similar to the process of immigrant naturalization). But many Indians and part Indians do not apply because they were treated worse than Blacks and had Bounties from 5 to 10 dollars put on their children who were forced to go to Government approved schools.

1893: Colorado state referendum grants full voting rights to women.

1896: Utah and Idaho grant full voting rights to women.

1901: Congress grants citizenship to Indians living in Indian Territory (Oklahoma).

1910: Washington state referendum approves full suffrage for women.

1911: California state referendum approves full voting rights for women.

1912: Oregon, Kansas and Arizona state referenda approve full voting rights for women.

1913: Alaska Territorial Legislature approves women's right to vote as its first official act.

1914: Montana and Nevada referenda approve full suffrage for women.

1918: South Dakota and Oklahoma referenda grant full

suffrage to women.

1919: American Indians who served in the military during World War I are granted U.S. citizenship.

1920: U.S. House of Representatives and Senate approve the 19th Amendment to grant suffrage (Right to Vote) to women. Amendment wins the necessary 2/3 ratification from state legislatures.

1922: Supreme Court rules, in Takao Ozawa v. United States, that people of Japanese heritage are not eligible to become naturalized citizens.

1924: The Indian Citizenship Act grants citizenship to American Indians, but many western states prohibited their voting.

1925: Filipinos barred from citizenship unless they have served three years in the U.S. Navy.

1943: Chinese Exclusion Act is repealed, making people of Chinese ancestry eligible for U.S. citizenship.

1946: Filipinos and indigenous people from India become eligible for U.S. citizenship.

1952: Walter-McCarran Act grants all people of Asian ancestry the right to become citizens.

1953: Full suffrage approved in New Mexico.

1965: The Voting Rights Act of 1965 suspends literacy tests in the Deep South and provides federal enforcement of black registration and voting rights where denied.

1970: The 1970 Voting Rights Act bans literacy tests in 20 states, including New York, Illinois, and California.

1971: The passage of the 26th Amendment expands full voting rights to 18 year-old citizens.

1975: 1975 Voting Rights Act provides language assistance to minority voters.

As you can see, not everyone had the Right to vote in America and only just within the last 45 years have the laws and limitations been lifted to allow all legal citizens in good standing, (Without Felonies or Crimes against the Country), a Right to vote. The irony in this is, less people choose to use the Right to Vote now that they have won the Right to do so, and 80% of those who vote believe just about anything they hear.

Another interesting fact is that when times are bad and people are out of work, the people with a little political knowledge will convince those who know nothing to vote for the Socialists so they can get free money i.e. "Entitlements" and when times are good and there are plenty of jobs and everyone is making plenty of money, people will convince those who know nothing to vote for Conservatives because they don't want to give the Government any of their money to pay for those entitlements. This impulse voting, without knowing what damage will be done, is why we are losing freedom. You need to be informed and know what the consequences are when you vote for more government.

"The policy of the American Government is to leave its citizens free, neither restraining them nor aiding them in their pursuits"
– Thomas Jefferson

No man escapes
When freedom fails,
The best men rot in filthy jails;
And they who cried: "Appease,
Appease!"
Are hanged by men they tried to
please.- Hiram Mann

Chapter Three
Laws, Rules and Actions that Cost Us Freedom

There are so many laws and rules on the books in this country that I could go on and on, so I will try and limit them to some of the most important ones that have cost us a lot of our freedom. Many of our freedoms were lost in just the last 35 years. Some of you younger readers may never have known we had these freedoms. That is because those who were against those freedoms never want you to know they were taken, or changed, to make you believe they are now a privilege and not a Right.

According to the Constitution the Inalienable Rights that were given to us can not legally be taken away by the government. But we allowed our government to pull the wool over our eyes while they added restrictions and changed the meaning of many of those Rights. This has been a major cause of our freedom lost. Unfortunately many of our Rights have turned into a Privilege or have just been totally ignored.

Most Americans think we have protection from an abusive government because of the Constitution and The Bill of Rights. Sadly we really have no protection at all. Our judges and police have no use for the Constitution or the Bill of Rights and routinely tell anyone who quotes any part of the document that they are out of order and to keep their mouth shut or they will be held in contempt of court and/or arrested for P.O.P. pissing off police! The majority of the people just cower in fear and allow themselves to be abused. Even when they know they are innocent and have inalienable Rights that the government can't take away, that was guaranteed in the Constitution. Unfortunately though, the people who stand their ground and bring up our Rights under the Constitution really make the Gestapo/police mad. The police know we have Rights and they can't stand it! They will try and twist our words around and then use them against us to abuse and arrest us. After you are arrested and put in jail, you will usually be threatened with a long jail sentence if you don't cop a plea to a crime that you never even commit. As outrageous as this sounds, it does not stop there. If you dare go to the press to let the public know the abuse of power that has been committed against you and take your case to court. The Court will paint you as the bad guy who does not know what they are talking about and persuade a jury to convict you. The Judge will come down hard on anyone who dares to try and show the people that the government thinks they are above the law. and does not respect our Constitutional or our inalienable Rights that the Constitution says the government can't take away from us! The Constitution and Bill of Rights gives us the Right to Question their Authority. But the government has chipped away those "Rights" the government has no Right to take away! The Constitution and Bill of Rights was created for us to use against the Government when it got out of hand. People often speak of their Constitutional Rights and this is technically untrue. The Constitution states we have "Inalienable Rights" as Humans given us by our creator that the government can never take from us. The Constitution placed restrictions on Government so they couldn't take away those inalienable rights, and gave us the power to stop them from abusing their power and your Rights. But inch by inch they have taken control over your lives in violation of the Constitution and Bill of Rights. Why and how did this happen?

I've learned a lot of what I wrote above from the many people who have come to me and shared their story of abuse of power by their city officials, when I was on the city council and the publisher of The Nor-Cal Paper. I published their story in my newspaper without judgment. I was an open forum newspaper where anyone could have a say. I attended many of the court hearings of the stories I published, and I witnessed first hand the abusive way the court would treat the people; and sometimes even me just for attending.

These are your Rights that you should never allow to be taken or changed into a privilege!

The First Amendment:

"Congress shall make no law respecting an establishment of religion, or prohibiting the free exercise thereof; or abridging the freedom of speech, or of the press; or the right of the people peaceably to assemble, and to petition the Government for a redress of grievances."

The Right of free speech and religion is a classic example of Rights that have been lost by added rules and laws governing those Rights. We no longer have the 1st Amendment as it was intended. Now you must follow certain rules and laws governing religion and speech or you can be arrested, fined and or imprisoned. A classic example was the arrest of two men who started to read the bible out loud in the parking lot of a DMV office in California several years ago. There was also the arrest and conviction a couple years ago of two brothers, Benjamin and Russell Bartholomew of Wheatland, Calif. who were protesting taxes in Yuba County, Calif. The Yuba County Sheriff and CHP saw a chance to get around their Constitutional right to protest by charging the two for wearing masks. The brothers had on masks as a form of political theater. It was the same mask that had become a symbol of revolt popularized in the movie V for Vendetta. The law states anyone who wears a mask while committing a crime is a violation; but these two were not committing a crime, they were Protesting Taxes. This was just

another tactic the Gestapo could use to detain them. The District Attorney knew this would not stand up in court, so after a lot of research, the charge was changed to detaining an Officer from performing their duties, PC148, which was also totally bogus.

The two brothers had videoed the whole incident with the sheriffs and CHP live via direct upload to their You Tube site; goodmendosomething.org and on You Tube at: http://www.youtube.com/watch?v=sG0rAkTJDmQ&feature=c4-overview-vl&list=PLE2114D1A87F51B0F

No one ever thought a jury would convict these two, but after the district attorney did his research and found a legal precedence that allowed them to arrest any protesters who Detained an Officer in the performance of their duties they charged and convicted the two young men because the Sheriff and CHP had to confront and harass the two protesters. This was a classic case of being charged with "P.O.P. - Pissing Off Police". The irony in all of this was a Yuba County Jury convicted the two brothers of basically Protesting Taxes, along with the crime Yuba County fabricated, which gave them a reason to arrest and charge the two, which was PC148. In the court trial one of the officers involved even stated under oath that he was wrong in arresting them for the charge, and yet the brainwashed jury still convicted these two brothers for what basically was protesting taxes. The Jury was not allowed to view the entire video and were basically told they had to convict the two young men, and that is exactly what they did. At their sentencing their father who was a Major in the USAF at that time, read a speech questioning what he was fighting for in America and stated his sons were doing more for freedom than he had in his whole time with the military. It was a speech reminiscent to Patrick Henry's Give me liberty or give me death and after he was done reading it, I applauded and was promptly thrown out of the Courtroom for my outburst of public courtroom disobedience. No longer can anyone in a courtroom move, speak out, talk, motion, nod, applaud or even wipe a runny nose without getting thrown out.

Justice in America has become a joke complete with little tin-gods that rule us as if they are God. No more order in the court spouted by the judge, just the 4 or 5 bailiffs with guns running over and forcefully removing the people who speak out or motion in any way. They surely don't want people to disagree with the judge and agree with the accused. Sadly most jurors have no idea what jury nullification is; (A Jury Voting Not Guilty if they don't agree with a crime against the defendant). Most jurors have no idea what abuse some Judges commit against a defendant and they really don't care. There are People that don't even know that a judge can be recalled by the citizens if they feel he or she isn't following the oath that the judge swore when they were elected. When they are sworn in, they promise to uphold the Constitution of the USA and the State they are in. The words "Blind Justice" now take on a whole new meaning in America.

Shortly after the two Brothers were sentenced and fined they

41

went back to the same place and performed the same Protest with an even larger Taxes=Theft sign. Only this time there were many more people with them and several Medias from newspapers to TV stations… and you know what? The local Law Enforcers did nothing this time!

This goes to show there is power in numbers and our laws in America are arbitrarily enforced or fabricated to suit the government. Unfortunately the brothers didn't appeal their conviction to a higher court because of unknown reasons. They were even told there were attorneys standing by pro-bono if they wanted to fight it. Well whatever the reason they still made an impact, because this is now a California precedent that can be quoted in other Protest cases.

About the same time this was going on back in 2011 and 2012, a former Marysville City Councilman was running for Yuba County Judge. This person had repeatedly called me a Nazi because of my depiction of any law enforcer that blatantly violates a citizen's Rights as a Gestapo...and because I was at the time the Chair of the Yuba County Libertarian Party, and was against him ever becoming a Judge. No One Should Ever Be Allowed To Sit On A Legal Bench who calls someone a Nazi for believing in Liberty and Justice For All! He even threatened the owner of the local AM Radio Station that was supporting my efforts and told him that he would never run any political ads with the station as long as he supported Nazi Libertarians like myself. The local newspapers knew about this and said nothing, they didn't want to lose ad revenue so they just didn't inform the public of the discriminating justice broker they were about to give a thrown to. This supposed honest and just person used Nazi propaganda to discredit my opinion of his performance while on the City Council, and because the local media wanted his ad money, they reported the news by omission and he won the election and is now a Yuba County Superior Court Judge/Justice Broker! I know... it's really scary to think anyone would allow this to happen and hard to believe, but people did elect Obama... twice! Unfortunately, most of the media both radio and printed omitted the negative information that would have or possibly could have lost him the election, but then again look what happened in Yuba County, California to those two young men protesting taxes.

Both Religion and Tax Protest cases clearly are a Right under the First Amendment, but the government sidestepped the Constitution by sighting other California Laws to charge the people with. Clearly doing an end run around the people's Rights alleging the California Laws supersede the Constitution and therefore canceling out the people's Constitutional Rights. Yet police/Gestapo, government attorneys and judges will argue these cases have nothing to do with Constitutional Rights, and claim they are legally justified to charge people and convict them. Sadly the majority of the sheeple believe them, and the people that don't believe will rarely speak out against them. let alone do anything to stop them.

If an individual that reads the Bible out loud and/or Protest taxes are not utilizing their Constitutional Right according to California Law Enforcers; then this would be a classic example of taking our First Amendment Right and turning it into a Privilege complete with rules and secondary laws to back up those rules, making the First Amendment void in California or at best arbitrarily allowed. This isn't a California issue alone by any means, it happens all across the Country. But California by far is one of the worst states destroying our Constitutional Rights in the Nation. They are closely followed by New Jersey and New York, which are some of the most populated states, so they set the stage for the federal government to change the meaning or down right ignore the Constitution and Bill of Rights. Those population figures, figure in Tax revenue, so it is all about the money and how much of your money they can steal.

Many of our States deliberately refuse to allow people to enjoy their Constitutional Rights, especially when the government in control disapproves of a Right Granted in the Bill of Rights such as the Second Amendment.

Second Amendment in the Bill of Rights:

You can judge for yourselves what our Founding Fathers had in mind when they wrote the Second Amendment.

As passed by Congress and preserved in the National Archives: "A well regulated Militia, being necessary to the security of a free State, the right of the people to keep and bear Arms, shall not be infringed."

This once guaranteed Right has now also been labeled a Privilege complete with laws and rules that totally go against the Second Amendment. Thirty years ago you could buy a hand gun or rifle from most anyone, anywhere in America. You could even walk down the end of a street in most parts of the Country into the fields, forest, deserts and wild lands with your gun to go hunting or target practice without anyone going through convulsions over it. Then the Progressives and Socialists got control and spat on the Constitution and started the Infringement of the Second Amendment. This really started in 1961, but didn't really escalate until the late 80s.

The Second Amendment clearly states that the "RIGHT" to bear arms "SHALL NOT BE INFRINGED" yet in California they recently passed a no open carry law against all Guns. This means if you openly carry a gun in public and show it, use it, sell it, or do not register or buy it through a STATE LICENSED DEALER; It can and will be used against you in a court of law that will make you out to look like a criminal, and then they will take away your RIGHT TO BEAR ARMS; But when you come to think about it we really have already lost that right! The politicians and law enforcers who work fervently to try and convince the people that this is not INFRINGING on their Rights honestly believe that The People are that stupid and will fall for it. Unfortunately they have been proven right, because the people really have done nothing to stop this Unconstitutional downright outward theft and abuse of our second amendment Right.

Elected officials like Dianne Feinstein a US Senator from California, and State Senator Darrel Steinberg, Obama, and other socialist leftists along with some of their progressive rightwing nuts really seem to hate the Constitution. They especially hate the Second Amendment. Elected officials like Feinstein and Steinberg have repeatedly tried to destroy the Second Amendment and Feinstein even admitted to it in a media interview; "If I could have gotten 51 votes in the Senate I would have said Mr. and Mrs. America turn in your guns."- Dianne Feinstein told the interviewer after her failed attempts to repeal the Second Amendment. They now are going after ammunition, and have passed a law banning lead bullets in California. How the hell can anyone say with a straight face that's not infringing on our Right to Bear Arms?

Let's look at some facts and recorded cause of deaths annually in the country according to our government's own statistics:

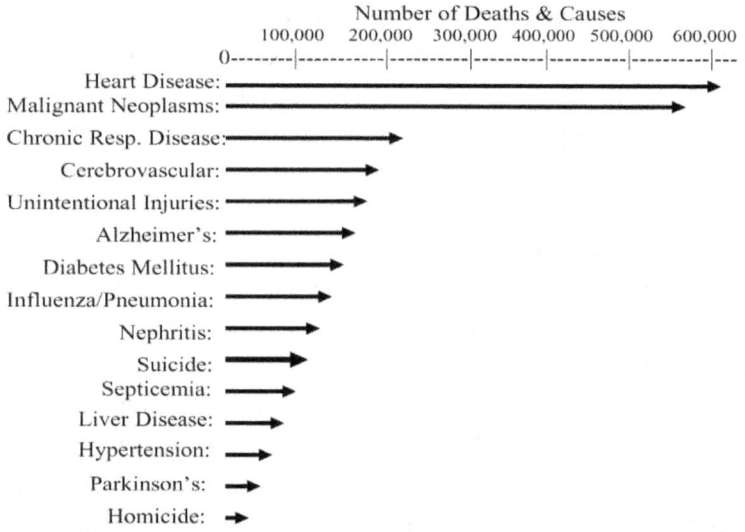

Number One Killer is Heart Disease 597,689 – Number Two: Cancer 574,743 – Number Three: Chronic lower Respiratory Disease 138,080 – Number Four: Stroke 129,476 – Number Five: Accidents 120,859 – Number Six: Alzheimer's 83,494 – Number Seven: Diabetes 69,071 – Number Eight: Nephritis

50,476 – Number Nine: Influenza & Pneumonia 50,097 – Number Ten: Suicide 38,364. The statistics above are from 2010. They were the most complete and available statistics that I could find. The total number of deaths by "guns" recorded back in 2010 was only 9,146 which also included people killed by law enforcers, suicide and self defense.

Knives, hands, feet and clubs account for more murders than rifles in America. Rifles only account for 384 deaths compared to 1,825 people who were killed by knives and sharp cutting tools. 801 people were killed by other people using their hands, fists and feet, 611 people were killed by blunt objects like bats, clubs, and hammers. There is a substantial difference when you compare all of this to the 384 people killed by rifles. I use the rifle statistics because the media and socialists in our government seem to be chipping away at our Second Amendment by using Rifles or (Assault Rifles) as they like to call them. They have successfully gained control of the hand guns with their laws that circumvent the Second Amendment which has made it too expensive and/or too regulated for most citizens to afford or be approved to legally bear those arms.

The US Government has totally ignored the Constitution when it comes to our Second Amendment Right. They have allowed States like California and New York to violate the Constitution with contempt. Many will argue that the Second Amendment is mostly still intact, but it is not! The 1968 Federal Gun Control Act which was part of a far larger conspiracy to "Disarm America", shown below, proves how the Second Amendment has been whittled down over the years:

"Under the United States Gun Control Act of 1968, any cartridge firearm made in or before 1898 ("pre-1899") is classified as an "antique", and is generally outside of Federal jurisdiction, as administered and enforced by the U.S. Bureau of

Alcohol, Tobacco, Firearms and Explosives (BATFE). The only exceptions to the Federal exemption are antique machineguns (such as the Maxim gun and Colt Model 1895 "Potato Digger") and antique cartridge rifles or shotguns firing shotgun shells that are classified as "short barreled" per the U.S. Gun Control Act of 1968, namely cartridge rifles with a barrel less than 16 inches long, or shotguns firing shotgun shells with a barrel less than 18 inches long, or either cartridge rifles or shotgun-shell-firing shotguns with an overall length of less than 26 inches. Muzzleloading guns, as replicas of antique guns, are not subject to Federal jurisdiction and are essentially classified the same as an antique gun. Hence, a muzzleloading black-powder shotgun is not subject to the short-barreled National Firearms Act of 1934 restrictions. Purchases of such modern-day manufactured replicas may be done outside of the normal Federal Firearms License (FFL) restrictions that otherwise exist when purchasing modern (post-1898) guns. Replicas of cartridge-firing rifles, however, are not classed the same as antiques, but must be purchased through FFL holders, although a true antique that was manufactured prior to 1899 firing the same cartridge as the replica would be legal for sale without the transfer being processed through an FFL. Furthermore, any rifle re-built on a receiver or frame that was manufactured prior to 1899 is considered antique, even if it has been re-barreled or even if every other part has been replaced.

The following is an excerpt from the portion of the Gun Control Act of 1968 (which modified Title 18, U.S. Code) that exempted pre-1899 guns from the Federal Firearms License paperwork requirements administered by the BATFE:

18 USC 921 (a)(16). (A) any firearm (including any firearm with a matchlock, flintlock, percussion cap, or similar type of ignition system) manufactured in or before 1898; and (B) any replica of any firearm described in subparagraph (A) if such

replica -- (i) is not designed or redesigned for using rimfire or conventional centerfire fixed ammunition, or (ii) uses rimfire or conventional centerfire fixed ammunition which is no longer manufactured in the United States and which is not readily available in the ordinary channels of commercial trade.

Within the United States, antique exemptions vary considerably from state to state.

Identifying pre-1899 antiques

The production of many cartridge firearms, such as the famous Winchester Model 1894 lever action rifle took place both before and after the December 31, 1898 cut-off date that delineates exempt antique status under U.S. law. Therefore, collectors rely on references such as The Pre-1899 Antique Guns FAQ by James Wesley Rawles to determine if a particular gun's serial number falls within the range of "antique" (pre-1899) production. For example, a Winchester Model 1894 with serial number 147,685 had its frame (or "receiver") made in December 1898 and it is hence classified as an "antique", but records show that a Winchester Model 1894 with serial number 147,686 had its frame made in January, 1899 and it is hence classified as "modern" by the BATFE therefore, black powder weapons are not firearms unless said black powder weapon can be converted to propel rim-fire ammunition.

Since it is the date of manufacture of the receiver that is relevant to identifying a gun as antique or modern, it is possible to have a weapon with date marks post-1898 but still be considered an antique gun. For example, some Finnish M39 (Ukko-Pekka) Mosin-Nagant rifles with hexagonal profile receivers are considered antique because some were built on receivers dated pre-1899, even though the rifle itself was adopted in 1939. Many of these were assembled using a mix of old round and "hex" receivers from then on, until as late as the 1970s. To be identified as pre-1899, however, Mosin-Nagants that have been re-barreled must be disassembled to see the date stamps on their tangs. A similar situation exists for 7.65mm Mauser Turkish Model 1893 bolt actions, most of which were re-arsenalized at the Ankara arsenal in the 1940s, and re-chambered to 8x57mm Mauser. Despite this re-arsenalization and re-chambering, they are still considered antiques under US law as all rifles of that model were manufactured between 1893 and 1896. Likewise, all firearms produced by Ludwig Loewe & Co. A.G., which are marked "Ludwig Loewe" or "Loewe, Berlin", are antiques. This is because Ludwig Loewe was merged into Deutsche Waffen und Munitionsfabriken in 1897, and the Loewe name was no longer used after the merger.

In the case United States vs. Kirvan, He was charged with Armed Robbery and a Felon in possession of a firearm while committing a felony. Kirvan was found guilty of the armed robbery but was found innocent of being a felon in possession of a firearm while committing a felony charge; due to the fact that a black powder weapon is not considered a firearm under the definition of federal gun laws. It was added that a black powder weapon that has never been used or shot before, classifies it as a display piece which does not consider it a firearm. Therefore the judge had to dismiss the charge.

So now only Black Powder guns are legal under the Second Amendment in the Constitution according to the Federal Government. They have been totally against what the Second Amendment stands for and have been trying to change the meaning of the Amendment for well over 150 years. After all their toiling with no surprise, they have successfully managed to change our second amendment and believe me they are not done yet!

In United States v. Cruikshank, 92 U.S. 542 (1875), the Supreme Court ruled that; "The right to bear arms is not granted by the Constitution; neither is it in any manner dependent upon that instrument for its existence. The Second Amendment means no more than that it shall not be infringed by Congress, and has no other effect than to restrict the powers of the 'National Government.'" This was shortly after the Civil War and the government was eager to limit the people's ability to wage war against the government ever again.

Other Supreme Court Cases that further confused the Second Amendment Right are: In the District of Columbia v. Heller, 554 U.S. 570 (2008), the Supreme Court ruled that the Second Amendment "Codified a pre-existing Right" and that it protects an individuals Right to possess a firearm unconnected with service in a militia, and to use that arm for traditional lawful purpose, such as self-defense within the home. It also stated; "that the right is not unlimited. It is not a right to keep and carry any weapon whatsoever in any manner whatsoever and for whatever purpose". They also clarified that many longstanding prohibitions and restrictions on firearm possession listed by the Court are consistent with the Second Amendment. Which is just manipulation of the Constitution to control your Right!

In McDonald v. Chicago, 561 U.S. 3025 (2010), the Supreme Court ruled that the Second Amendment limits state and local government to the same extent that it limits the federal government.

This hasn't stopped the State and Federal government from issuing laws and rules attached to our Constitutional Right under the Second Amendment. The government both federal and state, have for the most part ignored High Court rulings because they know it takes a lot of resource and a long time for anyone or any group to get a challenge to the Supreme Court, and by the time they do, most people will have excepted whatever illegal unconstitutional law that has been imposed and enforced on them. Only the Government (Federal & State) or large corporations with the financial resource are able to fight in the High Court arena, unless public outcry is widespread, and then the High Court may rule on the issue.

Our Government seems to be able to change so many of our rights at the drop of a dime. If it can help them win a case or they just want to exude their power and show us they are our masters, they will do whatever is necessary to win! We The Citizens of America need to be able to amend our Constitution to allow The Supreme Court Justice to be overruled if three fourths of the States disagree with their ruling. Then it should go to a vote of the people to either invalidate or ratify. This would give back the state their right that was granted them under the 10th Amendment of the Constitution; especially since we have seen totally Unconstitutional Laws/Taxes passed by the Supreme Court over the years. The Supreme Court Justice should have a term limit just as the President does, or some way to unseat them if they boldly and deliberately violate the Constitution, the reasoning behind this is pretty obvious. When an official is elected and they turn out to be bad and pass unconstitutional laws and regulations. We need to be able to get them out or have some solace in knowing that their time is limited. The President is only elected for a 4 year term and can do a lot of damage in that time, but we can choose to not elect them again in the next term. A Justice is in there for life and can really make some bad judgments that could shatter our Rights protected and guaranteed in Constitution, and when they do there is no way to get them out, or change their ruling!

This was the ratified wording from the States and authenticated by Thomas Jefferson, then Secretary of State: "A well regulated militia being necessary to the security of a free state, the right of the people to keep and bear arms shall not be infringed."

Free people should not have to ask for permission in a free country, especially when it comes down to your Guaranteed Amendment Rights! This is something you might think about if you ever have to ask permission from your government to use a Guaranteed Freedom that was clearly defined in the Bill of Rights as part of the Constitution. If any of your government officials laugh at you when you even mention your rights, ask them if they swore an oath to uphold the Constitution. If they did, then why are they laughing?

They have escalated this documented agenda of arms disarmament started in 1961 under the Kennedy Administration that most of you never knew about or were never told going to happen.

The United States Program for General and Complete Disarmament in a Peaceful World

U.S. DEPARTMENT OF STATE

DEPARTMENT OF STATE PUBLICATION
7277
Disarmament Series 5
Released September 1961

Office of Public Services
BUREAU OF PUBLIC AFFAIRS

INTRODUCTION

The revolutionary development of modern weapons within a world divided by serious ideological differences has produced a crisis in human history. In order to overcome the danger of nuclear war now confronting mankind, the United States has introduced at the Sixteenth General Assembly of the United Nations a Program for General and Complete Disarmament in a Peaceful World.

This new program provides for the progressive reduction of the war-making capabilities of nations and the simultaneous strengthening of international institutions to settle disputes and maintain the peace. It sets forth a series of comprehensive measures which can and should be taken in order to bring about a world in which there will be freedom from war and security for all states. It is based on three principles deemed essential to the achievement of practical progress in the disarmament field:

First, there must be immediate disarmament action:

A strenuous and uninterrupted effort must be made toward the goal of general and complete disarmament; at the same time, it is important that specific measures be put into effect as soon as possible.

Second, all disarmament obligations must be subject to effective international controls:

The control organization must have the manpower, facilities, and effectiveness to assure that limitations or reductions take place as agreed. It must also be able to certify to all states that retained forces and armaments do not exceed those permitted at any stage of the disarmament process.

Third, adequate peace-keeping machinery must be established:

There is an inseparable relationship between the scaling down of national armaments on the one hand and the building up of international peace-keeping machinery and institutions on the other. Nations are unlikely to shed their means of self-protection in the absence of alternative ways to safeguard their legitimate interests. This can only be achieved through the progressive strengthening of international institutions under the United Nations and by creating a United Nations Peace Force to enforce the peace as the disarmament process proceeds.

There follows a summary of the principal provisions of the United States Program for General and Complete Disarmament in a Peaceful World. The full text of the program is contained in an appendix to this pamphlet.

FREEDOM FROM WAR

THE UNITED STATES PROGRAM FOR GENERAL AND COMPLETE DISARMAMENT IN A PEACEFUL WORLD

SUMMARY

DISARMAMENT GOAL AND OBJECTIVES

The over-all goal of the United States is a free, secure, and peaceful world of independent states adhering to common standards of justice and international conduct and subjecting the use of force to the rule of law; a world which has achieved general and complete disarmament under effective international control; and a world in which adjustment to change takes place in accordance with the principles of the United Nations.

In order to make possible the achievement of that goal, the program sets forth the following specific objectives toward which nations should direct their efforts:

The disbanding of all national armed forces and the prohibition of their reestablishment in any form whatsoever other than those required to preserve internal order and for contributions to a United Nations Peace Force;

The elimination from national arsenals of all armaments, including all weapons of mass destruction and the means for their delivery, other than those required for a United Nations Peace Force and for maintaining internal order;

The institution of effective means for the enforcement of international agreements, for the settlement of disputes, and for the maintenance of peace in accordance with the principles of the United Nations;

The establishment and effective operation of an International Disarmament Organization within the framework of the United Nations to insure compliance at all times with all disarmament obligations.

TASK OF NEGOTIATING STATES

The negotiating states are called upon to develop the program into a detailed plan for general and complete disarmament and to continue their efforts without interruption until the whole program has been achieved. To this end, they are to seek the widest possible area of agreement at the earliest possible date. At the same time, and without prejudice to progress on the disarmament program, they are to seek agreement on those immediate measures that would contribute to the common security of nations and that could facilitate and form part of the total program.

GOVERNING PRINCIPLES

The program sets forth a series of general principles to guide the negotiating states in their work. These make clear that:

As states relinquish their arms, the United Nations must be progressively strengthened in order to improve its capacity to assure international security and the peaceful settlement of disputes;

Disarmament must proceed as rapidly as possible, until it is completed, in stages containing balanced, phased, and safeguarded measures;

Each measure and stage should be carried out in an agreed period of time, with transition from one stage to the next to take place as soon as all measures in the preceding stage have been carried out and verified and as soon as necessary arrangements for verification of the next stage have been made;

Inspection and verification must establish both that nations carry out scheduled limitations or reductions and that they do not retain armed forces and armaments in excess of those permitted at any stage of the disarmament process; and

Disarmament must take place in a manner that will not affect adversely the security of any state.

DISARMAMENT STAGES

The program provides for progressive disarmament steps to take place in three stages and for the simultaneous strengthening of international institutions.

FIRST STAGE

The first stage contains measures which would significantly reduce the capabilities of nations to wage aggressive war. Implementation of this stage would mean that:

The nuclear threat would be reduced:

All states would have adhered to a treaty effectively prohibiting the testing of nuclear weapons.

The production of fissionable materials for use in weapons would be stopped and quantities of such materials from past production would be converted to non-weapons uses.

States owning nuclear weapons would not relinquish control of such weapons to any nation not owning them and would not transmit to any such nation information or material necessary for their manufacture.

States not owning nuclear weapons would not manufacture them or attempt to obtain control of such weapons belonging to other states.

A Commission of Experts would be established to report on the feasibility and means for the verified reduction and eventual elimination of nuclear weapons stockpiles.

Strategic delivery vehicles would be reduced

Strategic nuclear weapons delivery vehicles of specified categories and weapons designed to counter such vehicles would be reduced to agreed levels by equitable and balanced steps; their production would be discontinued or limited; their testing would be limited or halted.

Arms and armed forces would be reduced:

The armed forces of the United States and the Soviet Union would be limited to 2.1 million men each (with appropriate levels not exceeding that amount for other militarily significant states); levels of armaments would be correspondingly reduced and their production would be limited.

An Experts Commission would be established to examine and report on the feasibility and means of accomplishing verifiable reduction and eventual elimination of all chemical, biological and radiological weapons.

Peaceful use of outer space would be promoted:

The placing in orbit or stationing in outer space of weapons capable of producing mass destruction would be prohibited.

States would give advance notification of space vehicle and missile launchings.

U.N. peace-keeping powers would be strengthened:

Measures would be taken to develop and strengthen United Nations arrangements for arbitration, for the development of international law, and for the establishment in Stage II of a permanent U.N. Peace Force.

An International Disarmament Organization would be established for effective verification of the disarmament program:

Its functions would be expanded progressively as disarmament proceeds.

It would certify to all states that agreed reductions have taken place and that retained forces and armaments do not exceed permitted levels.

It would determine the transition from one stage to the next.

States would be committed to other measures to reduce international tension and to protect against the chance of war by accident, miscalculation, or surprise attack:

States would be committed to refrain from the threat or use of any type of armed force contrary to the principles of the U.N. Charter and to refrain from indirect aggression and subversion against any country.

A U.N. peace observation group would be available to investigate any situation which might constitute a threat to or breach of the peace.

States would be committed to give advance notice of major military movements which might cause alarm; observation posts would be established to report on concentrations and movements of military forces.

SECOND STAGE

The second stage contains a series of measures which would bring within sight a world in which there would be freedom from war. Implementation of all measures in the second stage would mean:

Further substantial reductions in the armed forces, armaments, and military establishments of states, including strategic nuclear weapons delivery vehicles and countering weapons;

Further development of methods for the peaceful settlement of disputes under the United Nations;

Establishment of a permanent international peace force within the United Nations;

Depending on the findings of an Experts Commission, a halt in the production of chemical, bacteriological and radiological weapons and a reduction of existing stocks or their conversion to peaceful uses;

On the basis of the findings of an Experts Commission, a reduction of stocks of nuclear weapons;

The dismantling or the conversion to peaceful uses of certain military bases and facilities wherever located; and

The strengthening and enlargement of the International Disarmament Organization to enable it to verify the steps taken in Stage II and to determine the transition to Stage III.

THIRD STAGE

During the third stage of the program, the states of the world, building on the experience and confidence gained in successfully implementing the measures of the first two stages, would take final steps toward the goal of a world in which:

States would retain only those forces, non-nuclear armaments, and establishments required for the purpose of maintaining internal order; they would also support and provide agreed manpower for a U.N. Peace Force.

The U.N. Peace Force, equipped with agreed types and quantities of armaments, would be fully functioning.

The manufacture of armaments would be prohibited except for those of agreed types and quantities to be used by the U.N. Peace Force and those required to maintain internal order. All other armaments would be destroyed or converted to peaceful purposes.

The peace-keeping capabilities of the United Nations would be sufficiently strong and the obligations of all states under such arrangements sufficiently far-reaching as to assure peace and the just settlement of differences in a disarmed world.

Appendix

DECLARATION ON DISARMAMENT

THE UNITED STATES PROGRAM FOR GENERAL AND COMPLETE DISARMAMENT IN A PEACEFUL WORLD

The Nations of the world, conscious of the crisis in human history produced by the revolutionary development of modern weapons within a world divided by serious ideological differences;

Determined to save present and succeeding generations from the scourge of war and the dangers and burdens of the arms race and to create conditions in which all peoples can strive freely and peacefully to fulfill their basic aspirations;

Declare their goal to be: A free, secure, and peaceful world of independent states adhering to common standards of justice and international conduct and subjecting the use of force to the rule of law; a world where adjustment to change takes place in accordance with the principles of the United Nations; a world where there shall be a permanent state of general and complete disarmament under effective international control and where the resources of nations shall be devoted to man's material, cultural, and spiritual advance;

Set forth as the objectives of a program of general and complete disarmament in a peaceful world:

(a) The disbanding of all national armed forces and the prohibition of their reestablishment in any form whatsoever other than those required to preserve internal order and for contributions to a United Nations Peace Force;

(b) The elimination from national arsenals of all armaments, including all weapons of mass destruction and the means for their delivery, other than those required for a United Nations Peace Force and for maintaining internal order;

(c) The establishment and effective operation of an International Disarmament Organization within the framework of the United Nations to ensure compliance at all times with all disarmament obligations;

(d) The institution of effective means for the enforcement of international agreements, for the settlement of disputes, and for the maintenance of peace in accordance with the principles of the United Nations.

Call on the negotiating states:

(a) To develop the outline program set forth below into an agreed plan for general and complete disarmament and to continue their efforts without interruption until the whole program has been achieved;

(b) To this end to seek to attain the widest possible area of agreement at the earliest possible date;

(c) Also to seek --- without prejudice to progress on the disarmament program --- agreement on those immediate measures that would contribute to the common security of nations and that could facilitate and form a part of that program.

Affirm that disarmament negotiations should be guided by the following principles:

(a) Disarmament shall take place as rapidly as possible until it is completed in stages containing balanced, phased and safeguarded measures, with each measure and stage to be carried out in an agreed period of time.

(b) Compliance with all disarmament obligations shall be effectively verified from their entry into force. Verification arrangements shall be instituted progressively and in such a manner as to verify not only that agreed limitations or reductions take place but also that retained armed forces and armaments do not exceed agreed levels at any stage.

(c) Disarmament shall take place in a manner that will not affect adversely the security of any state, whether or not a party to an international agreement or treaty.

(d) As states relinquish their arms, the United Nations shall be progressively strengthened in order to improve its capacity to assure international security and the peaceful settlement of differences as well as to facilitate the development of international cooperation in common tasks for the benefit of mankind.

(e) Transition from one stage of disarmament to the next shall take place as soon as all the measures in the preceding stage have been carried out and effective verification is continuing and as soon as the arrangements that have been agreed to be necessary for the next stage have been instituted.

Agree upon the following outline program for achieving general and complete disarmament:

STAGE I

A. To Establish an International Disarmament Organization:

(a) An International Disarmament Organization (IDO) shall be established within the framework of the United Nations upon entry into force of the agreement. Its functions shall be expanded progressively as required for the effective verification of the disarmament program.

(b) The IDO shall have: (1) a General Conference of all the parties; (2) a Commission consisting of representatives of all the major powers as permanent members and certain other states on a rotating basis; and (3) an Administrator who will administer the Organization subject to the direction of the Commission and who will have the authority, staff, and finances adequate to assure effective impartial implementation of the functions of the Organization.

(c) The IDO shall: (1) ensure compliance with the obligations undertaken by verifying the execution of measures agreed upon; (2) assist the states in developing the details of agreed further verification and disarmament measures; (3) provide for the establishment of such bodies as may be necessary for working out the details of further measures provided for in the program and for such other expert study groups as may be required to give continuous study to the problems of disarmament; (4) receive reports on the progress of disarmament and verification arrangements and determine the transition from one stage to the next.

B. To Reduce Armed Forces and Armaments:

(a) Force levels shall be limited to 2.1 million each for the U.S. and U.S.S.R. and to appropriate levels not exceeding 2.1 million each for all other militarily significant states. Reductions to the agreed levels will proceed by equitable, proportionate, and verified steps.

(b) Levels of armaments of prescribed types shall be reduced by equitable and balanced steps. The reductions shall be accomplished by transfers of armaments to depots supervised by the IDO. When, at specified periods during the Stage I reduction process, the states party to the agreement have agreed that the armaments and armed forces are at prescribed levels, the armaments in depots shall be destroyed or converted to peaceful uses.

(c) The production of agreed types of armaments shall be limited.

(d) A Chemical, Biological, Radiological (CBR) Experts Commission shall be established within the IDO for the purpose of examining and reporting on the feasibility and means for accomplishing the verifiable reduction and eventual elimination of CBR weapons stockpiles and the halting of their production.

C. To Contain and Reduce the Nuclear Threat:

(a) States that have not acceded to a treaty effectively prohibiting the testing of nuclear weapons shall do so.

(b) The production of fissionable materials for use in weapons shall be stopped.

(c) Upon the cessation of production of fissionable materials for use in weapons, agreed initial quantities of fissionable materials from past production shall be transferred to non-weapons purposes.

(d) Any fissionable materials transferred between countries for peaceful uses of nuclear energy shall be subject to appropriate safeguards to be developed in agreement with the IAEA. (e) States owning nuclear weapons shall not relinquish control of such weapons to any nation not owning them and shall not transmit to any such nation information or material necessary for their manufacture. States not owning nuclear weapons shall not manufacture such weapons, attempt to obtain control of such weapons belonging to other states, or seek or receive information or materials necessary for their manufacture.

(f) A Nuclear Experts Commission consisting of representatives of the nuclear states shall be established within the IDO for the purpose of examining and reporting on the feasibility and means for accomplishing the verified reduction and eventual elimination of nuclear weapons stockpiles.

D. To Reduce Strategic Nuclear Weapons Delivery Vehicles:

(a) Strategic nuclear weapons delivery vehicles in specified categories and agreed types of weapons designed to counter such vehicles shall be reduced to agreed levels by equitable and balanced steps. The reduction shall be accomplished in each step by transfers to depots supervised by the IDO of vehicles that are in excess of levels agreed upon for each step. At specified periods during the Stage I reduction process, the vehicles that have been placed under supervision of the IDO shall be destroyed or converted to peaceful uses.

(b) Production of agreed categories of strategic nuclear weapons delivery vehicles and agreed types of weapons designed to counter such vehicles shall be discontinued or limited. (c) Testing of agreed categories of strategic nuclear weapons delivery vehicles and agreed types of weapons designed to counter such vehicles shall be limited or halted.

E. To Promote the Peaceful Use of Outer Space:

(a) The placing into orbit or stationing in outer space of weapons capable c,f producing mass destruction shall be prohibited.

(b) States shall give advance notification to participating states and to the IDO of launchings of space vehicles and missiles, together with the track of the vehicle.

F. To Reduce the Risks of War by Accident, Miscalculation, and Surprise Attack:

(a) States shall give advance notification to the participating states and to the IDO of major military movements and maneuvers, on a scale as may be agreed, which might give rise to misinterpretation or cause alarm and induce countermeasures. The notification shall include the geographic areas to be used and the nature, scale and time span of the event.

(b) There shall be established observation posts at such locations as major ports, railway centers, motor highways, and air bases to report on concentrations and movements of military forces.

(c) There shall also be established such additional inspection arrangements to reduce the danger of surprise attack as may be agreed.

(d) An international commission shall be established immediately within the IDO to examine and make recommendations on the possibility of further measures to reduce the risks of nuclear war by accident, miscalculation, or failure of communication.

G. To Keep the Peace:

(a) States shall reaffirm their obligations under the U.N. Charter to refrain from the threat or use of any type of armed force-- including nuclear, conventional, or CBR--contrary to the principles of the U.N. Charter.

(b) States shall agree to refrain from indirect aggression and subversion against any country.

(c) States shall use all appropriate processes for the peaceful settlement of disputes and shall seek within the United Nations further arrangements for the peaceful settlement of international disputes and for the codification and progressive development of international law.

(d) States shall develop arrangements in Stage I for the establishment in Stage II of a U.N. Peace Force.

(e) A U.N. peace observation group shall be staffed with a standing cadre of observers who could be dispatched to investigate any situation which might constitute a threat to or breach of the peace.

STAGE II

A. International Disarmament Organization:

The powers and responsibilities of the IDO shall be progressively enlarged in order to give it the capabilities to verify the measures undertaken in Stage II.

B. To Further Reduce Armed Forces and Armaments:

(a) Levels of forces for the U.S., U.S.S.R., and other militarily significant states shall be further reduced by substantial amounts to agreed levels in equitable and balanced steps. (b) Levels of armaments of prescribed types shall be further reduced by equitable and balanced steps. The reduction shall be accomplished by transfers of armaments to depots supervised by the IDO. When, at specified periods during the Stage II reduction process, the parties have agreed that the armaments and armed forces are at prescribed levels, the armaments in depots shall be destroyed or converted to peaceful uses.

(c) There shall be further agreed restrictions on the production of armaments.

(d) Agreed military bases and facilities wherever they are located shall be dismantled or converted to peaceful uses.

(e) Depending upon the findings of the Experts Commission on CBR weapons, the production of CBR weapons shall be halted, existing stocks progressively reduced, and the resulting excess quantities destroyed or converted to peaceful uses.

C. To Further Reduce the Nuclear Threat:

Stocks of nuclear weapons shall be progressively reduced to the minimum levels which can be agreed upon as a result of the findings of the Nuclear Experts Commission; the resulting excess of fissionable material shall be transferred to peaceful purposes.

D. To Further Reduce Strategic Nuclear Weapons Delivery Vehicles:

Further reductions in the stocks of strategic nuclear weapons delivery vehicles and agreed types of weapons designed to counter such vehicles shall be carried out in accordance with the procedure outlined in Stage I.

E. To Keep the Peace:

During Stage II, states shall develop further the peace-keeping processes of the United Nations, to the end that the United Nations can effectively in Stage III deter or suppress any threat or use of force in violation of the purposes and principles of the United Nations:

(a) States shall agree upon strengthening the structure, authority, and operation of the United Nations so as to assure that the United Nations will be able effectively to protect states against threats to or breaches of the peace.

(b) The U.N. Peace Force shall be established and progressively strengthened.

(c) States shall also agree upon further improvements and developments in rules of international conduct and in processes for peaceful settlement of disputes and differences.

STAGE III

By the time Stage II has been completed, the confidence produced through a verified disarmament program, the acceptance of rules of peaceful international behavior, and the development of strengthened international peace-keeping processes within the framework of the U.N. should have reached a point where the states of the world can move forward to Stage III. In Stage III progressive controlled disarmament and continuously developing principles and procedures of international law would proceed to a point where no state would have the military power to challenge the progressively strengthened U.N. Peace Force and all international disputes would be settled according to the agreed principles of international conduct.

The progressive steps to be taken during the final phase of the disarmament program would be directed toward the attainment of a world in which:

(a) States would retain only those forces, non-nuclear armaments, and establishments required for the purpose of maintaining internal order; they would also support and provide agreed manpower for a U.N Peace Force.

(b) The U.N. Peace Force, equipped with agreed types and quantities of armaments, would be fully functioning.

(c) The manufacture of armaments would be prohibited except for those of agreed types and quantities to be used by the U.N. Peace Force and those required to maintain internal order. All other armaments would be destroyed or converted to peaceful purposes.

(d) The peace-keeping capabilities of the United Nations would be sufficiently strong and the obligations of all states under such arrangements sufficiently far-reaching as to assure peace and the just settlement of differences in a disarmed world.

U.S. GOVERNMENT PRINTING OFFICE: 1961 O 609147

If you read the document closely you see to achieve their goal we all must be disarmed, except the government and UN.

The Third Amendment:

"No Soldier shall, in time of peace be quartered in any house, without the consent of the Owner, nor in time of war, but in a manner to be prescribed by law."

The Third Amendment to the United States Constitution places restrictions on the quartering of soldiers in private homes without the owner's consent, forbidding the practice in peace time. The amendment is a response to Quartering Acts passed by the British parliament during the American Revolutionary War that allowed the British Army to lodge soldiers in private residences. Basically they would take a persons home and use it for as long as it was in their interest and loot it and many times burn it to the ground.

But today the government can easily get around the Third Amendment by declaring marshal law against an unknown terrorist which they claim they are at war with.

Fourth Amendment:

"The right of the people to be secure in their persons, houses, papers, and effects, against unreasonable searches and seizures, shall not be violated, and no Warrants shall issue, but upon probable cause, supported by Oath or affirmation, and particularly describing the place to be searched, and the persons or things to be seized."

The Fourth Amendment governing search and seizure has been shredded and is basically just words with no meaning as far as the government is concerned. It is supposed to prohibit unreasonable search and seizure and requires a warrant to be judicially sanctioned by a Judge and supported by probable cause. It was adopted in response to the abuse of the writ of assistance, a type of general search warrant issued by the British Government and a major source of tension in pre-Revolutionary America. The government of today has reintroduced the Writ of

Assistance by allowing a Judge to sign a blank warrant that law enforcers can use without contacting a judge. These warrants are a Blanket Warrant that covers everything and anything, just like the Gestapo used in Nazi Germany.

This very important Right is ignored by most of the States and the Federal Government, and of all the Amendments I think this one has been abused the most by our government. Sadly it is each and every one of our faults, because we have done nothing to stop the abuse. We allow these liars and power hungry manipulators to stay in power, even after they have proven they have no intention of representing the people that they were elected to represent or protect the Constitution... Whenever an honest person does manage to get elected and they try to do the right things that an elected official is suppose to do, they are bad mouthed in the socialist media and by every anti-constitutional and communist group infesting this Country! Even other politicians will bad mouth the honest politician if they rock the boat and upset their gravy train. Consequently it is the honest politicians who don't last long in politics, and that is the biggest shame, because the uninformed and ignorant people believe the lies and they side with the tyrants.

The Fifth Amendment:

"No person shall be held to answer for a capital, or otherwise infamous crime, unless on a presentment or indictment of a Grand Jury, except in cases arising in the land or naval forces, or in the Militia, when in actual service in time of War or public danger; nor shall any person be subject for the same offence to be twice put in jeopardy of life or limb; nor shall be compelled in any criminal case to be a witness against himself, nor be deprived of life, liberty, or property, without due process of law; nor shall private property be taken for public use, without just compensation."

The Fifth Amendment has been ignored and has been deemed as Not a Defense in court after court. This Amendment is extremely important to Freedom and people have stood aside and said nothing, allowing it to become null and void. I have seen people attempt to use their 4th and 5th Amendment Rights when being abused by Law Enforcers. These law enforcers who swore an oath to uphold the Constitution and Bill of Rights, just laugh between each other and say, Ha, he thinks he knows his Rights, we'll show him how much he knows." Then they arrest that person without just cause. The Gestapo calls this a P.O.P. charge as I stated earlier, which if you forgot means (Pissing Off Police).

Judges have totally thrown out the 5th Amendment defense in most cases and force people to talk by intimidation of contempt, jail time and fines. I have heard judges tell defendants who try and use the 5th Amendment that it doesn't apply in their case and they had to talk or they would be jailed for contempt of court. On the other hand I have also heard defense attorneys say that they have to see the same Judges in their courtroom day after day, so they have to watch what they say, even if the Judge is totally wrong and the defendant has the 5th Amendment Right on their side. The attorney does not want to piss off the judge by objecting. I have come to the realization that if you want an attorney who will not be scared of pissing off the judge, you have to go outside your local area to find one.

The Sixth Amendment:

"In all criminal prosecutions, the accused shall enjoy the right to a speedy and public trial, by an impartial jury of the State and district wherein the crime shall have been committed, which district shall have been previously ascertained by law, and to be informed of the nature and cause of the accusation; to be confronted with the witnesses against him; to have compulsory process for obtaining witnesses in his favor, and to have the Assistance of Counsel for his defense."

I don't think you have to look too far to see this Amendment has also been shredded and twisted to serve the courts and not those accused of a crime. Since the advent of the cell phone and video cameras, more and more people are video taping crimes by both citizen and law enforcers, and time and time again police seize the recording device and erase or destroy them which is directly in violation of the 1st, 4th and 5th Amendments. The Courts are also refusing to allow many of these recorded violations to be seen, especially if it shows law enforcers are the ones breaking the law with civil Rights violations.

The Seventh Amendment:

"In Suits at common law, where the value in controversy shall exceed twenty dollars, the right of trial by jury shall be preserved, and no fact tried by a jury, shall be otherwise re-examined in any Court of the United States, than according to the rules of the common law."

Once again the 7th Amendment is also ignored and maybe the most ignored by far. Anytime you see "mandatory arbitration" in any warrantee on any item you buy, or when signing up for telephone service, cable, gas and electric, or even signing to be seen by a doctor, or buying a new car, you are signing away your 7th Amendment Right, and the odds are stacked against you. Most times you have no recourse to appeal a decision and it's stated that all decisions are final.

The right to file a civil complaint in federal court has been shredded by the Supreme Court's decision on Iqbal and the Twombly cases. I have to wonder if this wasn't deliberate since it created new harder standards for filing a civil suit against a corporation, and it will no doubt get worse with the new interpretations/rewriting of the 7th Amendment each time one of the appeal courts get to it. The 7th shredding started in 1950 with a Supreme Court decision that pretty much gives governments and government contractors exemption from being sued for negligence. Trying to recover from negligence at the hands of the government or military or a government contractor with billions of dollars in government contracts probably isn't going to happen no matter how blatant the negligence was. So the Corporate Government has made sure it's protected from the people by changing the rules contrary to what the 7th Amendment of the Constitution clearly states… And once again the people are complacently apathetic about all this manipulation of the Bill of Rights.

The Eighth Amendment:

"Excessive bail shall not be required, nor excessive fines imposed, nor cruel and unusual punishments inflicted."

This Amendment is gone altogether since President Obama signed into law a bill that lets the government imprison American Citizens deemed to be a possible combatant without Bail or Trial forever if they want. On December 31, 2011, President Barack Obama signed the National Defense Authorization Act, NDAA, that was ratified in 2013 when it passed the Senate with a 98-0 vote. The authorization gave the government the ability to be able to detain American Citizens without a trial indefinitely, eliminating habeas corpus for the American people.

The Ninth Amendment:

"The enumeration in the Constitution, of certain rights, shall not be construed to deny or disparage others retained by the people."

The Ninth Amendment was supposed to give Rights you never knew you had. But it too has been ignored by the government, and since few people know about the Ninth Amendment, which reaffirms in pretty broad terms the rights "retained by the people"; Those in power have pretend that it really doesn't exist. The right to die, or what you can do to or with your own body, and the right to do whatever you want with your own property were "Unremunerated" Rights including, the right to privacy The Founding Fathers were trying to acknowledge some of the rights that no government could deny free people. But of course that didn't stop the government from denying freedom to all the people.

The Tenth Amendment:

"The powers not delegated to the United States by the Constitution, nor prohibited by it to the States, are reserved to the States respectively, or to the people."

Well of course this is another Right ignored and abused. Wikipedia sums it up: "The Tenth Amendment is similar to an earlier provision of the Articles of Confederation: "Each state retains its sovereignty, freedom, and independence, and every power, jurisdiction, and right, which is not by this Confederation expressly delegated to the United States, in Congress assembled." After the Constitution was ratified, some wanted to add a similar amendment limiting the federal government to powers "expressly" delegated, which would have denied implied powers. However, the word "expressly" ultimately did not appear in the Tenth Amendment as ratified, and therefore the Tenth Amendment did not reject the powers implied by the Necessary and Proper Clause."

When James Madison introduced the Tenth Amendment in Congress, he explained that many states were eager to ratify this amendment, despite critics who deemed the amendment superfluous or unnecessary: *"I find, from looking into the amendments proposed by the State conventions, that several are particularly anxious that it should be declared in the Constitution, that the powers not therein delegated should be reserved to the several States. Perhaps words which may define this more precisely than the whole of the instrument now does, may be considered as superfluous. I admit they may be deemed unnecessary: but there can be no harm in making such a declaration, if gentlemen will allow that the fact is as stated. I am sure I understand it so, and do therefore propose it"*- James Madison.

I think it's interesting to note that the 1st, 2nd, 4th, 5th, 6th, 8th, 9th, and 10th Amendments were originally shred by President (Honest Abe) Lincoln during the Civil War. One of the great things he is known for is freeing the black slaves, but he unwittingly then helped enslave us all, by deliberately ignoring parts of Constitution that got in his way and set the precedent for future presidents to further shred the Bill of Rights.

Honest Abe was given his name facetiously by people who really knew his two faced side, in the same way the biggest kid in school is called tiny. Honest Abe threatened anyone who invoked the Constitution during the Civil War. A classic example is the threats that were aimed at former President Franklin Pierce by the Lincoln Administration, when President Pierce denounced Lincoln for ignoring the Constitutional Rights and the people of the States. Lincoln basically told Pierce he better stop or else, meaning Lincoln would charge him with treason. But former President Pierce ignored the threats and kept on sighting the Constitution as the foundation of Freedom in the U.S.

From Lincoln on, just about every President since, has ignored parts of the Constitution that got in their way. Now the original 10 Amendments of the Constitutional Bill of Rights have little meaning or respect by our Government or the complacent and apathetic American people. It is no longer the Land of the Free and Home of the Brave. It has become the Land of the Few Free and Home of the Humble.

Chapter Four
Public Serpents & Conflict of Interest

Did you know that many of our local, state and federal public and elected officials have proposed and passed laws and regulations while in office, that benefited a business or corporation that they wind up going to work for after they leave public office? Sounds like a conflict of interest doesn't it, and most likely is, but proving it is almost impossible unless you have a paper trail that goes back far enough proving that elected official was offered a job before he or she created legislation or pushed for legislation to create a law that benefited the business they go to work for after they leave office. Yet some are so blatant that any dummy could see the collusion some of these public serpents bake up. Like this little slice for instance; From 2005 and 2009, Rapiscan spent $1,678,500 on lobbying, according to data compiled at the Center for Responsive Politics (OpenSecrets.org) for creating regulation for the TSI to install Xray-body scanners, that they manufacture. They hired former legislative aides and even the former head of DHS as consultants. Three other companies American Science & Engineering, Tek84 Engineering Group, also have Michael Chertoff, former head of the Department of Homeland Security, as a paid consultant, all are associated with Rapiscan. On January 26, 2010, Congresswoman Jane Harman a colleague of Michael Chertoff, wrote to Janet Napolitano, head of Homeland Security, noting that Rapiscan was a company in the Congresswoman's district. She urged or coerced Ms. Napolitano to "expedite installation of scanning machines in key airports." Congresswoman Harman closed with: "If you need additional funds, I am ready to help." Jane Harman represented the aerospace center of California during nine terms in Congress, and she served on all the major security committees, six years on

Armed Services, eight years on Intelligence, and eight on Homeland Security. She also accepted political contributions from Rapiscan. Of course she contends it had nothing to do with her enthusiasm to *"expedite installation of (Rapiscan) scanning machines in key airports."*

Rapiscan Systems Inc. went all out with its lobbying on Capitol Hill. It opened a Washington, D.C. office in 2006 and better than tripled their lobbying expenditures, from $130,000 in 2006 to more than $400,000 in 2008. They also hired former legislative aides to Rep. David Price, D-N.C. who was chairman of the homeland security appropriations subcommittee, and also hired aides that worked for Senator Trent Lott, R-Miss. Rapiscan contributing heavily to David Price, Bennie Thompson, D-Miss., head of the homeland security committee, and Jane Harman, D-Calif. who was also on that committee; and Sen. Thad Cochran, R-Miss., the top Republican on the Senate appropriations committee. Rapiscan also opened a North Carolina plant in David Price's district and expanded its operations in Ocean Springs, Mississippi, Bennie Thompson, Thad Cochran and Trent Lott's State, and expanded its headquarters in Torrance, Calif., in Jane Harman's district... And for all Rapiscan's enthusiasm for our politic process they won a $9.1 million dollar Department of Defense contract.

If you're thinking these are isolated cases, you are living the great American illusion, along with all the others who refuse to see the obvious.

Benjamin Franklin — *'When the people find that they can vote themselves money that will herald the end of the republic.'*

The only way we can try and stop this, is to make it unprofitable for elected officials and public employees. We need a clause put in place that stipulates they cannot work for any industry they helped by a vote or proxy for a 4 year period. This would insure enough time goes by so things would have changed in the government and in that industry they helped with their legislature. Or if they have any notion or indication that a company their vote would benefit wants to hire them after their term or employment ends, they would have to abstain from voting on or working on any legislation regarding that company or corporation. Otherwise the 4 year clause would be retro active. We have to take the profit out of this or the public serpents will continue to vote themselves money. Now I am not talking about a standing legislator or bureaucrat working on, or, proposing a bill or law that affects all business or all industry, just those laws passed that benefit one particular business or industry that they help financially, like those I have pointed out. There are States that have laws in place like the one I have proposed, but most are for a 1 year period and are vague or not well defined, and say little or nothing about Public Employees or Administrators and bureaucrats that have benefited a business or industry through their direct influence. All Public Officials should be held to the same accountability, because in many cases the public employees and bureaucrats are really the ones in charge of creating laws, licensing, fees and ordinances, by working within the system to benefit an industry or business.

Unfortunately not many politicians are held accountable for their crimes against your Rights and the Constitution. The reason being, if they were held accountable they could never again hold public office. Under existing laws any person in office convicted of Federal law regulating oath of office, which in part is to uphold the Constitution and defend it, by government officials, is divided into four parts along with an executive order which further defines the law for purposes of enforcement. 5 U.S.C. 3331, provides the text of the actual oath of office for elected members who are required to take before assuming office. 5

U.S.C. 3333 requires members to sign an affidavit that they have taken the oath of office required by 5 U.S.C. 3331 and have not or will not violate that oath of office during their tenure of office as defined by the third part of the law, 5 U.S.C. 7311 which explicitly makes it a federal criminal offense (and a violation of oath of office) for anyone employed in the United States Government (including members of Congress) to overthrow or over rule our Constitutional form of government". The fourth federal law, 18 U.S.C. 1918 provides penalties for violation of oath office described in 5 U.S.C. 7311 which include: (1) removal from office and; (2) confinement or a fine, the judicial invalidation of them upon proper findings of fact and conclusions of law, that they did indeed knowingly violate with contempt, their oath of office.

I am going to print up the states conflict of interest laws and also some of the officials that have been convicted of crimes. You can look at your State's Conflict of Interest laws and regulations. It is essential to know what your elected officials can and can't do under the existing conflict laws in your state, or any state you might do business in. Otherwise they will tell you whatever they think you will believe, legal or not! You also need to know who has already been convicted of crimes against you and the Constitution so you don't inadvertently elect them to another position, as you will see has happened with Alcee Hastings (D-Florida), a Federal District court judge that was impeached by the House and convicted by the Senate of soliciting a bribe, "corrupt conspiracy". Now you are going to be reading the general conflict laws in the States and Territories and you may want to check if the conflict laws have been amended or changed, because they do change from time to time. These are verbatim as they were written.

Here are some of our officials that were convicted of, abuse of power, conspiracy, racketeering, extortion, money laundering and other crimes.

Michael Grimm (R-NY) pleaded guilty of felony tax evasion. This was the 4th count in a 20 count indictment brought against him for improper use of campaign funds. The guilty plea has the maximum sentence of 3 years. He was sentenced to three months in prison in 2015.

Trey Radel (R-FL) was convicted of possession of cocaine in November 2013. As a first time offender, he was sentenced to one year probation and fined $250. Radel announced he would take a leave of absence, but did not resign. Later, under pressure from a number of Republican leaders, he announced through a spokesperson he would resign and did so in January of 2014. Trey Radel voted for Republican legislation that would allow states to make food stamp recipients pee in cups to prove they're not on drugs.

Rick Renzi (R-AZ) was found guilty on 17 of 32 counts against him June 12, 2013, including wire fraud, conspiracy, extortion, racketeering, money laundering and making false statements to insurance regulators. (2013)

Jesse Jackson, Jr. (D-IL) pleaded guilty February 20, 2013, to one count of wire and mail fraud in connection with his misuse of $750,000 in campaign funds. Jackson was sentenced to two and one-half years imprisonment. (2013)

Lewis Libby (R) Chief of Staff to Vice President Dick Cheney (R). 'Scooter' was convicted of perjury and obstruction of justice in the Plame Affair on March 6, 2007 and was sentenced to 30 months in prison and fined $250,000. His sentence was commuted by George W. Bush (R) on July 1, 2007.

William J. Jefferson (D-LA) was charged in August 2005 after the FBI seized $90,000 in cash from his home freezer. He was re-elected to the House in 2006, but lost in 2008. He was convicted November 13, 2009, of 11 counts of bribery and sentenced to 13 years in prison. (2009) Jefferson's Chief of Staff Brett Pfeffer, was sentenced to 84 months for bribery. (2006)

Jack Abramoff CNMI scandal involves the efforts of Abramoff to influence Congressional action concerning U.S. immigration and minimum wage laws.

Congressmen convicted in the Abramoff scandal include: **Bob Ney** (R-OH) pleaded guilty to conspiracy and making false statements as a result of his receiving trips from Abramoff in exchange for legislative favors. Ney received 30 months in prison. (2007)

Duke Cunningham (R-CA) pleaded guilty November 28, 2005, to charges of conspiracy to commit bribery, mail fraud, wire fraud and tax evasion in what came to be called the Cunningham scandal and was sentenced to over eight years in prison. (2005)

Frank Ballance (D-NC) admitted to federal charges of money laundering and mail fraud in October 2005 and was sentenced to four years in prison. (2005)

Bill Janklow (R-SD) was convicted of second-degree manslaughter for running a stop sign and killing a motorcyclist. Resigned from the House and given 100 days in the county jail and three years probation. (2003)

Jim Traficant (D-OH) was found guilty on ten felony counts of financial corruption, sentenced to eight years in prison and expelled from the House of Representatives. (2002)

Wade Sanders (D), Deputy Assistant United States Secretary of the Navy, for Reserve Affairs, was sentenced to 37 months in prison on one charge of possession of child pornography. (2009)

Mel Reynolds (D-IL) was convicted on 12 counts of sexual assault, obstruction of justice and solicitation of child pornography. (1997) He was later convicted of 12 counts of bank fraud. (1999)

Walter R. Tucker III (D-CA) was sentenced to 27 months in prison in 1996 for extortion and tax evasion. (1995)

Wes Cooley (R-OR), was convicted of having lied on the 1994 voter information pamphlet about his service in the Army. He was fined and sentenced to two years probation (1997) After leaving office, Cooley was convicted of income tax fraud connected to an investment scheme. He was sentenced to one year in prison and to pay restitution of $3.5 million to investors and $138,000 to the IRS.

Austin Murphy (D-PA) was convicted of one count of voter fraud for filling out absentee ballots for members of a nursing home. (1999)

House banking scandal. The House of Representatives Bank found that 450 members had overdrawn their checking accounts, but not been penalized. Six were convicted of charges, most only tangentially related to the House Bank itself. Twenty two more of the most prolific over-drafters were singled out by the House Ethics Committee. (1992)

Buz Lukens (R-Ohio) convicted of bribery and conspiracy.

Carl C. Perkins (D-Kentucky) pleaded guilty to a check kiting scheme involving several financial institutions (including the House Bank).

Carroll Hubbard (D-Kentucky) was convicted of illegally funneling money to his wife's 1992 campaign to succeed him in congress.

Mary Rose Oakar (D-Ohio) pleaded guilty to a misdemeanor campaign finance charge not related to the House Bank.

Walter Fauntroy (D-District of Columbia) was convicted of filing false disclosure forms to hide unauthorized income.

Congressional Post Office scandal (1991–1995) was a conspiracy to embezzle House Post Office money through stamps and postal vouchers to congressmen.

Dan Rostenkowski (D-IL) was convicted and sentenced to 18 months in prison, in 1995.

Joe Kolter (D-Pennsylvania) pleaded guilty to one count of conspiracy and sentenced to 6 months in prison.

Jay Kim (R-CA) accepted $250,000 in illegal 1992 campaign contributions and was sentenced to two months house arrest and a $5,000 fine. (1992)

Catalina Vasquez Villalpando, (R) Treasurer of the United States, pleaded guilty to obstruction of justice and tax evasion. (1992)

Nicholas Mavroules (D-Massachusetts) was convicted of extortion, accepting illegal gifts and failing to report them on congressional disclosure and income tax forms. Mavroules pleaded guilty to fifteen counts in April 1993 and was sentenced to a fifteen-month prison term. (1993)

Albert Bustamante (D-Texas) was convicted of accepting bribes and sentenced to three and one-half years in prison. (1993)

David Durenberger Senator (R-Minnesota) denounced by

Senate for unethical financial transactions and then disbarred (1990). He pleaded guilty to misuse of public funds and given one year probation (1995)

Housing and Urban Development Scandal was a controversy concerning bribery by selected contractors for low income housing projects.

James G. Watt (R) United States Secretary of the Interior 1981–1983, was charged with 25 counts of perjury and obstruction of justice. Sentenced to five years probation, fined $5,000 and 500 hours of community service.

Wedtech scandal... Wedtech Corporation was convicted of bribery in connection with Defense Department contracts.

Mario Biaggi (D-New York) sentenced to 2½ years. (1987)

Robert Garcia (D-New York) sentenced to 2½ years.

Mario Biaggi (D-New York), Convicted of obstruction of justice and accepting illegal gratuities he was sentenced to 2½ years in prison and fined $500K for his role in the Wedtech scandal. Just before expulsion from the House, he resigned. The next year he was convicted of another 15 counts of obstruction and bribery. (1988)

Iran-Contra Affair (1985–1986); A secret sale of arms to Iran, to secure the release of hostages and allow U.S. intelligence agencies to fund the Nicaraguan Contras, in violation of the Boland Amendment.

Elliott Abrams (R) Assistant Secretary of State for Inter-American Affairs, convicted of withholding evidence. Given 2 years probation. Later pardoned by President George H. W. Bush.

Michael Deaver (R) White House Deputy Chief of Staff to Ronald Reagan 1981–85, pleaded guilty to perjury related to lobbying activities and was sentenced to 3 years probation and fined $100,000

Donald E. "Buz" Lukens (R-Ohio), was convicted of two counts of bribery and conspiracy. (1996)

Abscam FBI sting involving fake 'Arabs' trying to bribe 31 congressmen.(1980) The following Congressmen were convicted:

Harrison A. Williams Senator (D-New Jersey) Convicted on 9 counts of bribery and conspiracy. Sentenced to 3 years in prison.

John Jenrette Representative (D-South Carolina) sentenced to two years in prison for bribery and conspiracy.

Richard Kelly (R-Florida) Accepted $25K and then claimed he was conducting his own investigation into corruption. Served 13 months.

Raymond Lederer (D-Pennsylvania) "I can give you me" he said after accepting $50K. Sentenced to 3 years.

Michael Myers (D-Pennsylvania) Accepted $50K saying, "...money talks and bullshit walks." Sentenced to 3 years and was expelled from the House.

Frank Thompson (D-New Jersey) Sentenced to 3 years.

John M. Murphy (D-New York) Served 20 months of a 3-year sentence.

Pat Swindall (R-Georgia) convicted of 6 counts of perjury. (1989)

George V. Hansen (R-Idaho) censured for failing to file out disclosure forms. Spent 15 months in prison.

Frederick W. Richmond (D-New York), Convicted of tax evasion and possession of marijuana. Served 9 months (1982)

Dan Flood (D-Pennsylvania) censured for bribery. After a trial ended in a deadlocked jury, pleaded guilty and was sentenced to a year's probation.

Joshua Eilberg (D-Pennsylvania) pleaded guilty to conflict-of-interest charges. In addition, he convinced President Carter to fire the U.S. Attorney investigating his case.

Fred Richmond (D-New York) – Convicted of tax fraud and possession of marijuana. Served 9 months in prison. Charges of soliciting sex from a 16-year-old boy were dropped after he submitted to counseling. (1978)

Charles Diggs (D-Michigan), convicted on 29 charges of mail fraud and filing false payroll forms which formed a kickback scheme with his staff. Sentenced to 3 years (1978)

Michael Myers (D-Pennsylvania) Received suspended six-month jail term after pleading no contest to disorderly conduct charged stemming from an incident at a Virginia bar in which he allegedly attacked a hotel security guard and a cashier.

Frank M. Clark (D-Pennsylvania) pleaded guilty to mail fraud and tax evasion on June 12, 1979 and sentenced to two years in prison.

Richard Tonry (D-Louisiana) pleaded guilty to receiving illegal campaign contributions.

James F. Hastings (R-New York), convicted of kickbacks and mail fraud, he also took money from his employees for personal use. Served 14 months at Allenwood penitentiary. (1976)

John V. Dowdy (D-Texas), Allegedly tried to stop a federal investigation of a construction firm. He served 6 months in prison for perjury. (1973)

Bertram Podell (D-New York), pleaded guilty to conspiracy and conflict of interest. He was fined $5,000 and served four months in prison. (1974)

Frank Brasco (D-New York) Sentenced to three months in jail and fined $10,000 for conspiracy to accept bribes from a reputed Mafia figure who sought truck leasing contracts from the Post Office and loans to buy trucks.

Richard T. Hanna (D-CA), convicted in an influence-buying scandal. (1974)

Watergate (1972–1973) Republican 'bugging' of the Democratic Party National Headquarters at the Watergate Hotel led to a burglary which was discovered. The cover up of the affair by President Richard Nixon (R) and his staff resulted in 69 government officials being charged and 48 pleading guilty, including 7 for actual burglary. Eventually, Nixon resigned his position.

John N. Mitchell (R) former Attorney General, convicted of perjury.

Spiro Agnew (R) Former Vice President, convicted of income-tax evasion.

Cornelius Gallagher (D-New Jersey) pleaded guilty to tax evasion, and served two years in prison.

J. Irving Whalley (R-Pennsylvania) Received suspended three-year sentence and fined $11,000 in 1973 for using mails to deposit staff salary kickbacks and threatening an employee to prevent her from giving information to the FBI.

Martin B. McKneally (R-New York) Placed on one-year probation and fined $5,000 in 1971 for failing to file income tax return. He had not paid taxes for many years prior.

James Fred Hastings (R-NY) Resigned on January 20, 1976 after being convicted of kickbacks and mail fraud. He served 14 months at Allenwood penitentiary (1976).

Ted Kennedy Senator (D-Massachusetts) drove his car into the channel between Chappaquiddick Island and Martha's Vineyard, killing passenger Mary Jo Kopechne. Kennedy pleaded guilty to leaving the scene of an accident and received a suspended sentence of two months in (1969)

Daniel Brewster (D-Maryland) Senator pleaded no contest to accepting "an unlawful gratuity without corrupt intent ".

Frank W. Boykin Congressman (D-AL) was convicted of conspiracy and conflict of interest in July 1963.

Thomas F. Johnson (D-Maryland) was convicted of conspiracy and conflict of interest regarding the receipt of illegal gratuities.

Frank Boykin (D-Alabama) Was placed on probation and fined $40,000 following conviction in a case involving a conflict of interest and conspiracy to defraud the government. He was pardoned by President Lyndon Johnson in 1965.

Thomas J. Lane (D-Massachusetts) convicted for evading taxes on his congressional income. Served 4 months in prison, but was re-elected three more times, before his 1962 defeat due to re-districting. (1956)

Ernest K. Bramblett (R-California) Received a suspended sentence and a $5,000 fine in 1955 for making false statements in connection with payroll padding and kickbacks from congressional employees.

Walter E. Brehm (R-Ohio) convicted of accepting contributions illegally from one of his employees. Received a 15-month suspended sentence and a $5,000 fine.

J. Parnell Thomas (R-New Jersey): a member of the House Committee on Un-American Activities (HUAC), was convicted of salary fraud and given an 18-month sentence and a fine, resigning from Congress in 1950. He was imprisoned in Danbury Prison with two of the Hollywood Ten he had helped put there. After serving his 18 months he was pardoned by Truman (D) in 1952,

Andrew J. May (D-Kentucky) Convicted of accepting bribes in 1947 from a war munitions manufacturer. Was sentenced to 9 months in prison, after which he was pardoned by Truman (D) in 1952.

James M. Curley (D-Massachusetts) fined $1,000 and served six-months for fraud before Harry S. Truman commuted the rest of his sentence.

John H. Hoeppel (D-CA) convicted in 1936 of selling an appointment to the West Point Military Academy. He was fined $1,000 and sentenced to 4–12 months in jail.

Harry E. Rowbottom, (R-IN) was convicted in Federal court of accepting bribes from persons who sought post office appointments. He served one year in Leavenworth.(1931)

John W. Langley (R-KY) Resigned from the US Congress in January 1926, after losing an appeal to set aside his conviction of violating the Volstead Act (Prohibition). He'd also been caught trying to bribe a Prohibition officer. He was sentenced to two years after which, his wife ran for Congress in his place and won two full terms.

The Harding administration was marred by scandals stemming from his appointment of men in his administration whom he had known in Ohio. They came to be known as the Ohio Gang. They include; **Albert Fall** (R) Secretary of the Interior who was bribed by Harry F. Sinclair for control of the Teapot Dome federal oil reserves in Wyoming. He was the first U.S. cabinet member to ever be convicted; he served two years in prison. (1922)

Henry B. Cassel (R-Pennsylvania) was convicted of fraud related to the construction of the Pennsylvania State Capitol (1909).

John Hipple Mitchell Senator (R-Oregon) was involved with the Oregon land fraud scandal, for which he was indicted and convicted while a sitting U.S. Senator. (1905)

Joseph R. Burton Senator (R-Kansas) was convicted of accepting a $2500 bribe in 1904.

Oregon US Federal District Attorney John Hicklin Hall (R) was appointed by President William McKinley. In 1903, Hall was ordered to investigate land fraud in what became known as the Oregon land fraud scandal and was put on trial for failing to prosecute land companies engaging in fraudulent activities, and for using his knowledge of illegal activities to blackmail his political opponents. On February 8, 1908, a jury found Hall guilty of the charges. (1907) He was later pardoned by President William Howard Taft.

Matthew Lyon (Democratic Republican Kentucky). First Congressman to be recommended for censure after spitting on Roger Griswold (Federalist-Connecticut). The censure failed to pass. Also found guilty of violating Alien and Sedition Acts and sentenced to four months in jail, during which he was re-elected (1798)

Federal Judges that have been convicted

Samuel B. Kent (R), Federal District Judge of the Galveston Division of the U.S. Southern District of Texas, was sentenced May 11, 2009, to 33 months in prison for having lied about sexually harassing two female employees. (2009)

Thomas Porteous (D), Federal Judge of the U.S. Eastern District of Louisiana was impeached, convicted and removed from office December 8, 2010, on charges of bribery and lying to Congress. (2010)

Senior Federal U.S. District Court Jack Camp (R) was arrested in an undercover drug bust while trying to purchase cocaine from an FBI agent. Judge Jack T. Camp resigned his position after pleading guilty to three criminal charges. He was sentenced to 30 days in jail, 400 community service hours and fined.

Robert Frederick Collins (D), Judge of the United States District Court for the Eastern District of Louisiana, was convicted of bribery and sentenced to six years, ten months.

Walter Nixon (D) Judge of the United States District Court for the Southern District of Mississippi was impeached by the House and convicted by the Senate for perjury November 3, 1989.

Alcee Hastings (D-Florida), Federal District court judge impeached by the House and convicted by the Senate of soliciting a bribe, "corrupt conspiracy" to extort a $150,000 bribe (1989). Subsequently and ironically elected to the U.S. House of Representatives in 1992 by the very people he sold out. Just goes to show how uninformed people are.

Harry Claiborne (D-Nebraska), Federal District court Judge impeached by the House and convicted by the Senate on two counts of tax evasion. He served over one year in prison.

Conflict of Interest Laws for States and U.S. Territories

Alabama: § 36-25-1

(8) Conflict of interest. A conflict on the part of a public official or public employee between his or her private interests and the official responsibilities inherent in an office of public trust. A conflict of interest involves any action, inaction, or decision by a public official or public employee in the discharge of his or her official duties which would materially affect his or her financial interest or those of his or her family members or any business with which the person is associated in a manner different from the manner it affects the other members of the class to which he or she belongs. A conflict of interest shall not include any of the following:

a. A loan or financial transaction made or conducted in the ordinary course of business.

b. An occasional non-pecuniary award publicly presented by an organization for performance of public service.

c. Payment of or reimbursement for actual and necessary expenditures for travel and subsistence for the personal attendance of a public official or public employee at a convention or other meeting at which he or she is scheduled to meaningfully participate in connection with his or her official duties and for which attendance no reimbursement is made by the state.

d. Any campaign contribution, including the purchase of tickets to, or advertisements in journals, for political or testimonial dinners, if the contribution is actually used for political purposes and is not given under circumstances from which it could reasonably be inferred that the purpose of the contribution is to substantially influence a public official in the performance of his or her official duties.

§ 36-25-5

(f) A conflict of interest shall exist when a member of a legislative body, public official, or public employee has a substantial financial interest by reason of ownership of, control of, or the exercise of power over any interest greater than five percent of the value of any corporation, company, association, or firm, partnership, proprietorship, or any other business entity of any kind or character which is uniquely affected by proposed or pending legislation; or who is an officer or director for any such corporation, company, association, or firm, partnership, proprietorship, or any other business entity of any kind or character which is uniquely affected by proposed or pending legislation.

Alaska: § 24.60.030

Prohibitions related to conflicts of interest and unethical conduct.

(a) A legislator or legislative employee may not; (1) solicit, agree to accept, or accept a benefit other than official compensation for the performance of public duties; this paragraph may not be construed to prohibit lawful solicitation for and acceptance of campaign contributions or the acceptance of a lawful gratuity under AS 24.60.080;

(2) use public funds, facilities, equipment, services, or another government asset or resource for a non-legislative purpose, for

involvement in or support of or opposition to partisan political activity, or for the private benefit of either the legislator, legislative employee, or another person; this paragraph does not prohibit

(A) limited use of state property and resources for personal purposes if the use does not interfere with the performance of public duties and either the cost or value related to the use is nominal or the legislator or legislative employee reimburses the state for the cost of the use; (B) the use of mailing lists, computer data, or other information lawfully obtained from a government agency and available to the general public for non-legislative purposes; (C) telephone or facsimile use that does not carry a special charge; (D) the legislative council, notwithstanding AS 24.05.190 , from designating a public facility for use by legislators and legislative employees for health or fitness purposes; when the council designates a facility to be used by legislators and legislative employees for health or fitness purposes, it shall adopt guidelines governing access to and use of the facility; the guidelines may establish times in which use of the facility is limited to specific groups; or (E) a legislator from using the legislator's private office in the capital city during a legislative session, and for the five days immediately before and the five days immediately after a legislative session, for non-legislative purposes if the use does not interfere with the performance of public duties and if there is no cost to the state for the use of the space and equipment, other than utility costs and minimal wear and tear, or the legislator promptly reimburses the state for the cost; an office is considered a legislator's private office under this subparagraph if it is the primary space in the capital city reserved for use by the legislator, whether or not it is shared with others;

(3) knowingly seek, accept, use, allocate, grant, or award public funds for a purpose other than that approved by law, or make a

false statement in connection with a claim, request, or application for compensation, reimbursement, or travel allowances from public funds;

(4) require a legislative employee to perform services for the private benefit of the legislator or employee at any time, or allow a legislative employee to perform services for the private benefit of a legislator or employee on government time; it is not a violation of this paragraph if the services were performed in an unusual or infrequent situation and the person's services were reasonably necessary to permit the legislator or legislative employee to perform official duties;

(5) use or authorize the use of state funds, facilities, equipment, services, or another government asset or resource for the purpose of political fund raising or campaigning; this paragraph does not prohibit

(A) limited use of state property and resources for personal purposes if the use does not interfere with the performance of public duties and either the cost or value related to the use is nominal or the legislator or legislative employee reimburses the state for the cost of the use; (B) the use of mailing lists, computer data, or other information lawfully obtained from a government agency and available to the general public for non-legislative purposes; (C) telephone or facsimile use that does not carry a special charge; (D) storing or maintaining, consistent with (b) of this section, election campaign records in a legislator's office; or (E) a legislator from using the legislator's private office in the capital city during a legislative session, and for the five days immediately before and the five days immediately after a legislative session, for non-legislative purposes if the use does not interfere with the performance of public duties and if there is no cost to the state for the use of the space and equipment, other than utility costs and minimal wear and tear, or the legislator promptly reimburses the state for the cost; an office is considered a legislator's private office under this subparagraph if it is the primary space in the capital city reserved for use by the legislator, whether or not it is shared with others.

(b) A legislative employee may not on government time assist in political party or candidate activities, campaigning, or fund raising. A legislator may not require an employee to perform an act in violation of this subsection.

(f) A legislative employee may not serve in a position that requires confirmation by the legislature. A legislator or legislative employee may serve on a board of an organization, including a governmental entity, that regularly has a substantial interest in the legislative activities of the legislator or employee if the legislator or employee discloses the board membership to the committee. A legislator or legislative employee who is required to make a disclosure under this subsection shall file the disclosure with the committee by the deadlines set out in AS 24.60.105 stating the name of each organization on whose board the person serves. The committee shall maintain a public record of the disclosure and forward the disclosure to the appropriate house for inclusion in the journal. This subsection does not require a legislator or legislative employee who is appointed to a board by the presiding officer to make a disclosure of the appointment to the committee if the appointment has been published in the appropriate legislative journal during the calendar year.

(g) Unless required by the Uniform Rules of the Alaska State Legislature, a legislator may not vote on a question if the legislator has an equity or ownership interest in a business, investment, real property, lease, or other enterprise if the interest is substantial and the effect on that interest of the action to be voted on is greater than the effect on a substantial class of persons to which the legislator belongs as a member of a profession, occupation, industry, or region.

Arizona: § 38-503

A. Any public officer or employee of a public agency who has, or whose relative has, a substantial interest in any contract, sale, purchase or service to such public agency shall make known that interest in the official records of such public agency and shall refrain from voting upon or otherwise participating in any manner as an officer or employee in such contract, sale or purchase.

B. Any public officer or employee who has, or whose relative has, a substantial interest in any decision of a public agency shall make known such interest in the official records of such public agency and shall refrain from participating in any manner as an officer or employee in such decision.

C. Notwithstanding the provisions of subsections A and B of this section, no public officer or employee of a public agency shall supply to such public agency any equipment, material, supplies or services, unless pursuant to an award or contract let after public competitive bidding, except that: 1. A school district governing board may purchase, as provided in sections 15-213 and 15-323, supplies, materials and equipment from a school board member. 2. Political subdivisions other than school districts may purchase through their governing bodies, without using public competitive bidding procedures, supplies, materials and equipment not exceeding three hundred dollars in cost in any single transaction, not to exceed a total of one thousand dollars annually, from a member of the governing body if the policy for such purchases is approved annually.

D. Notwithstanding subsections A and B of this section and as provided in sections 15-421 and 15-1441, the governing board of a school district or a community college district may not employ a person who is a member of the governing board or who is the spouse of a member of the governing board.

§ 38-502

3. "Make known" means the filing of a paper which is signed by a public officer or employee and which fully discloses a substantial interest or the filing of a copy of the official minutes of a public agency which fully discloses a substantial interest. The filing shall be in the special file established pursuant to section 38-509.

10. "Remote interest" means:

(a) That of a non-salaried officer of a nonprofit corporation.

(b) That of a landlord or tenant of the contracting party.

(c) That of an attorney of a contracting party.

(d) That of a member of a nonprofit cooperative marketing association.

(e) The ownership of less than three per cent of the shares of a corporation for profit, provided the total annual income from dividends, including the value of stock dividends, from the corporation does not exceed five per cent of the total annual income of such officer or employee and any other payments made to him by the corporation do not exceed five per cent of his total annual income.

(f) That of a public officer or employee in being reimbursed for his actual and necessary expenses incurred in the performance of official duty.

(g) That of a recipient of public services generally provided by the incorporated city or town, political subdivision or state department, commission, agency, body or board of which he is a public officer or employee, on the same terms and conditions as if he were not an officer or employee.

(h) That of a public school board member when the relative involved is not a dependent, as defined in section 43-1001, or a spouse.

(i) That of a public officer or employee, or that of a relative of a public officer or employee, unless the contract or decision involved would confer a direct economic benefit or detriment upon the officer, employee or his relative, of any of the following:

(i) Another political subdivision.

(ii) A public agency of another political subdivision.

(iii) A public agency except if it is the same governmental entity.

(j) That of a member of a trade, business, occupation, profession or class of persons consisting of at least ten members which is no greater than the interest of the other members of that trade, business, occupation, profession or class of persons.

11. "Substantial interest" means any pecuniary or proprietary interest, either direct or indirect, other than a remote interest.

House Rule 35 (E)(2) & Senate Rule 30 (E)(2)

A personal financial interest exists if it is reasonably foreseeable that an action in the discharge of his official duties will have a material financial benefit or detriment either directly or indirectly on the member, his spouse or any minor child of whom he has legal custody, except that no personal financial interest exists if the legislator or such member of his household is a member of a class of persons and it reasonably appears that a majority of the total membership of that class is to be affected by such action.

Arkansas: § 21-8-803

(a) A legislator who is required to take an action in the discharge of his or her official duties that may affect his or her financial interest or cause financial benefit or detriment to him, or a business in which he or she is an officer, director, stockholder owning more than ten percent (10%) of the stock of the company, owner, trustee, partner, or employee, which is distinguishable from the effects of the action on the public generally or a broad segment of the public, shall:

(1) Prepare a written statement describing the matter requiring action and stating the potential conflict; and (2) (A) Deliver a copy of the statement to the appropriate official to be filed with the statement of financial interest. (B) The copy of the statement may be delivered in person by the public official, by mail, or by a person authorized by the public official to deliver the copy.

(b) The obligation to report a potential conflict of interest under this section arises as soon as the legislator is aware of the conflict.(c) If the statement of financial interest filed by the legislator makes the conflict readily apparent, then no report need be filed.

California: Joint Rule 44

A person subject to this rule (recusal) has an interest that is in substantial conflict with the proper discharge of his or her duties in the public interest and of his or her responsibilities as prescribed by the laws of this state, or a personal interest, arising from any situation, within the scope of this rule, if he or she has reason to believe or expect that he or she will derive a direct monetary gain or suffer a direct monetary loss, as the case may be, by reason of his or her official activity. He or she does not have an interest that is in substantial conflict with the proper discharge of his or her duties in the public interest and of his or her responsibilities as prescribed by the laws of this state, or a personal interest, arising from any situation, within the scope of this rule, if any benefit or detriment accrues to him or her as a member of a business, profession, occupation, or group to no greater extent than any other member of the business, profession, occupation, or group....

GOVERNMENT CODE; Title 9. Political Reform; Chapter 7. Conflicts of Interest; Article

1. General Prohibition § 87100. Prohibition because of financial interest.
No public official at any level of state or local government shall make, participate in making or in any way attempt to use his official position to influence a governmental decision in which he knows or has reason to know he has a financial interest.

GOVERNMENT CODE; Title 9. Political Reform; Chapter 7. Conflicts of Interest; Article 1. General Prohibition § 87101. Exception when participation in decision required.

Section 87100 does not prevent any public official from making or participating in the making of a governmental decision to the extent his participation is legally required for the action or decision to be made. The fact that an official's vote is needed to break a tie does not make his participation legally required for purposes of this section.

GOVERNMENT CODE; Title 9. Political Reform; Chapter 7. Conflicts of Interest; Article 1.

General Prohibition § 87102.5. Application of remedies of Fair Political Practices Act.

(a) The remedies provided in Chapter 3 (commencing with Section 83100) shall apply to any Member of the Legislature who makes, participates in making, or in any way attempts to use his or her official position to influence any of the following governmental decisions in which he or she knows or has reason to know that he or she has a financial interest:

(1) Any state governmental decision, other than any action or decision before the Legislature, made in the course of his or her duties as a member.

(2) Approval, modification, or cancellation of any contract to which either house or a committee of the Legislature is a party.

(3) Introduction as a lead author of any legislation that the member knows or has reason to know is non-general legislation.

(4) Any vote in a legislative committee or subcommittee on what the member knows or has reason to know is non-general legislation.

(5) Any roll call vote on the Senate or Assembly floor on an item which the member knows is non-general legislation.

(6) Any action or decision before the Legislature in which all of the following occur:

(A) The member has received any salary, wages, commissions, or similar earned income within the preceding 12 months from a lobbyist employer.

(B) The member knows or has reason to know the action or decision will have a direct and significant financial impact on the lobbyist employer.

(C) The action or decision will not have an impact on the public generally or a significant segment of the public in a similar manner.

(7) Any action or decision before the Legislature on legislation that the member knows or has reason to know will have a direct and significant financial impact on any person, distinguishable from its impact on the public generally or a significant segment of the public, from whom the member has received any compensation within the preceding 12 months for the purpose of appearing, agreeing to appear, or taking any other action on behalf of that person, before any local board or agency.

(b) For purposes of this section, all of the following apply:

(1) "Any action or decision before the Legislature" means any vote in a committee or subcommittee, or any roll call vote on the floor of the Senate or Assembly.

(2) "Financial interest" means an interest as defined in Section 87103.

(3) "Legislation" means a bill, resolution, or constitutional amendment.

(4) "Non-general legislation" means legislation that is described in Section 87102.6 and is not of a general nature pursuant to Section 16 of Article IV of the Constitution.

(5) A Member of the Legislature has reason to know that an action or decision will have a direct and significant financial impact on a person with respect to which disqualification may be required pursuant to subdivision (a) if either of the following apply:

(A) With the knowledge of the member, the person has attempted to influence the vote of the member with respect to the action or decision.

(B) Facts have been brought to the member's personal attention indicating that the action or decision will have a direct and significant impact on the person.

(6) The prohibitions specified in subdivision (a) do not apply to a vote on the Budget Bill as a whole, or to a vote on a consent calendar, a motion for reconsideration, a waiver of any legislative rule, or any purely procedural matter.

(7) A Member of the Legislature has reason to know that legislation is non-general legislation if facts have been brought to his or her personal attention indicating that it is non-general legislation.
(8) Written advice given to a Member of the Legislature regarding his or her duties under this section by the Legislative Counsel shall have the same effect as advice given by the commission pursuant to subdivision (b) of Section 83114 if both of the following apply:

(A) The member has made the same written request based on the same material facts to the commission for advice pursuant to Section 83114 as to his or her duties under this section, as the written request and facts presented to the Legislative Counsel.

(B) The commission has not provided written advice pursuant to the member's request prior to the time the member acts in good faith reliance on the advice of the Legislative Counsel.

GOVERNMENT CODE; Title 9. Political Reform; Chapter 7. Conflicts of Interest; Article 1.

General Prohibition § 87102.6. "Non-general legislation".

(a) "Non-general legislation" means legislation as to which both of the following apply:

(1) It is reasonably foreseeable that the legislation will have direct and significant financial impact on one or more identifiable persons, or one or more identifiable pieces of real property.

(2) It is not reasonably foreseeable that the legislation will have a similar impact on the public generally or on a significant segment of the public.

(b) For purposes of this section and Section 87102.5, all of the following apply:

(1) "Legislation" means a bill, resolution, or constitutional amendment.

(2) "Public generally" includes an industry, trade, or profession.

(3) Any recognized subgroup or specialty of the industry, trade, or profession constitutes a significant segment of the public.

(4) A legislative district, county, city, or special district constitutes a significant segment of the public.

(5) More than a small number of persons or pieces of real property is a significant segment of the public.

(6) Legislation, administrative action, or other governmental action impacts in a similar manner all members of the public, or all members of a significant segment of the public, on which it has a direct financial effect, whether or not the financial effect on individual members of the public or the significant segment of the public is the same as the impact on the other members of the public or the significant segment of the public.

(7) The Budget Bill as a whole is not non-general legislation.

(8) Legislation that contains at least one provision that constitutes non-general legislation is non-general legislation, even if the legislation also contains other provisions that are

general and do not constitute non-general legislation.

GOVERNMENT CODE; Title 9. Political Reform; Chapter 7. Conflicts of Interest; Article

1. General Prohibition § 87102.8. Use of official position to influence governmental decision in which official has financial interest.

(a) No elected state officer, as defined in subdivision (f) of Section 14 of Article v. of the California Constitution, shall make or participate in the making of, or use his or her official position to influence, any governmental decision before the agency in which the elected state officer serves, where he or she knows or has reason to know that he or she has a financial interest.

(b) An elected state officer knows or has reason to know that he or she has a financial interest in any action by, or a decision before the agency in which he or she serves where either of the following occur:

(1) The action or decision will have a direct and significant financial impact on a lobbyist employer from which the officer has received any salary, wages, commissions, or similar earned income within the preceding 12 months and the action or decision will not have an impact on the public generally or a significant segment of the public in a similar manner.

(2) The action or decision will have a direct and significant financial impact on any person, distinguishable from its impact on the public generally or a significant segment of the public, from whom the officer has received any compensation within the preceding 12 months for the purpose of appearing, agreeing to appear, or taking any other action on behalf of that person, before any local board or agency.

(c) The definitions of "public generally" and "significant segment of the public" contained in Section 87102.6 shall apply to this section.

(d) Notwithstanding Section 87102, the remedies provided in Chapter 3 (commencing with Section 83100) shall apply to violations of this section.

GOVERNMENT CODE; Title 9. Political Reform; Chapter 7. Conflicts of Interest, Article 1. General Prohibition § 87103. Financial interest.

A public official has a financial interest in a decision within the meaning of Section 87100 if it is reasonably foreseeable that the decision will have a material financial effect, distinguishable from its effect on the public generally, on the official, a member of his or her immediate family, or on any of the following:

(a) Any business entity in which the public official has a direct or indirect investment worth two thousand dollars ($2,000) or more.

(b) Any real property in which the public official has a direct or indirect interest worth two thousand dollars ($2,000) or more.

(c) Any source of income, except gifts or loans by a commercial lending institution made in the regular course of business on terms available to the public without regard to official status, aggregating five hundred dollars ($500) or more in value provided or promised to, received by, the public official within 12 months prior to the time when the decision is made. (d) Any business entity in which the public official is a director, officer, partner, trustee, employee, or holds any position of management.

(e) Any donor of, or any intermediary or agent for a donor of, a gift or gifts aggregating two hundred fifty dollars ($250) or more in value provided to, received by, or promised to the public official within 12 months prior to the time when the decision is made. The amount of the value of gifts specified by this subdivision shall be adjusted biennially by the commission to equal the same amount determined by the commission pursuant to subdivision (f) of Section 89503.

For purposes of this section, indirect investment or interest means any investment or interest owned by the spouse or dependent child of a public official, by an agent on behalf of a public official, or by a business entity or trust in which the official, the official's agents, spouse, and dependent children own directly, indirectly, or beneficially a 10-percent interest or greater.

Colorado: Colo. Const. Art. 5, § 43

A member who has a personal or private interest in any measure or bill proposed or pending before the general assembly, shall disclose the fact to the house of which he is a member, and shall not vote thereon.

House Rule 21

"A member who has an immediate personal or financial interest in any bill or measure proposed or pending before the General Assembly shall disclose the fact to the House, and shall not vote upon such bill or measure."

Senate Rule 17

"Any Senator having a personal or private interest in any question or bill pending, shall disclosure such fact to the Senate and shall not vote thereon, and if the vote be by ayes or noes, such fact shall be entered in the journal."

Senate Rule 41

(b) Conflicts of interest - personal or private interests versus public interest - definition.

(1) Subject to article V, section 43, of the state constitution, a Senator has the right to vote upon all questions before the Senate and to participate in the business of the Senate and its committees, and, in so doing, is presumed to act in good faith and in the public interest. When a personal interest conflicts with the public interest and tends to affect the Senator's independence of judgment, legislative activities are subject to limitations. Where any such conflict exists, it disqualifies the Senator from voting upon any question and from attempting to influence any legislation to which it relates.

(2) A question arises as to whether a personal or private interest tends to affect a Senator's independence of judgment if the Senator:

(A) Has or acquires a substantial economic interest by reason of the Senator's personal situation, distinct from that held generally by members of the same occupation, profession, or business, in a measure proposed or pending before the General Assembly; or has a close relative or close economic associate with such an interest.

(B) Has or acquires a financial interest in an enterprise, direct or indirect, which enterprise or interest would be affected by proposed legislation differently from like enterprises.
(C) Has or acquires a close economic association with, or is a close relative of, a person who has a financial interest in an enterprise, direct or indirect, which enterprise or interest would be affected by proposed legislation differently from like enterprises.

(D) Has or acquires a close economic association with, or is a close relative of, a person who is a lobbyist or who employs or has employed a lobbyist to propose legislation or to influence proposed legislation on which the Senator has or may be expected to vote.

(E) Accepts a gift, loan, service, or economic opportunity of significant value from a person who would be affected by or who has an interest in an enterprise which would be affected by proposed legislation. This provision shall likewise apply where such gift, loan, service, or opportunity is accepted by a close relative of the Senator. It shall not normally apply in the following cases: A commercially reasonable loan made in the ordinary course of business by an institution authorized by the laws of this state to engage in the business of making loans; an occasional non-pecuniary gift, insignificant in value; a non-pecuniary award publicly presented by a nonprofit organization in recognition of public service; or payment of or reimbursement for actual and necessary expenditures for travel and subsistence for personal attendance at a convention or other meeting at which the Senator is scheduled to participate and for which attendance no reimbursement is made by the state of Colorado.

Connecticut: TITLE 1 PROVISIONS OF GENERAL APPLICATION ; CHAPTER 10 CODES OF ETHICS; PART I CODE OF ETHICS FOR PUBLIC OFFICIALS § 1-85. (Formerly Sec. 1-68). Interest in conflict with discharge of duties.

A public official, including an elected state official, or state employee has an interest which is in substantial conflict with the proper discharge of his duties or employment in the public interest and of his responsibilities as prescribed in the laws of this state, if he has reason to believe or expect that he, his spouse, a dependent child, or a business with which he is associated will derive a direct monetary gain or suffer a direct monetary loss, as the case may be, by reason of his official activity. A public official, including an elected state official, or state employee does not have an interest which is in substantial conflict with the proper discharge of his duties in the public interest and of his responsibilities as prescribed by the laws of this state, if any benefit or detriment accrues to him, his spouse, a dependent child, or a business with which he, his spouse or such dependent child is associated as a member of a profession, occupation or group to no greater extent than any other member of such profession, occupation or group. A public official, including an elected state official or state employee who has a substantial conflict may not take official action on the matter.

Delaware: TITLE 29. STATE GOVERNMENT; PART II. THE GENERAL ASSEMBLY; CHAPTER 10. LEGISLATIVE CONFLICTS OF INTEREST § 1002. Restrictions relating to personal or private interest.

(a) A legislator who has a personal or private interest in any measure or bill pending in the General Assembly shall disclose the fact to the House of which he or she is a member and shall not participate in the debate nor vote thereon; provided, that upon the request of any other member of the House or Senate, as the case may be, a legislator who has such a personal or private interest may nevertheless respond to questions concerning any such measure or bill. A personal or private interest in a measure or bill is an interest which tends to impair a legislator's independence of judgment in the performance of his or her legislative duties with respect to that measure or bill.

(b) A legislator has an interest which tends to impair his or her independence of judgment in the performance of his or her legislative duties with regard to any bill or measure when:

(1) The enactment or defeat of the measure or bill would result in a financial benefit or detriment to accrue to the legislator or a close relative to a greater extent than such benefit or detriment would accrue to others who are members of the same class or group of persons; or;

(2) The legislator or a close relative has a financial interest in a private enterprise which enterprise or interest would be affected by a measure or bill to a lesser or greater extent than like enterprises or other interests in the same enterprise; or;

(3) A person required to register as a legislative agent pursuant to Chapter 16 of this title is a close relative of the legislator and that person acts to promote, advocate, influence or oppose the measure or bill.

(c) Disclosure required under subsection (a) of this section shall be made in open session:

(1) Prior to the vote on the measure or bill by any committee of which the legislator is a member; and;

(2) Prior to the vote on the measure or bill in the House of which the legislator is a member.

(d) A legislator who violates the provisions of this section shall be subject to such sanction as shall be prescribed by the House of which he or she is a member pursuant to rules adopted under article II, § 9 of the Delaware Constitution.

District of Columbia: TITLE 1. GOVERNMENT ORGANIZATION; CHAPTER 11. ELECTION CAMPAIGNS; LOBBYING; CONFLICT OF INTEREST; SUBCHAPTER I. GENERAL PROVISIONS; PART F. CONFLICT OF INTEREST AND DISCLOSURE

§ 1-1106.01. Conflict of interest [Formerly § 1-1461].

(a) The Congress declares that elective and public office is a public trust, and any effort to realize personal gain through official conduct is a violation of that trust.

(b) No public official shall use his or her official position or office to obtain financial gain for himself or herself, any member of his or her household, or any business with which he or she or a member of his or her household is associated, other than that compensation provided by law for said public official. This subsection shall not affect a vote by a public official: (1) On any matter which affects a class of persons (such a class shall include no less than 50 persons) of which such public official is a member if the financial gain to be realized is de minimis; (2) on any matter relating to such public official's compensation as authorized by law; or (3) regarding any elections law. If an action is taken by any department, agency, board, or commission of the District of Columbia, except by the Council of the District of Columbia, in violation of this section, such action may be set aside and declared void and of no effect, upon a proper order of a court of competent jurisdiction.

(c) No person shall offer or give to a public official or a member of a public official's household, and no public official shall solicit or receive anything of value, including a gift, favor, service, loan gratuity, discount, hospitality, political contribution, or promise of future employment, based on any understanding that such public official's official actions or judgment or vote would be influenced thereby, or where it could reasonably be inferred that the thing of value would influence the public official in the discharge of his or her duties, or as a reward, except for political contributions publicly reported pursuant to § 1-1102.06 and transactions made in the ordinary course of business of the person offering or giving the thing of value.

(d) No person shall offer or pay to a public official, and no public official shall solicit or receive any money, in addition to that lawfully received by the public official in his or her official capacity, for advice or assistance given in the course of the public official's employment or relating to his or her employment.

(e) No public official shall use or disclose confidential information given in the course of or by reason of his or her official position or activities in any way that could result in financial gain for himself or herself or for any other person.

(f) No member or employee of the Council of the District of Columbia or Board of Education of the District of Columbia shall accept assignment to serve on a committee the jurisdiction of which consists of matters (other than of a de minimis nature) in which he or she or a member of his or her family or a business with which he or she is associated, has financial interest.

(g) Any public official who, in the discharge of his or her official duties, would be required to take an action or make a decision that would affect directly or indirectly his or her financial interests or those of a member of his or her household, or a business with which he or she is associated, or must take an official action on a matter as to which he or she has a conflict situation created by a personal, family, or client interest, shall:

(1) Prepare a written statement describing the matter requiring action or decision, and the nature of his or her potential conflict of interest with respect to such action or decision;

(2) Cause copies of such statement to be delivered to the District of Columbia Board of Elections and Ethics (referred to in this subchapter as the "Board"), and to his or her immediate superior,

if any;

(3) If he or she is a member of the Council of the District of Columbia or member of the Board of Education of the District of Columbia, or employee of either, deliver a copy of such statement to the Chairman thereof, who shall cause such statement to be printed in the record of proceedings, and, upon request of said member or employee, shall excuse the member from votes, deliberations, and other action on the matter on which a potential conflict exists;

(4) If he or she is not the Mayor or a member of the Council of the District of Columbia, his or her superior, if any, shall assign the matter to another employee who does not have a potential conflict of interest, or, if he or she has no immediate superior, except the Mayor, he or she shall take such steps as the Board prescribes through rules and regulations to remove himself or herself from influence over actions and decisions on the matter on which potential conflict exists; and;

(5) During a period when a charge of conflict of interest is under investigation by the Board, if he or she is not the Mayor or a member of the Council of the District of Columbia or a member of the Board of Education, his or her superior, except the Mayor, if any, shall have the arbitrary power to assign the matter to another employee who does not have a potential conflict of interest, or if he or she has no immediate superior, he or she shall take such steps as the Board shall prescribe through rules and regulations to remove himself or herself from influence over actions and decisions on the matter on which there is a conflict of interest.

(h) Neither the Mayor nor any member of the Council of the District of Columbia may represent another person before any regulatory agency or court of the District of Columbia while serving in such office. The preceding sentence does not apply to an appearance by such an official before any such agency or court in his or her official capacity or to the appearance by a member of the Council (not the Chairman) licensed to practice law in the District of Columbia, before any court or non-District of Columbia regulatory agency in any matter which does not affect his or her official position.

(h-1)

(1) No member of a board or commission shall be eligible for appointment by the members of that board or commission to any paid office or position under the supervision of that board or commission.

(2) No former member of a board or commission shall be eligible for appointment to any paid office or position under the supervision of the board or commission on which he or she served, unless;

(A) At least 45 days have passed since the date of termination of his or her service as a member of the board or commission; and;

(B) He or she has followed the same employment application requirements required of other applicants for the paid office or position.

(i) As used in this section, the term:

(1) "Public official" means any person required to file a financial statement under § 1-1106.02.

(2) "Business" means any corporation, partnership, sole proprietorship, firm, enterprise, franchise, association, organization, self-employed individual, holding company, joint stock, trust, and any legal entity through which business is conducted for profit.

(3) "Business with which he or she is associated" means any business of which the person or member of his or her household is a director, officer, owner, employee, or holder of stock worth $ 1,000 or more at fair market value, and any business which is a client of that person.

(4) "Household" means the public official and his or her immediate family.

(5) "Immediate family" means the public official's spouse and any parent, brother, or sister, or child of the public official, and the spouse of any such parent, brother, sister, or child.

Florida: § 112.3143. Voting conflicts...

(2) No state public officer is prohibited from voting in an official capacity on any matter. However, any state public officer voting in an official capacity upon any measure which would inure to the officer's special private gain or loss; which he or she knows would inure to the special private gain or loss of any principal by whom the officer is retained or to the parent organization or subsidiary of a corporate principal by which the officer is retained; or which the officer knows would inure to the special private gain or loss of a relative or business associate of the public officer shall, within 15 days after the vote occurs, disclose the nature of his or her interest as a public record in a memorandum filed with the person responsible for recording the minutes of the meeting, who shall incorporate the memorandum in the minutes.

§ 112.312. Definitions....

(8) Conflict or conflict of interest means a situation in which regard for a private interest tends to lead to disregard of a public duty or interest.

Georgia: § **45-10-3**. Code of ethics for members of boards, commissions, and authorities -- Establishment and text.

Notwithstanding any provisions of law to the contrary, each member of all boards, commissions, and authorities created by general statute shall:

(9) Never take any official action with regard to any matter under circumstances in which he knows or should know that he has a direct or indirect monetary interest in the subject matter of such matter or in the outcome of such official action.

§ 45-10-90. Definitions. As used in this part, the term:

(1) "Abuse of official power" means threatening to use the powers or personnel of a state entity for personal purposes of coercion, retaliation, or punishment.

(4) "Conflict of interest" means an individual has multiple interests and uses his or her official position to exploit, in some way, his or her position for his or her own direct, unique, pecuniary, and personal benefit.

(6) "Improper conduct" means a member of the General Assembly:

   (A) Engages in conduct that is a conflict of interest;
   (B) Engages in conduct that is an abuse of official power; or

   (C) Illegally uses an employee in a political campaign.

House Rule 133

Members are expected to abstain from voting if they are "immediately and particularly interested."

Senate Rule 1-4.1

(d) No Senator shall vote upon any question if the Senator or any member of the Senator's immediate family has a direct pecuniary interest in the result of such vote which interest is distinct, unique or peculiar to the Senator or the Senator's immediate family.

Senate Rule 1-4.3

(a) Senators and staff shall avoid financial conflicts of interest and close economic associations where official action or decisions are motivated not by public duty but by economic self-interest or association. "Financial conflicts of interest and close economic associations" are defined as those financial interests or interests arising from close economic associations with other persons or entities which are so material, direct, distinct, unique, and peculiar to the Senator or staff that it might reasonably be expected that impartial official judgment could not be exercised.

Guam: TITLE 4. PUBLIC OFFICERS AND EMPLOYEES; CHAPTER 15. STANDARD OF CONDUCT FOR ELECTED OFFICERS, APPOINTED OFFICERS, AND PUBLIC EMPLOYEES OF THE GOVERNMENT OF GUAM; ARTICLE 2. SPECIFIED STANDARDS

§ 15205. Conflicts of Interest.

(a) No employee shall take any official action directly affecting:

(1) business or other undertaking in which the employee has a financial interest; or
(2) private undertaking in which the employee is engaged as legal counsel, advisor, consultant, representative, or other agency capacity. A department head who is unable to be disqualified on any matter described in item (1) or (2) of this Subsection may be in violation of this Subsection even if the individual has complied with the disclosure requirements of § 15208; and a

person whose position on a board, commission or committee is mandated by statute, resolution or executive order to have particular qualifications shall only be prohibited from taking official action that directly and specifically affects a business or undertaking in which such person has a financial interest; provided that the financial interest is related to the member's particular qualifications.

(b) No employee shall acquire financial interests in any business or other undertaking which the employee has reason to believe may be directly involved in official action to be taken by the employee.

(c) No employee shall assist any person or business or act in a representative capacity before any territorial agency for any compensation in any transaction involving the Territory.

(d) No employee shall assist any person or business or act in a representative capacity for a fee or other compensation to secure passage of a bill or to obtain a contract, claim, or other transaction or proposal in which the employee has participated or will participate as an employee, nor shall the employee assist any person, or business, or act in a representative capacity for a fee or other compensation on such bill, contract, claim, or other transaction or proposal before the Legislature or territorial agency of which the individual is an employee.

(e) No employee shall assist any person or business or act in a representative capacity before a territorial agency for a fee or other compensation, on any bill, contract, claim, or other transaction or proposal involving official action by the agency if the employee has official authority over that agency unless such employee has complied with the disclosure requirements of § 15208.

(f) Nothing herein shall preclude an employee from having

outside business interests or employment so long as such interests or employment do not interfere with performance of official duties and is not otherwise in direct conflict with this Chapter.

Hawaii: § 84-14. Conflicts of interests.

(a) No employee shall take any official action directly affecting:

(1) A business or other undertaking in which he has a substantial financial interest; or(2) A private undertaking in which he is engaged as legal counsel, advisor, consultant, representative, or other agency capacity. A department head who is unable to disqualify himself on any matter described in items (1) and (2) above will not be in violation of this subsection if he has complied with the disclosure requirements of section 84-17; and a person whose position on a board, commission, or committee is mandated by statute, resolution, or executive order to have particular qualifications shall only be prohibited from taking official action that directly and specifically affects a business or undertaking in which he has a substantial financial interest; provided that the substantial financial interest is related to the member's particular qualifications.

(b) No employee shall acquire financial interests in any business or other undertaking which he has reason to believe may be directly involved in official action to be taken by him.

(c) No legislator or employee shall assist any person or business or act in a representative capacity before any State or county agency for a contingent compensation in any transaction involving the State.

(d) No legislator or employee shall assist any person or business or act in a representative capacity for a fee or other compensation to secure passage of a bill or to obtain a contract, claim, or other transaction or proposal in which he has participated or will participate as a legislator or employee, nor shall he assist any person or business or act in a representative capacity for a fee or other compensation on such bill, contract, claim, or other transaction or proposal before the legislature or agency of which he is an employee or legislator.

(e) No employee shall assist any person or business or act in a representative capacity before a state or county agency for a fee or other consideration on any bill, contract, claim, or other transaction or proposal involving official action by the agency if he has official authority over that state or county agency unless he has complied with the disclosure requirements of section 84-17.

Idaho: § 59-703. Definitions.

(4) "Conflict of interest" means any official action or any decision or recommendation by a person acting in a capacity as a public official, the effect of which would be to the private pecuniary benefit of the person or a member of the person's household, or a business with which the person or a member of the person's household is associated, unless the pecuniary benefit arises out of the following:

(a) An interest or membership in a particular business, industry, occupation or class required by law as a prerequisite to the holding by the person of the office or position;

(b) Any action in the person's official capacity which would affect to the same degree a class consisting of an industry or occupation group in which the person, or a member of the person's household or business with which the person is associated, is a member or is engaged;

(c) Any interest which the person has by virtue of his profession, trade or occupation where his interest would be affected to the same degree as that of a substantial group or class of others similarly engaged in the profession, trade or occupation;

(d) Any action by a public official upon any revenue measure, any appropriation measure or any measure imposing a tax, when similarly situated members of the general public are affected by the outcome of the action in a substantially similar manner and degree.

5) "Economic gain" means increase in pecuniary value from sources other than lawful compensation as a public official.

§ 59-704. Required action in conflicts.

A public official shall not take any official action or make a formal decision or formal recommendation concerning any matter where he has a conflict of interest and has failed to disclose such conflict as provided in this section. Disclosure of a conflict does not affect an elected public official's authority to be counted for purposes of determining a quorum and to debate and to vote on the matter, unless the public official requests to be excused from debate and voting at his or her discretion. In order to determine whether a conflict of interest exists relative to any matter within the scope of the official functions of a public official, a public official may seek legal advice from the attorney representing that governmental entity or from the attorney general or from independent counsel. If the legal advice is that no real or potential conflict of interest exists, the public official may proceed and shall not be subject to the prohibitions of this chapter. If the legal advice is that a real or potential conflict may exist, the public official:

(1) If he is an elected legislative public official, he shall disclose the nature of the potential conflict of interest and/or be subject to the rules of the body of which he/she is a member and shall take

all action required under such rules prior to acting on the matter. If a member requests to be excused from voting on an issue which involves a conflict or a potential conflict, and the body of which he is a member does not excuse him, such failure to excuse shall exempt that member from any civil or criminal liability related to that particular issue.

(2) If he is an elected state public official, he shall prepare a written statement describing the matter required to be acted upon and the nature of the potential conflict, and shall file such statement with the secretary of state prior to acting on the matter. A public official may seek legal advice from the attorney representing that agency or from the attorney general or from independent counsel. The elected public official may then act on the advice of the agency's attorney, the attorney general or independent counsel.

(3) If he is an appointed or employed state public official, he shall prepare a written statement describing the matter to be acted upon and the nature of the potential conflict, and shall deliver the statement to his appointing authority. The appointing authority may obtain an advisory opinion from the attorney general or from the attorney representing that agency. The public official may then act on the advice of the attorney general, the agency's attorney or independent counsel.

(4) If he is an elected public official of a county or municipality, he shall disclose the nature of a potential conflict of interest prior to acting on a matter and shall be subject to the rules of the body of which he/she is a member and take all action required by the rules prior to acting on the matter. If a member requests to be excused from voting on an issue which involves a conflict or a potential conflict, and the body of which he is a member does not excuse him, such failure to excuse shall exempt that member from any civil or criminal liability related to that particular issue.

The public official may obtain an advisory opinion from the attorney general or the attorney for the county or municipality or from independent counsel. The public official may then act on the advice of the attorney general or attorney for the county or municipality or his independent counsel.

(5) If he is an appointed or employed public official of a county or municipality, he shall prepare a written statement describing the matter required to be acted upon and the nature of the potential conflict, and shall deliver the statement to his appointing authority. The appointing authority may obtain an advisory opinion from the attorney for the appointing authority, or, if none, the attorney general. The public official may then act on the advice of the attorney general or attorney for the appointing authority or independent counsel.

(6) Nothing contained herein shall preclude the executive branch of state government or a political subdivision from establishing an ethics board or commission to perform the duties and responsibilities provided for in this chapter. Any ethics board or commission so established shall have specifically stated powers and duties including the power to:

(a) Issue advisory opinions upon the request of a public official within its jurisdiction;

(b) Investigate possible unethical conduct of public officials within its jurisdiction and conduct hearings, issue findings, and make recommendations for disciplinary action to a public official's appointing authority;

(c) Accept complaints of unethical conduct from the public and take appropriate action.

Illinois: § 5 ILCS 420/3-202. [Conflict situations; abstention]

When a legislator must take official action on a legislative matter as to which he has a conflict situation created by a personal, family, or client legislative interest, he should consider the possibility of eliminating the interest creating the conflict situation. If that is not feasible, he should consider the possibility of abstaining from such official action. In making his decision as to abstention, the following factors should be considered;

a. whether a substantial threat to his independence of judgment has been created by the conflict situation;

b. the effect of his participation on public confidence in the integrity of the legislature;

c. whether his participation is likely to have any significant effect on the disposition of the matter;

d. the need for his particular contribution, such as special knowledge of the subject matter, to the effective functioning of the legislature.

He need not abstain if he decides to participate in a manner contrary to the economic interest which creates the conflict situation.

If he does abstain, he should disclose that fact to his respective legislative body.

§ 5 ILCS 420/3-203. [Public interest to prevail]

When, despite the existence of a conflict situation, a legislator chooses to take official action on a matter, he should serve the public interest, and not the interest of any person.

Indiana: § 35-44-1-3. Conflicts of interest -- Public servants.

(a) A public servant who knowingly or intentionally:

(1) has a pecuniary interest in; or

(2) derives a profit from;

a contract or purchase connected with an action by the governmental entity served by the public servant commits conflict of interest, a Class D felony.

(b) This section does not prohibit a public servant from receiving compensation for:

(1) services provided as a public servant; or

(2) expenses incurred by the public servant as provided by law.

(c) This section does not prohibit a public servant from having a pecuniary interest in or deriving a profit from a contract or purchase connected with the governmental entity served under any of the following conditions:

(1) If the:

(A) public servant is not a member or on the staff of the governing body empowered to contract or purchase on behalf of the governmental entity; (B) functions and duties performed by the public servant for the governmental entity are unrelated to the contract or purchase; and (C) public servant makes a disclosure under subsection (d)(1) through (d)(6).

(2) If the contract or purchase involves utility services from a utility whose rate structure is regulated by the state or federal government.

(3) If the public servant:

(A) is an elected public servant or a member of the board of trustees of a state supported college or university; and (B) makes a disclosure under subsection (d)(1) through (d)(6).

(4) If the public servant:

(A) was appointed by an elected public servant or the board of trustees of a state supported college or university; and (B) makes a disclosure under subsection (d)(1) through (d)(7).

(5) If the public servant:

(A) acts in only an advisory capacity for a state supported college or university; and (B) does not have authority to act on behalf of the college or university in a matter involving a contract or purchase.

(6) If the public servant:

(A) is employed by the governing body of a school corporation and the contract or purchase involves the employment of a dependent or the payment of fees to a dependent; and (B) makes a disclosure under subsection (d)(1) through (d)(6).

(7) If the public servant is under the jurisdiction of the state ethics commission as provided in IC 4-2-6-2.5 and obtains from the state ethics commission, following full and truthful disclosure, written approval that the public servant will not or does not have a conflict of interest in connection with the contract or purchase under IC 4-2-6 and this section. The approval required under this subdivision must be:

(A) granted to the public servant before action is taken in connection with the contract or purchase by the governmental entity served; or (B) sought by the public servant as soon after the contract or purchase as the public servant becomes aware of the facts that give rise to a question of conflict of interest.

(d) A disclosure required by this section must:

(1) be in writing;

(2) describe the contract or purchase to be made by the governmental entity;

(3) describe the pecuniary interest that the public servant has in the contract or purchase;

(4) be affirmed under penalty of perjury;

(5) be submitted to the governmental entity and be accepted by the governmental entity in a public meeting of the governmental entity prior to final action on the contract or purchase;

(6) be filed within fifteen (15) days after final action on the contract or purchase with:

(A) the state board of accounts; and (B) if the governmental entity is a governmental entity other than the state or a state supported college or university, the clerk of the circuit court in the county where the governmental entity takes final action on the contract or purchase; and

(7) contain, if the public servant is appointed, the written approval of the elected public servant (if any) or the board of trustees of a state supported college or university (if any) that appointed the public servant.

(e) The state board of accounts shall forward to the state ethics commission a copy of all disclosures filed with the board under IC 16-22-2 through IC 16-22-5, IC 16-23-1, or this section.

(f) The state ethics commission shall maintain an index of all disclosures received by the commission. The index must contain a listing of each public servant, setting forth the disclosures received by the commission made by that public servant.

(g) A public servant has a pecuniary interest in a contract or purchase if the contract or purchase will result or is intended to result in an ascertainable increase in the income or net worth of:

(1) the public servant; or

(2) a dependent of the public servant who:

(A) is under the direct or indirect administrative control of the public servant; or (B) receives a contract or purchase order that is reviewed, approved, or directly or indirectly administered by the public servant.

(h) It is a defense in a prosecution under this section that the public servant's interest in the contract or purchase and all other contracts and purchases made by the governmental entity during the twelve (12) months before the date of the contract or purchase was two hundred fifty dollars ($250) or less.

(i) Notwithstanding subsection (d), a member of the board of trustees of a state supported college or university, or a person appointed by such a board of trustees, complies with the disclosure requirements of this chapter with respect to the member's or person's pecuniary interest in a particular type of contract or purchase which is made on a regular basis from a particular vendor if the member or person files with the state board of accounts and the board of trustees a statement of pecuniary interest in that particular type of contract or purchase made with that particular vendor. The statement required by this subsection must be made on an annual basis.

(j) This section does not apply to members of the governing board of a hospital organized or operated under IC 16-22-1 through IC 16-22-5 or IC 16-23-1.

(k) As used in this section, "dependent" means any of the following:

(1) The spouse of a public servant.

(2) A child, stepchild, or adoptee (as defined in IC 31-9-2-2) of a public servant who is:

(A) un-emancipated; and (B) less than eighteen (18) years of age.

(3) Any individual more than one-half (1/2) of whose support is provided during a year by the public servant.

Senate Rules 87-96

VII. ETHICS.

87. It is declared that high moral and ethical standards among State Senators are essential to the conduct of free government; that the Senate believes that a code of ethics for the guidance of State Senators will help them avoid conflicts of interest in public office, will improve standards of public service, and will promote and strengthen the faith and confidence of the people of Indiana. The code is intended to protect the individual Senators while providing guidelines for all members of the Senate. Recognizing that service in the Indiana General Assembly is a part-time endeavor and that members of the General Assembly are individuals who are active in the affairs of their localities and elsewhere and that it is necessary that they maintain a livelihood and source of income apart from their legislative compensation, the following guidelines are adopted to assist the members in the conduct of their legislative duties.

88. A Senator who is offered;

(1) an economic or investment opportunity; or

(2) a loan, gratuity, discount, favor, hospitality, or other goods or services; by a person, shall consider, in determining whether or not to accept the offer, whether the Senator's acceptance of the offer may affect the Senator's independent legislative judgment. In so considering, the Senator shall take into account the following:

(A) whether the opportunity is being offered with the intent to influence the Senator's conduct in the performance of legislative duties; or (B) whether acceptance of the offer would have a unique, direct, and material effect on the non-legislative income of the Senator, a member of the Senator's immediate family or those of a partnership, corporation or business in which the Senator holds a legal or equitable interest. Should the Senator determine that, by acceptance of the offer, the Senator's independent legislative judgment may be affected, the Senator shall refuse the offer.

89. A Senator who has a direct personal or pecuniary interest in a piece of legislation which is so substantial as to affect the Senator's independent legislative judgment is not precluded from participating in committee and floor debate on the legislation, if the Senator publicly proclaims that interest.

90. During the course of a legislative session, a Senator may be placed in a position where the Senator has the obligation to vote on legislation in which the Senator has a direct personal or pecuniary interest. In making this decision pursuant to Rule 4 of the Standing Rules of the Senate and Orders for Government relative to the Senator's activity on the legislation, the Senator shall consider the following:

(1) Whether the Senator's interest in the legislation is so substantial as to affect the Senator's independence of judgment with respect to the legislation.(2) To what extent the Senator's

interest in the legislation mirrors the interest of the citizenry to which the Senator is directly responsible.(3) The effect of the Senator's participation in the voting on the legislation on public confidence in the integrity of the legislature.(4) The need of the Senator's particular contribution, such as special knowledge of the subject matter, to the effective functioning of the legislature.(5) Whether the legislation would have a unique, direct, and material effect on the non-legislative income of the Senator, a member of the Senator's immediate family or those of a partnership, corporation, or business in which the Senator holds a legal or equitable interest.

91. A Senator may request the assistance of the Senate Legislative Ethics Committee (established pursuant to IC 2-2.1-3-5) in determining the propriety of the Senator's:

(1) proposed acceptance of an offer;

(2) participation in upcoming debate; or

(3) participation in an upcoming vote.

92. Under Rule 91, the Senator shall:

(1) Prepare a written statement describing the matter requiring action or decision by the Senator and the nature of the Senator's potential conflict of interest; and

(2) Deliver a copy of the statement to the Chairman of the Senate Legislative Ethics Committee. If the Chairman is unavailable, a copy of the statement may be delivered to the President Pro Tempore.

93. If a Senator requests the assistance of the Senate Legislative Ethics Committee under Rule 91, and there is insufficient time to comply with Rule 92, the Senator shall orally inform the Chairman of the Senate Legislative Ethics Committee of the

potential conflict. The matter shall then be immediately referred to the Legislative Ethics Committee for its recommendation. The Committee shall issue an oral recommendation to the Senator making the request as soon as possible after considering the request. The Committee shall follow the oral recommendation with a written report as required by Senate Rule 95.

94. The Legislative Ethics Committee shall meet as soon as possible and render an advisory opinion on the question raised. Should the committee vote result in a tie, the effect will be to make no recommendation.

95. The written report of the Legislative Ethics Committee shall be forwarded to the President Pro Tempore of the Senate and the Senate Minority Leader. Copies of the report and the written statement of the Senator making the request shall be maintained in the offices of the Majority Attorney and the Minority Attorney. The committee's written report and the written statement of the Senator making the request under Rule 92 shall remain confidential unless the Senator making the request consents to their disclosure.

96. In addition to any meetings held under Rule 94, the Senate Legislative Ethics Committee shall meet and may recommend amendments to the code of ethics for the Senate not later than thirty (30) days after the first session day of each legislative session, pursuant to IC 2-2.1-3-6.

House Code of Ethics

Every member of the House of Representatives shall, to the best of his or her ability, be fully objective when considering a proposition upon which he or she must act, keeping the welfare of all of the citizens of the state in mind at all times.

No member of the House of Representatives shall sponsor or cast a vote on any legislative matter, except budget or general revenue bills, that might reasonably be expected to directly result in a substantial increase of his or her non-legislative income. Any member of the House of Representatives not voting for this reason shall be considered present for the purpose of determining a quorum. If a significant number of members are so affected, the House of Representatives or a committee thereof, as the case may be, may, by a vote of two-thirds of those voting, permit such members to vote.

Every member shall give freely of his or her particular expertise during a discussion or debate upon a given proposition; in doing so the member shall, insofar as it is possible, present the positions of all sides of the proposition.

Iowa: § 68B.2A Conflicts of interest -- outside employment and activities.

1. Any person who serves or is employed by the state or a political subdivision of the state shall not engage in any outside employment or activity which is in conflict with the person's official duties and responsibilities. In determining whether particular outside employment or activity creates an unacceptable conflict of interest, situations in which an unacceptable conflict shall be deemed to exist shall include, but not to be limited to, any of the following:

a. The outside employment or activity involves the use of the state's or the political subdivision's time, facilities, equipment, and supplies or the use of the state or political subdivision badge, uniform, business card, or other evidences of office or employment to give the person or member of the person's immediate family an advantage or pecuniary benefit that is not available to other similarly situated members or classes of members of the general public. This paragraph does not apply to off-duty peace officers who provide private duty security or fire fighters or emergency medical care providers certified under chapter 147A who provide private duty fire safety or emergency medical services while carrying their badge or wearing their official uniform, provided that the person has secured the prior approval of the agency or political subdivision in which the person is regularly employed to engage in the activity. For purposes of this subsection, a person is not "similarly situated" merely by being or being related to a person who serves or is employed by the state or a political subdivision of the state.

b. The outside employment or activity involves the receipt of, promise of, or acceptance of money or other consideration by the person, or a member of the person's immediate family, from anyone other than the state or the political subdivision for the performance of any act that the person would be required or expected to perform as a part of the person's regular duties or during the hours during which the person performs service or work for the state or political subdivision of the state.

c. The outside employment or activity is subject to the official control, inspection, review, audit, or enforcement authority of the person, during the performance of the person's duties of office or employment.

2. If the outside employment or activity is employment or activity described in subsection 1, paragraph "a" or "b", the person shall immediately cease the employment or activity. If the outside employment or activity is employment or activity described in subsection 1, paragraph "c", or constitutes any other unacceptable conflict of interest, unless otherwise provided by law, the person shall take one of the following courses of action:

a. Cease the outside employment or activity.

b. Publicly disclose the existence of the conflict and refrain from taking any official action or performing any official duty that would detrimentally affect or create a benefit for the outside employment or activity. For purposes of this paragraph, "official action" or "official duty" includes, but is not limited to, participating in any vote, taking affirmative action to influence any vote, granting any license or permit, determining the facts or law in a contested case or rulemaking proceeding, conducting any inspection, or providing any other official service or thing that is not available generally to members of the public in order to further the interests of the outside employment or activity.

3. Unless otherwise specifically provided the requirements of this section shall be in addition to, and shall not supersede, any other rights or remedies provided by law.

Kansas: § 46-229. "Substantial interest" and "client or customer" defined.

"Substantial interest" means any of the following:

(a) If an individual or an individual's spouse, either individually or collectively, has owned within the preceding 12 months a legal or equitable interest exceeding $ 5,000 or 5% of any business, whichever is less, the individual has a substantial interest in that business.

(b) If an individual or an individual's spouse, either individually or collectively, has received during the preceding calendar year compensation which is or will be required to be included as taxable income on federal income tax returns of the individual and spouse in an aggregate amount of $ 2,000 from any business or combination of businesses, the individual has a substantial interest in that business or combination of businesses.

(c) If an individual or an individual's spouse, either individually or collectively, has received directly or indirectly in the preceding 12 months, gifts or honoraria having an aggregate value of $ 500 or more from any person, the individual has a substantial interest in that person. If a gift is received for which the value is unknown, the individual shall be deemed to have a substantial interest in the donor. A substantial interest does not exist under this subsection by reason of: (1) A gift or bequest received as the result of the death of the donor; (2) a gift from a spouse, parent, grandparent, sibling, aunt or uncle; or (3) acting as a trustee of a trust for the benefit of another.

(d) If an individual or an individual's spouse holds the position of officer, director, associate, partner or proprietor of any business, the individual has a substantial interest in that business, irrespective of the amount of compensation received by the individual or individual's spouse.

(e) If an individual or an individual's spouse receives compensation which is a portion or percentage of each separate fee or commission paid to a business or combination of businesses, the individual has a substantial interest in any client or customer who pays fees or commissions to the business or combination of businesses from which fees or commissions the individual or the individual's spouse, either individually or collectively, received an aggregate of $ 2,000 or more in the preceding calendar year.

As used in this subsection, "client or customer" means a business or combination of businesses.

Kentucky: Kentucky Constitution, Section 57

A member who has a personal or private interest in any measure or bill proposed or pending before the General Assembly, shall disclose the fact to the House of which he is a member, and shall not vote thereon upon pain of expulsion.

Kentucky Revised Statutes, 6.731. General standards of conduct.

Penalties.

A legislator, by himself or through others, shall not intentionally:

(1) Use or attempt to use his influence as a member of the General Assembly in any matter which involves a substantial conflict between his personal interest and his duties in the public interest. Violation of this subsection is a Class A misdemeanor;

(2) Use his official position or office to obtain financial gain for himself, any members of the legislator's family, or a business associate of the legislator. Violation of this subsection is a Class D felony;

(3) Use or attempt to use his official position to secure or create privileges, exemptions, advantages, or treatment for himself or others in direct contravention of the public interest at large. Violation of this subsection is a Class A misdemeanor;

(4) Use public funds, time, or personnel for his private gain or that of another, unless the use is authorized by law. Violation of this subsection is a Class A misdemeanor...

Louisiana: LOUISIANA REVISED STATUTES

§ 42:1120. Recusal from voting.

If any elected official, in the discharge of a duty or responsibility of his office or position, would be required to vote on a matter which vote would be a violation of R.S. 42:1112, he shall recuse himself from voting. An elected official who recuses himself from voting pursuant to this Section shall not be prohibited from participating in discussion and debate concerning the matter, provided that he verbally discloses the nature of the conflict or potential conflict during his participation in the discussion or debate and prior to any vote taken on the matter.

LOUISIANA REVISED STATUTES

§ 42:1112. Participation in certain transactions involving the governmental entity.

A. No public servant, except as provided in R.S. 42:1120, shall participate in a transaction in which he has a personal substantial economic interest of which he may be reasonably expected to know involving the governmental entity.

B. No public servant, except as provided in R.S. 42:1120, shall participate in a transaction involving the governmental entity in which, to his actual knowledge, any of the following persons has a substantial economic interest:

(1) Any member of his immediate family.

(2) Any person in which he has a substantial economic interest of which he may reasonably be expected to know.

(3) Any person of which he is an officer, director, trustee, partner, or employee.

(4) Any person with whom he is negotiating or has an arrangement concerning prospective employment.

(5) Any person who is a party to an existing contract with such public servant, or with any legal entity in which the public servant exercises control or owns an interest in excess of twenty-five percent, or who owes any thing of economic value to such public servant, or to any legal entity in which the public servant exercises control or owns an interest in excess of twenty-five percent, and who by reason thereof is in a position to affect directly the economic interests of such public servant.

C. Every public employee, excluding an appointed member of any board or commission, shall disqualify himself from participating in a transaction involving the governmental entity when a violation of this Part would result. The procedures for such disqualification shall be established by regulations issued pursuant to R.S. 42:1134(1).

D. No appointed member of any board or commission, except as otherwise provided in R.S. 42:1120.1, 1120.2, or 1120.3, shall participate or be interested in any transaction involving the agency when a violation of this Part would result.

Maine: TITLE 1. GENERAL PROVISIONS

§ 1014. Conflict of interest.

1. Situations involving conflict of interest. A Legislator engages in a violation of legislative ethics if that Legislator votes on a question in connection with a conflict of interest in committee or in either body of the Legislature or attempts to influence the outcome of that question unless a presiding officer in accordance with the Joint Rules of the Legislature requires a Legislator to vote or advises the Legislator that there is no conflict in accordance with section 1013, subsection 2, paragraph K. A conflict of interest includes:

A. Where a Legislator or a member of his immediate family has or acquires a direct substantial personal financial interest, distinct from that of the general public, in an enterprise which would be financially benefited by proposed legislation, or derives a direct substantial personal financial benefit from close economic association with a person known by the Legislator to have a direct financial interest in an enterprise affected by proposed legislation.

B. Where a Legislator or a member of his immediate family accepts gifts, other than campaign contributions duly recorded as required by law, from persons affected by legislation or who have an interest in a business affected by proposed legislation, where it is known or reasonably should be known that the purpose of the donor in making the gift is to influence the Legislator in the performance of his official duties or vote, or is intended as a reward for action on his part.

C. Receiving compensation or reimbursement not authorized by law for services, advice or assistance as a Legislator.

D. Appearing for, representing or assisting another in respect to a claim before the Legislature, unless without compensation and for the benefit of a citizen.

E. Where a Legislator or a member of his immediate family accepts or engages in employment which could impair the Legislator's judgment, or where the Legislator knows that there is a substantial possibility that an opportunity for employment is being afforded him or a member of his immediate family with intent to influence his conduct in the performance of his official duties, or where the Legislator or a member of his immediate family stands to derive a personal private gain or loss from employment, because of legislative action, distinct from the gain or losses of other employees or the general community.

F. Where a Legislator or a member of his immediate family has an interest in legislation relating to a profession, trade, business or employment in which the Legislator or a member of his immediate family is engaged, where the benefit derived by the Legislator or a member of his immediate family is unique and distinct from that of the general public or persons engaged in similar professions, trades, businesses or employment.

2-A. Undue influence. It is a violation of legislative ethics for a Legislator to engage in conduct that constitutes the exertion of undue influence, including, but not limited to:

A. Appearing for, representing or advocating for another person in a matter before a state agency or authority, for compensation other than compensation as a Legislator, if the Legislator makes reference to that Legislator's legislative capacity, communicates with the agency or authority on legislative stationery or makes threats or implications relating to legislative action;

B. Appearing for, representing or advocating for another person in a matter before a state agency or authority if the Legislator oversees the policies of the agency or authority as a result of the Legislator's committee responsibilities, unless:

(1) The appearance, representation or advocacy is provided without compensation and for the benefit of a constituent;

(2) The Legislator is engaged in the conduct of the Legislator's profession and is in good standing with a licensing board, if any, that oversees the Legislator's profession;

(3) The appearance, representation or advocacy is provided before a court or office of the judicial branch; or

(4) The representation consists of filing records or reports or performing other routine tasks that do not involve the exercise of discretion on the part of the agency or authority; and
C. Representing or assisting another person in the sale of goods or services to the State, a state agency or a state authority, unless the transaction occurs after public notice and competitive bidding.

3. ABUSE OF OFFICE OR POSITION. It is presumed that a conflict of interest exists where a Legislator abuses his office or position, including but not limited to the following cases.

A. Where a Legislator or a member of his immediate family has a direct financial interest or an interest through a close economic association in a contract for goods or services with the State, a state agency or authority in a transaction not covered by public notice and competitive bidding or by uniform rates established by the State, a state agency, authority or other governmental entity or by a professional association or organization.

B. Granting or obtaining special privilege, exemption or preferential treatment to or for oneself or another, which privilege, exemption or treatment is not readily available to members of the general community or class to which the beneficiary belongs.

C. Use or disclosure of confidential information obtained because of office or position for the benefit of self or another.

Maryland: § 15-511. Disqualification -- Presumption of conflict.

(a) "Close economic association" defined.

(1) In this section, "close economic association" means:

(i) a legislator's: 1. employer; 2. employee; or 3. partner in a business or professional enterprise;

(ii) a partnership, limited liability partnership, or limited liability company in which a legislator has invested capital or owns an interest;

(iii) a corporation in which a legislator owns the lesser of: 1. 10% or more of the outstanding capital stock; or 2. capital stock with a cumulative value of $ 25,000 or more; and (iv) a corporation in which the legislator is an officer, director, or agent.

(2) "Close economic association" does not mean stock owned directly through a mutual fund, retirement plan, or other similar

commingled investment vehicle the individual investments of which the legislator does not control or manage.

(b) Disqualification.

(1) An interest of a member of the General Assembly conflicts with the public interest if the legislator's interest tends to impair the legislator's independence of judgment

(2) The conflict disqualifies the legislator from participating in any legislative action, or otherwise attempting to influence any legislation, to which the conflict relates.

(c) Presumption of conflict. -- It is presumed that an interest disqualifies a legislator from participating in legislative action in any of the following circumstances:

(1) having or acquiring a direct interest in an enterprise which would be affected by the legislator's vote on proposed legislation, unless the interest is common to all members of:

(i) a profession or occupation of which the legislator is a member; or

(ii) the general public or a large class of the general public;

(2) benefiting financially from a close economic association with a person whom the legislator knows has a direct interest in an enterprise or interest which would be affected by the legislator's participation in legislative action, differently from other like enterprises or interests;

(3) benefiting financially from a close economic association with a person who is lobbying for the purpose of influencing legislative action; or

(4) soliciting, accepting, or agreeing to accept a loan, other than

a loan from a commercial lender in the normal course of business, from a person who would be affected by or has an interest in an enterprise which would be affected by the legislator's participation in legislative action.

Massachusetts: Senate Rule 10. No member, officer, or employee shall use or attempt to use improper means to influence an agency, board, authority, or commission of the Commonwealth or any political subdivision of the Commonwealth. No member, officer, or employee of the Senate shall receive compensation or permit compensation to accrue to the member, officer or employee's beneficial interest by virtue of influence improperly exerted from the member, officer or employee's position in the Senate. Every reasonable effort shall be made to avoid situations where it might appear that the member, officer or employee is making such use of the member, officer or employee's official position. Members, officers, and employees should avoid accepting or retaining an economic interest or opportunity which represents a threat to their independence of judgment.

Senate Rule 16A. (1.) While members, officers and employees should not be denied those opportunities available to all other citizens to acquire and retain private, economic and other interests, members, officers, and employees should exercise prudence in any and all such endeavors and make every reasonable effort to avoid transactions, activities, or obligations, which are in substantial conflict with or will substantially impair their independence of judgment.

(4.) No member, officer or employee shall receive any compensation or permit any compensation to accrue to his or her beneficial interest by virtue of influence improperly exerted from his or her official position in the House.

Chapter 268A Conduct of Public Officials and Employees

§ 6A. Notifying State Ethics Commission of Conflict of Interest.

Any public official, as defined by section one of chapter two hundred and sixty-eight B, who in the discharge of his official duties would be required knowingly to take an action which would substantially affect such official's financial interests, unless the effect on such an official is no greater than the effect on the general public, shall file a written description of the required action and the potential conflict of interest with the state ethics commission.

Michigan: § 15.302. Prohibition of substantial conflict of interest.

Sec. 2. No member of the legislature, herein referred to as a "legislator", nor any state officer shall be interested directly or indirectly in any contract with the state or any political subdivision thereof which shall cause a substantial conflict of interest.

§ 15.304 Pecuniary interest; cases in which there is no substantial conflict of interest.

Sec. 4. (1) As used in section 2, "interested" means a pecuniary interest.

(2) If there is a conflict of interest on the part of a legislator or state officer in respect to a contract with the state or a political subdivision of the state, to be prohibited by this act his or her personal interest must be of such substance as to induce action on his or her part to promote the contract for his or her own personal benefit.

(3) In the following cases, there is no substantial conflict of interest:

(a) A contract between the state or a political subdivision of the state and any of the following:

(i) A corporation in which a legislator or state officer is a stockholder owning 1% or less of the total stock outstanding in any class if the stock is not listed on a stock exchange or the stock has a present market value of $25,000.00 or less if the stock is listed on a stock exchange.

(ii) A corporation in which a trust, where a legislator or state officer is a beneficiary under the trust, owns 1% or less of the total stock outstanding in any class if the stock is not listed on a stock exchange or the stock has a present market value of $25,000.00 or less if the stock is listed on a stock exchange.

(iii) A professional limited liability company organized pursuant to the Michigan limited liability company act, Act No. 23 of the Public Acts of 1993, being sections 450.5101 to 450.6200 of the Michigan Compiled Laws, if a legislator or state officer is an employee but not a member of the company.

(b) A contract between the state or a political subdivision of the state and any of the following:

(i) A corporation in which a legislator or state officer is a stockholder owning more than 1% of the total stock outstanding in any class if the stock is not listed on a stock exchange or the stock has a present market value in excess of $25,000.00 if the stock is listed on a stock exchange or a director, officer, or employee.

(ii) A firm, partnership, or other unincorporated association, in which a legislator or state officer is a partner, member, or employee.

(iii) A corporation or firm that has an indebtedness owed to a legislator or state officer.

(iv) A trustee or trustees under a trust in which a legislator or state officer is a beneficiary or trustee or a corporation in whose stock the trust funds are invested, if the investment includes more than 1% of the total stock outstanding in any class if the stock is not listed on a stock exchange or if the stock has a present market value in excess of $25,000.00 if the stock is listed on a stock exchange, if the legislator or state officer does not solicit the contract, takes no part in the negotiations for or in the approval of the contract or any amendment to the contract, and does not in any way represent either party in the transaction and the contract is not with or authorized by the department or agency of the state or a political subdivision with which the state officer is connected.

(c) A contract between the state and a political subdivision of the state or between political subdivisions of the state.

(d) A contract awarded to the lowest qualified bidder, upon receipt of sealed bids pursuant to a published notice for bids provided the notice does not bar, except as authorized by law, any qualified person, firm, corporation, or trust from bidding. This subdivision does not apply to amendments or renegotiations of a contract or to additional payments under the contract which were not authorized by the contract at the time of award.

(e) A contract for public utility services where the rates for the services are regulated by the state or federal government.

Senate Rule 1.303. Improper influence. A Senator shall not accept anything that will influence his or her official act, decision, or vote.

1.305. A Senator shall not use his or her influence in any matter that involves substantial conflict between his or her personal interest and his or her duties in the public interest.

1.306. A personal, private, or professional interest in a bill is an interest that would provide a benefit particular to a Senator or a benefit particular to any individual or entity to whom the Senator is financially or legally obligated or is personally related.

House Rule 47. A Member shall not use his or her position in any manner to solicit or obtain anything of value for himself or herself, House employees or any other Member which tends to influence the manner in which the Member performs his or her official duties.

Minnesota: § 10A.07 CONFLICTS OF INTEREST.

A public official or a local official elected to or appointed by a metropolitan governmental unit who in the discharge of official duties would be required to take an action or make a decision that would substantially affect the official's financial interests or those of an associated business, unless the effect on the official is no greater than on other members of the official's business classification, profession, or occupation, must take the following actions:

(1) prepare a written statement describing the matter requiring action or decision and the nature of the potential conflict of interest;

(2) deliver copies of the statement to the official's immediate superior, if any; and

(3) if a member of the legislature or of the governing body of a metropolitan governmental unit, deliver a copy of the statement to the presiding officer of the body of service.

If a potential conflict of interest presents itself and there is insufficient time to comply with clauses (1) to (3), the public or local official must orally inform the superior or the official body of service or committee of the body of the potential conflict.

Subd. 2. Required actions.

If the official is not a member of the legislature or of the governing body of a metropolitan governmental unit, the superior must assign the matter, if possible, to another employee who does not have a potential conflict of interest. If there is no immediate superior, the official must abstain, if possible, in a manner prescribed by the board from influence over the action or decision in question. If the official is a member of the legislature, the house of service may, at the member's request, excuse the member from taking part in the action or decision in question. If the official is not permitted or is otherwise unable to abstain from action in connection with the matter, the official must file a statement describing the potential conflict and the action taken. A public official must file the statement with the board and a local official must file the statement with the governing body of the official's political subdivision. The statement must be filed within a week of the action taken.

Subd. 3. Interest in contract; local officials.

This section does not apply to a local official with respect to a matter governed by sections 471.87 and 471.88.

§ 471.87 PUBLIC OFFICERS, INTEREST IN CONTRACT; PENALTY

Except as authorized in section 471.88, a public officer who is authorized to take part in any manner in making any sale, lease, or contract in official capacity shall not voluntarily have a personal financial interest in that sale, lease, or contract or personally benefit financially there from. Every public officer who violates this provision is guilty of a gross misdemeanor.

Mississippi: § 25-4-105.

Certain actions, activities and business relationships prohibited or authorized; contracts in violation of section voidable; penalties.

(1) No public servant shall use his official position to obtain or attempt to obtain pecuniary benefit for himself other than that compensation provided for by law, or to obtain or attempt to obtain pecuniary benefit for any relative or any business with which he is associated.

(2) No public servant shall be interested, directly or indirectly, during the term for which he shall have been chosen, or within one (1) year after the expiration of such term, in any contract with the state, or any district, county, city or town thereof, authorized by any law passed or order made by any board of which he may be or may have been a member.

(3) No public servant shall:

(a) Be a contractor, subcontractor or vendor with the governmental entity of which he is a member, officer, employee or agent, other than in his contract of employment, or have a material financial interest in any business which is a contractor, subcontractor or vendor with the governmental entity of which he is a member, officer, employee or agent.

(b) Be a purchaser, direct or indirect, at any sale made by him in his official capacity or by the governmental entity of which he is an officer or employee, except in respect of the sale of goods or services when provided as public utilities or offered to the general public on a uniform price schedule.

(c) Be a purchaser, direct or indirect, of any claim, certificate, warrant or other security issued by or to be paid out of the treasury of the governmental entity of which he is an officer or employee.

(d) Perform any service for any compensation during his term of office or employment by which he attempts to influence a decision of the authority of the governmental entity of which he is a member.

(e) Perform any service for any compensation for any person or business after termination of his office or employment in relation to any case, decision, proceeding or application with respect to which he was directly concerned or in which he personally participated during the period of his service or employment.

(4) Notwithstanding the provisions of subsection (3) of this section, a public servant or his relative:

(a) May be an officer or stockholder of banks or savings and loan associations or other such financial institutions bidding for bonds, notes or other evidences of debt or for the privilege of keeping as depositories the public funds of a governmental entity thereof or the editor or employee of any newspaper in which legal notices are required to be published in respect to the publication of said legal notices.

(b) May be a contractor or vendor with any authority of the governmental entity other than the authority of the governmental entity of which he is a member, officer, employee or agent or have a material financial interest in a business which is a contractor or vendor with any authority of the governmental entity other than the authority of the governmental entity of which he is a member, officer, employee or agent where such contract is let to the lowest and best bidder after competitive bidding and three (3) or more legitimate bids are received or where the goods, services or property involved are reasonably available from two (2) or fewer commercial sources, provided such transactions comply with the public purchases laws.

(c) May be a subcontractor with any authority of the governmental entity other than the authority of the governmental entity of which he is a member, officer, employee or agent or have a material financial interest in a business which is a subcontractor with any authority of the governmental entity other than the authority of the governmental entity of which he is a member, officer, employee or agent where the primary contract is let to the lowest and best bidder after competitive bidding or where such goods or services involved are reasonably available from two (2) or fewer commercial sources, provided such transactions comply with the public purchases laws.

(d) May be a contractor, subcontractor or vendor with any authority of the governmental entity of which he is a member, officer, employee or agent or have a material financial interest in a business which is a contractor, subcontractor or vendor with any authority of the governmental entity of which he is a member, officer, employee or agent: (i) where such goods or services involved are reasonably available from two (2) or fewer commercial sources, provided such transactions comply with the public purchases laws; or (ii) where the contractual relationship involves the further research, development, testing, promotion or merchandising of an intellectual property created by the public servant.

(e) May purchase securities issued by the governmental entity of which he is an officer or employee if such securities are offered to the general public and are purchased at the same price as such securities are offered to the general public.

(f) May have an interest less than a material financial interest in a business which is a contractor, subcontractor or vendor with any governmental entity.

(g) May contract with the Mississippi Veteran's Home Purchase Board, Mississippi Housing Finance Corporation, or any other state loan program, for the purpose of securing a loan; however, public servants shall not receive favored treatment.

(h) May be employed by or receive compensation from an authority of the governmental entity other than the authority of the governmental entity of which the public servant is an officer or employee.

(i) If a member of the Legislature or other public servant employed on less than a full-time basis, may represent a person or organization for compensation before an authority of the governmental entity other than an authority of the governmental entity of which he is an officer or employee.

(j) If a constable, may be employed and receive compensation as a deputy sheriff or other employee of the county for which he serves as constable.

(5) No person may intentionally use or disclose information gained in the course of or by reason of his official position or employment as a public servant in any way that could result in pecuniary benefit for himself, any relative, or any other person, if the information has not been communicated to the public or is not public information.

(6) Any contract made in violation of this section may be declared void by the governing body of the contracting or selling authority of the governmental subdivision or a court of competent jurisdiction and the contractor or subcontractor shall retain or receive only the reasonable value, with no increment for profit or commission, of the property or the services furnished prior to the date of receiving notice that the contract has been

voided.

(7) Any person violating the provisions of this section shall be punished as provided for in Sections 25-4-109 and 25-4-111.

25-4-103

(k) "Material financial interest" means a personal and pecuniary interest, direct or indirect, accruing to a public servant or spouse, either individually or in combination with each other. Notwithstanding the foregoing, the following shall not be deemed to be a material financial interest with respect to a business with which a public servant may be associated:

(i) Ownership of any interest of less than ten percent (10%) in a business where the aggregate annual net income to the public servant there from is less than One Thousand Dollars ($ 1,000.00);

(ii) Ownership of any interest of less than two percent (2%) in a business where the aggregate annual net income to the public servant there from is less than Five Thousand Dollars ($ 5,000.00);

(iii) The income as an employee of a relative if neither the public servant or relative is an officer, director or partner in the business and any ownership interest would not be deemed material pursuant to subparagraph (i) or (ii) herein; or;

(iv) The income of the spouse of a public servant when such spouse is a contractor, subcontractor or vendor with the governmental entity that employs the public servant and the public servant exercises no control, direct or indirect, over the contract between the spouse and such governmental entity.

(l) "Pecuniary benefit" means benefit in the form of money, property, commercial interests or anything else the primary significance of which is economic gain. Expenses associated with social occasions afforded public servants shall not be deemed a pecuniary benefit.

§ 25-4-119. Officials not to derive pecuniary benefits as result of official duties; penalties

No elected or appointed official shall derive any pecuniary benefit, directly or indirectly, as a result of such elected or appointed official's duties under Sections 21-19-33, 27-109-1, 27-109-3, 27-109-7, 27-109-9, 67-1-71, 87-1-5, 95-3-25, 97-33-1, 97-33-7, 97-33-9, 97-33-17, 97-33-25, and 97-33-27. Any person convicted of a violation of this section shall be punished pursuant to the provisions of this article.

NOTE: the statutes mentioned deal with municipal government, gaming, taxation and finance, among others.

Missouri: § 105.452. Prohibited acts by elected and appointed public officials and employees.

No elected or appointed official or employee of the state or any political subdivision thereof shall:

(1) Act or refrain from acting in any capacity in which he is lawfully empowered to act as such an official or employee by reason of any payment, offer to pay, promise to pay, or receipt of anything of actual pecuniary value paid or payable, or received or receivable, to himself or any third person, including any gift or campaign contribution, made or received in relationship to or as a condition of the performance of an official act, other than compensation to be paid by the state or political subdivision; or

(2) Use confidential information obtained in the course of or by reason of his employment or official capacity in any manner with intent to result in financial gain for himself, his spouse, his dependent child in his custody, or any business with which he is associated;

(3) Disclose confidential information obtained in the course of or by reason of his employment or official capacity in any manner with intent to result in financial gain for himself or any other person;

(4) Favorably act on any matter that is so specifically designed so as to provide a special monetary benefit to such official or his spouse or dependent children, including but not limited to increases in retirement benefits, whether received from the state of Missouri or any third party by reason of such act. For the purposes of this subdivision, "special monetary benefit" means being materially affected in a substantially different manner or degree than the manner or degree in which the public in general will be affected or, if the matter affects only a special class of persons, then affected in a substantially different manner or degree than the manner or degree in which such class will be affected. In all such matters such officials must recuse themselves from acting and shall not be relieved by reason of the provisions of section 105.460, except that such official may act on increases in compensation subject to the restrictions of section 13 of article VII of the Missouri Constitution; or;

(5) Use his decision-making authority for the purpose of obtaining a financial gain which materially enriches himself, his spouse or dependent children by acting or refraining from acting for the purpose of coercing or extorting from another anything of actual pecuniary value.

Montana: § 2-2-112 Ethical requirements for legislators.

(1) The requirements in this section are intended as rules for legislator conduct, and violations constitute a breach of the public trust of legislative office.

(2) A legislator has a responsibility to the legislator's

constituents to participate in all matters as required in the rules of the legislature. A legislator concerned with the possibility of a conflict may briefly present the facts to the committee of that house that is assigned the determination of ethical issues. The committee shall advise the legislator as to whether the legislator should disclose the interest prior to voting on the issue pursuant to the provisions of subsection (5). The legislator may, subject to legislative rule, vote on an issue on which the legislator has a conflict, after disclosing the interest.

(3) When a legislator is required to take official action on a legislative matter as to which the legislator has a conflict created by a personal or private interest that would directly give rise to an appearance of impropriety as to the legislator's influence, benefit, or detriment in regard to the legislative matter, the legislator shall disclose the interest creating the conflict prior to participating in the official action, as provided in subsections (2) and (5) and the rules of the legislature. In making a decision, the legislator shall consider:

(a) whether the conflict impedes the legislator's independence of judgment;

(b) the effect of the legislator's participation on public confidence in the integrity of the legislature;

(c) whether the legislator's participation is likely to have any significant effect on the disposition of the matter; and

(d) whether a pecuniary interest is involved or whether a potential occupational, personal, or family benefit could arise from the legislator's participation.

(4) A conflict situation does not arise from legislation or legislative duties affecting the membership of a profession, occupation, or class.

(5) A legislator shall disclose an interest creating a conflict, as provided in the rules of the legislature. A legislator who is a member of a profession, occupation, or class affected by legislation is not required to disclose an interest unless the class contained in the legislation is so narrow that the vote will have a direct and distinctive personal impact on the legislator. A legislator may seek a determination from the appropriate committee provided for in 2-2-135.

Nebraska: § 49-1499. Legislature; discharge of official duties; potential conflict; actions required.

(1) A member of the Legislature who would be required to take any action or make any decision in the discharge of his or her official duties that may cause financial benefit or detriment to him or her, a member of his or her immediate family, or a business with which he or she is associated, which is distinguishable from the effects of such action on the public generally or a broad segment of the public, shall take the following actions as soon as he or she is aware of such potential conflict or should reasonably be aware of such potential conflict, whichever is sooner:

(a) Prepare a written statement describing the matter requiring action or decision and the nature of the potential conflict, and if he or she will not abstain from voting, deliberating, or taking other action on the matter, the statement shall state why, despite the potential conflict, he or she intends to vote or otherwise participate; and

(b) Deliver a copy of the statement to the commission and to the Speaker of the Legislature who shall cause the statement to be filed with the Clerk of the Legislature to be held as a matter of public record.

(2) Nothing in this section shall prohibit any member of the Legislature from voting, deliberating, or taking other action on any matter that comes before the Legislature.

(3) The member of the Legislature may abstain from voting, deliberating, or taking other action on the matter on which the potential conflict exists. He or she may have the reasons for the abstention recorded in the Legislative Journal.

Nevada: A public officer or employee shall not use the public officer's or employee's position in government to secure or grant unwarranted privileges, preferences, exemptions or advantages for the public officer or employee, any business entity in which the public officer or employee has a significant pecuniary interest, or any person to whom the public officer or employee has a commitment in a private capacity to the interests of that person. As used in this subsection "unwarranted" means without justification or adequate reason. 281A.400 NRS

281A.420: (DOES NOT APPLY TO LEGISLATORS - see part 7)

Except as otherwise provided in this section, a public officer or employee shall not approve, disapprove, vote, abstain from voting or otherwise act upon a matter: (a   1.Regarding which the public officer or employee has accepted a gift or loan;   )In which the public officer or employee has a significant pecuniary interest; or (b)Which would reasonably be affected by the public officer's or employee's commitment in a private capacity to the interests of another person, without disclosing information concerning the gift or loan, significant pecuniary interest or commitment in a private capacity to the interests of the person that is sufficient to inform the public of the potential effect of the action or abstention upon the person who provided the gift or loan, upon the public officer's or employee's significant pecuniary interest, or upon the person to whom the public officer or employee has a commitment in a private capacity. Such a disclosure must be made at the time the matter is considered. If the public officer or employee is a member of a body which makes decisions, the public officer or employee shall make the disclosure in public to the chair and other members of the body. If the public officer or employee is not a member of such a body and holds an appointive office, the public officer or employee shall make the disclosure to the supervisory head of the public officer's or employee's organization or, if the public officer holds an elective office, to the general public in the area from which the public officer is elected... (c)

3. Except as otherwise provided in this section, in addition to the requirements of subsection 1, a public officer shall not vote upon or advocate the passage or failure of, but may otherwise participate in the consideration of, a matter with respect to which the independence of judgment of a reasonable person in the public officer's situation would be materially affected by:

The public officer's commitment in a private capacity to the interests of another person. The public officer's significant pecuniary interest; or (c) The public officer's acceptance of a gift or loan; (b) (a)

4.In interpreting and applying the provisions of subsection 3:

It must be presumed that the independence of judgment of a reasonable person in the public officer's situation would not be materially affected by the public officer's acceptance of a gift or loan, significant pecuniary interest or commitment in a private capacity to the interests of another person where the resulting benefit or detriment accruing to the public officer, or if the public officer has a commitment in a private capacity to the interests of another person, accruing to the other person, is not greater than that accruing to any other member of any general business, profession, occupation or group that is affected by the matter. The presumption set forth in this paragraph does not affect the applicability of the requirements set forth in subsection 1 relating to the disclosure of the acceptance of a gift or loan, significant pecuniary interest or commitment in a private capacity to the interests of another person. (a)

The Commission must give appropriate weight and proper deference to the public policy of this State which favors the right of a public officer to perform the duties for which the public officer was elected or appointed and to vote or otherwise act upon a matter, provided the public officer has properly disclosed the public officer's acceptance of a gift or loan, significant pecuniary interest or commitment in a private capacity to the interests of another person in the manner required by subsection 1. Because abstention by a public officer disrupts the normal course of representative government and deprives the public and the public officer's constituents of a voice in governmental affairs, the provisions of this section are intended to require abstention only in clear cases where the independence of judgment of a reasonable person in the public officer's situation would be materially affected by the public officer's acceptance of a gift or loan, significant pecuniary interest or commitment in a private capacity to the interests of another person. (b)

5. Except as otherwise provided in NRS 241.0355, if a public officer declares to the body or committee in which the vote is to be taken that the public officer will abstain from voting because of the requirements of this section, the necessary quorum to act upon and the number of votes necessary to act upon the matter, as fixed by any statute, ordinance or rule, is reduced as though the member abstaining were not a member of the body or committee.

6. The provisions of this section do not, under any circumstances, apply to State Legislators or allow the Commission to exercise jurisdiction or authority over State Legislators. The responsibility of a State Legislator to make disclosures concerning gifts, loans, interests or commitments and the responsibility of a State Legislator to abstain from voting upon or advocating the passage or failure of a matter are governed by the Standing Rules of the Legislative Department of State Government which are adopted, administered and enforced exclusively by the appropriate bodies of the Legislative Department of State Government pursuant to Section 6 of Article 4 of the Nevada Constitution.

281.221. Contracts in which state officer has interest prohibited; exceptions; penalties.

Except as otherwise provided in this section and 1. NRS 281A.430, it is unlawful for a state officer, who is not a member of the Legislature subject to the restrictions set forth in NRS 218A.970, to:

Become a contractor under any contract or order for supplies or other kind of contract authorized by or for the State or any of its departments, or the Legislature or either of its houses, or to be interested, directly or indirectly, as principal, in any kind of contract so authorized. (a)

Be interested in any contract made by the officer or to be a purchaser or interested in any purchase under a sale made by the officer in the discharge of the officer's official duties. (b)

2. A member of any board, commission or similar body who is engaged in the profession, occupation or business regulated by the board, commission or body may supply or contract to supply, in the ordinary course of his or her business, goods, materials or services to any state or local agency, except the board,

commission or body of which he or she is a member, if the member has not taken part in developing the contract plans or specifications and the member will not be personally involved in opening, considering or accepting offers.

3. A full- or part-time faculty member in the Nevada System of Higher Education may bid on or enter into a contract with a governmental agency, or may benefit financially or otherwise from a contract between a governmental agency and a private entity, if the contract complies with the policies established by the Board of Regents of the University of Nevada pursuant to NRS 396.255.

4. A state officer, other than an officer described in subsection 2 or 3, may bid on or enter into a contract with a governmental agency if the contracting process is controlled by rules of open competitive bidding, the sources of supply are limited, the officer has not taken part in developing the contract plans or specifications and the officer will not be personally involved in opening, considering or accepting offers.

5. Any contract made in violation of this section may be declared void at the instance of the State or of any other person interested in the contract except an officer prohibited from making or being interested in the contract.

6. A person who violates this section is guilty of a gross misdemeanor and shall forfeit his or her office.

Senate Rule 23 and Assembly Rule 23: Senate Rule 23: 8. In determining whether a Legislator has a conflict of interest, the Legislator should consider whether the independence of judgment of a reasonable person in his or her situation upon the matter in question would be materially affected by the Legislator's:

(a) Acceptance of a gift or loan; (b) Private economic interest; or (c) Commitment to a member of his or her household or immediate family.

In interpreting and applying the provisions of this subsection, it must be presumed that the independence of judgment of a reasonable person in the Legislator's situation would not be materially affected by the Legislator's private economic interest or the Legislator's commitment to a member of his or her household or immediate family where the resulting benefit or detriment accruing to the Legislator, or if the Legislator has a commitment to a member of his or her household or immediate family, accruing to those other persons, is not greater than that accruing to any other member of the general business, profession, occupation or group that is affected by the matter.

New Hampshire: Per the General Court's Ethics Guidelines § 2, pt. 2. "Conflict of Interest" is the condition in which a legislator has a financial interest in any official activity.

If participation in an official activity creates a conflict of interest not disclosed in the financial disclosure forms, legislators must complete and file a Declaration of Intent Form in accordance with section 5 of the Ethics Guidelines. Even if legislators disclose a financial interest on this form, he may still have to file a separate Declaration of Intent Form on a particular bill.

New Jersey: § 52:13D-13. Definitions...

(g) "Interest" means (1) the ownership or control of more than 10% of the profits or assets of a firm, association, or partnership, or more than 10% of the stock in a corporation for profit other than a professional service corporation organized under the "Professional Service Corporation Act," P.L. 1969, c. 232 (C. 14A:17-1 et seq.); or (2) the ownership or control of more than

1% of the profits of a firm, association, or partnership, or more than 1% of the stock in any corporation, which is the holder of, or an applicant for, a casino license or in any holding or intermediary company with respect thereto, as defined by the "Casino Control Act," P.L. 1977, c. 110 (C. 5:12-1 et seq.). The provisions of this act governing the conduct of individuals are applicable to shareholders, associates or professional employees of a professional service corporation regardless of the extent or amount of their shareholder interest in such a corporation.

§ 52:13D-23. Codes of ethics.

(a) (1) The head of each State agency, or the principal officer in charge of a division, board, bureau, commission or other instrumentality within a department of State Government designated by the head of such department for the purposes hereinafter set forth, shall within six months from the date of enactment, promulgate a code of ethics to govern and guide the conduct of the members of the Legislature...

(e) A code of ethics for officers and employees of a State agency shall conform to the following general standards:

(1) No State officer or employee or special State officer or employee should have any interest, financial or otherwise, direct or indirect, or engage in any business or transaction or professional activity, which is in substantial conflict with the proper discharge of his duties in the public interest.

(2) No State officer or employee or special State officer or employee should engage in any particular business, profession, trade or occupation which is subject to licensing or regulation by a specific agency of State Government without promptly filing notice of such activity with the State Ethics Commission, if he is an officer or employee in the Executive Branch, or with the Joint Legislative Committee on Ethical Standards, if he is an officer or

employee in the Legislative Branch.

(3) No State officer or employee or special State officer or employee should use or attempt to use his official position to secure unwarranted privileges or advantages for himself or others.

(4) No State officer or employee or special State officer or employee should act in his official capacity in any matter wherein he has a direct or indirect personal financial interest that might reasonably be expected to impair his objectivity or independence of judgment.

(5) No State officer or employee or special State officer or employee should undertake any employment or service, whether compensated or not, which might reasonably be expected to impair his objectivity and independence of judgment in the exercise of his official duties.

(6) No State officer or employee or special State officer or employee should accept any gift, favor, service or other thing of value under circumstances from which it might be reasonably inferred that such gift, service or other thing of value was given or offered for the purpose of influencing him in the discharge of his official duties.

(7) No State officer or employee or special State officer or employee should knowingly act in any way that might reasonably be expected to create an impression or suspicion among the public having knowledge of his acts that he may be engaged in conduct violative of his trust as a State officer or employee or special State officer or employee.

(8) Rules of conduct adopted pursuant to these principles should recognize that under our democratic form of government public officials and employees should be drawn from all of our society,

that citizens who serve in government cannot and should not be expected to be without any personal interest in the decisions and policies of government; that citizens who are government officials and employees have a right to private interests of a personal, financial and economic nature; that standards of conduct should separate those conflicts of interest which are unavoidable in a free society from those conflicts of interest which are substantial and material, or which bring government into disrepute.

(f) The code of ethics for members of the Legislature shall conform to subsection (e) hereof as nearly as may be possible.

New Jersey Legislative Code of Ethics.

For the purpose of this section a "personal interest" means the member of the Legislature, or a member of his immediate family, believes or has reason to believe he will derive a direct monetary gain or suffer a direct monetary loss by the enactment or defeat of the legislation; a "personal interest" does not mean that by enactment or defeat of the legislation no benefit or detriment could be expected to accrue to him, or to a member of his immediate family, as a member of a business, profession, occupation or group, to any greater extent than any such benefit or detriment could be expected to accrue to any other member of such business, profession, occupation or group (C.52:13D-18).

New Mexico: § 10-16-2. Definitions.

F. "financial interest" means an interest held by an individual or the individual's family that is: (1) an ownership interest in business or property; or (2) any employment or prospective employment for which negotiations have already begun;

H. "official act" means an official decision, recommendation, approval, disapproval or other action that involves the use of discretionary authority;

J. "standards" means the conduct required by the Governmental Conduct Act;

L. "substantial interest" means an ownership interest that is greater than twenty percent.

§ 10-16-3. Ethical principles of public service; certain official acts prohibited; penalty.

A. A legislator or public officer or employee shall treat the legislator's or public officer's or employee's government position as a public trust. The legislator or public officer or employee shall use the powers and resources of public office only to advance the public interest and not to obtain personal benefits or pursue private interests.

B. Legislators and public officers and employees shall conduct themselves in a manner that justifies the confidence placed in them by the people, at all times maintaining the integrity and discharging ethically the high responsibilities of public service.

C. Full disclosure of real or potential conflicts of interest shall be a guiding principle for determining appropriate conduct. At all times, reasonable efforts shall be made to avoid undue influence and abuse of office in public service.

D. No legislator or public officer or employee may request or receive, and no person may offer a legislator or public officer or employee, any money, thing of value or promise thereof that is conditioned upon or given in exchange for promised performance of an official act. Any person who knowingly and willfully violates the provisions of this subsection is guilty of a fourth degree felony and shall be sentenced pursuant to the provisions of Section 31-18-15 NMSA 1978.

Senate and House Rule 26-1: A. Members of the senate shall conduct themselves in a manner that justifies the confidence placed in them by the people. The members shall not use their offices for private gain and shall at all times maintain the integrity and discharge ethically the high responsibilities of their legislative positions. Full disclosure of real or potential conflicts of interest shall be a guiding principle for determining appropriate conduct of the members.

B. To avoid a potential conflict of interest:

(1) a senator shall not accept anything of value that improperly influences an official act, decision or vote;

(2) a senator shall attempt to ensure that his private employment does not impair his impartiality and independence of judgment in the exercise of official duties;

(3) a senator shall not receive compensation or reimbursement not authorized by law for rendering services, advice or assistance as a legislator;

(4) a senator shall not accept gifts, other than lawfully collected and reported campaign contributions, from persons affected by legislation or from persons who have an interest in a business affected by proposed legislation, where it is known or reasonably should be known that the purpose of the donor in making the gift is to influence the senator in the performance of his official duties or vote or is intended as a reward for action on his part;

(5) a senator shall not accept or engage in employment if the senator knows it is being afforded him with the intent to influence his conduct in the performance of his official duties

New York: PUBLIC OFFICERS LAW; ARTICLE 4. POWERS AND DUTIES OF PUBLIC OFFICERS

§ 74. Code of ethics.

Rule with respect to conflicts of interest. No officer or employee of a state agency, member of the legislature or legislative employee should have any interest, financial or otherwise, direct or indirect, or engage in any business or transaction or professional activity or incur any obligation of any nature, which is in substantial conflict with the proper discharge of his duties in the public interest.

North Carolina: § 138A-35. Other rules of conduct.

(a) A public servant shall make a due and diligent effort before taking any action, including voting or participating in discussions with other public servants on a board on which the public servant also serves, to determine whether the public servant has a conflict of interest. If the public servant is unable to determine whether or not a conflict of interest may exist, the public servant has a duty to inquire of the Commission as to that conflict.

(b) A public servant shall continually monitor, evaluate, and manage the public servant's personal, financial, and professional affairs to ensure the absence of conflicts of interest.

(c) A public servant shall obey all other civil laws, administrative requirements, and criminal statutes governing conduct of State government applicable to appointees and employees.

138A-3. Definitions.

(14c) Financial benefit. – A direct pecuniary gain or loss to the legislator, the public servant, or a person with which the legislator or public servant is associated, or a direct pecuniary loss to a business competitor of the legislator, the public servant, or a person with which the legislator or public servant is associated.

North Dakota: § 44-04-22. Conflict of interest law.

A person acting in a legislative or quasi-legislative or judicial or quasi-judicial capacity for a political subdivision of the state who has a direct and substantial personal or pecuniary interest in a matter before that board, council, commission, or other body, must disclose the fact to the body of which that person is a member, and may not participate in or vote on that particular matter without the consent of a majority of the rest of the body.

Ohio: § 102.02. Duty to file disclosure statement with ethics commission.

(10)(B) The Ohio ethics commission shall examine each disclosure statement required to be kept confidential to determine whether a potential conflict of interest exists for the person who filed the disclosure statement. A potential conflict of interest exists if the private interests of the person, as indicated by the person's disclosure statement, might interfere with the public interests the person is required to serve in the exercise of the person's authority and duties in the person's office or position of employment. If the commission determines that a potential conflict of interest exists, it shall notify the person who filed the disclosure statement and shall make the portions of the disclosure statement that indicate a potential conflict of interest subject to public inspection in the same manner as is provided for other disclosure statements. Any portion of the disclosure statement that the commission determines does not indicate a potential conflict of interest shall be kept confidential by the commission and shall not be made subject to public inspection, except as is necessary for the enforcement of Chapters 102. and 2921. of the Revised Code and except as otherwise provided in this division.

Oklahoma: TITLE 74. STATE GOVERNMENT; CHAPTER 62.

APPENDIX. TITLE 257. ETHICS COMMISSION CHAPTER 20. ETHICS AND CONFLICTS OF INTEREST 257:20-1-7.

Votes, deliberations, and discussions by legislators or statewide elective officers.

(a) A legislator or statewide elective officer shall not introduce or cause to have introduced, request the introduction of, promote, or vote on any legislation if the statewide elective officer or legislator or a child adopted child, step-child or spouse of the officer or legislator or a business or entity with which the legislator or officer or a member of the immediate family of the legislator or officer is associated has: (1) a pecuniary interest in; or (2) a reasonably foreseeable benefit from; the legislation. A reasonably foreseeable benefit includes detriment to a business competitor to the legislator or statewide elective officer, to a business competitor of a member of the immediate family of the legislator or officer, or to a business competitor of a business or entity with which the legislator or officer or child, adopted child, step-child or spouse of the legislator or officer is associated.(b) A legislator or statewide elective officer may introduce or cause to have introduced, request the introduction of, promote, or vote on legislation if the only pecuniary interest or reasonably foreseeable benefit that may accrue to the legislator or officer, child, adopted child, step-child or spouse of the legislator or officer, or business or entity with which a legislator or officer or a child, adopted child, step-child or spouse of a legislator or officer is associated is incidental to the legislator's or officer's, child's, adopted child's, step-child's, or spouse's or business or entity's position, or which accrues to the legislator or officer, child, adopted child, step-child or spouse of the legislator or officer, or business or entity as a member of a profession, occupation, or large class, whichever is applicable, to no significantly greater extent than the pecuniary interest or potential benefit could reasonably be foreseen to accrue to all other members of the profession, occupation, or large class.(c) Nothing in this subsection shall allow a legislator or a member of the immediate family of a legislator, a statewide elective officer, or a business or entity with which the legislator or statewide elective officer is associated to contract with a governmental entity except as provided in Subsection (b) of Section 10 of this chapter.

Oregon: 244.020. Definitions.

(1) "Actual conflict of interest" means any action or any decision or recommendation by a person acting in a capacity as a public official, the effect of which would be to the private pecuniary benefit or detriment of the person or the person's relative or any business with which the person or a relative of the person is associated unless the pecuniary benefit or detriment arises out of circumstances described in subsection (12) of this section.

(12) "Potential conflict of interest" means any action or any decision or recommendation by a person acting in a capacity as a public official, the effect of which could be to the private pecuniary benefit or detriment of the person or the person's relative, or a business with which the person or the person's relative is associated, unless the pecuniary benefit or detriment arises out of the following:

(a) An interest or membership in a particular business, industry, occupation or other class required by law as a prerequisite to the holding by the person of the office or position.

(b) Any action in the person's official capacity which would affect to the same degree a class consisting of all inhabitants of the state, or a smaller class consisting of an industry, occupation or other group including one of which or in which the person, or the person's relative or business with which the person or the person's relative is associated, is a member or is engaged.

(c) Membership in or membership on the board of directors of a nonprofit corporation that is tax-exempt under section 501(c) of the Internal Revenue Code.

Pennsylvania: PENNSYLVANIA CONSOLIDATED STATUTES; TITLE 65. PUBLIC OFFICERS; PART II. ACCOUNTABILITY; CHAPTER 11. ETHICS STANDARDS AND FINANCIAL DISCLOSURE § 1102. Definitions 65 Pa.C.S. § 1102

"Conflict" or "conflict of interest." Use by a public official or public employee of the authority of his office or employment or any confidential information received through his holding public office or employment for the private pecuniary benefit of himself, a member of his immediate family or a business with which he or a member of his immediate family is associated. The term does not include an action having a de minimis economic impact or which affects to the same degree a class consisting of the general public or a subclass consisting of an industry, occupation or other group which includes the public official or public employee, a member of his immediate family or a business with which he or a member of his immediate family is associated.

Puerto Rico: TITLE 3. EXECUTIVE; CHAPTER 65. ETHICS IN GOVERNMENT ACT; SUBCHAPTER III. CODE OF ETHICS FOR THE EXECUTIVE, LEGISLATIVE AND JUDICIAL BRANCHES;

RESTRICTIONS ON FORMER PUBLIC SERVANTS §
1822. Prohibitions--Generally

(a) No public official or employee, whether personally or acting as a public servant, shall disregard the laws in effect, or the summons or orders of the Courts of Justice, the Legislative Branch or the agencies of the Executive Branch thus empowered.

(b) No public official or employee shall delay the rendering of services that the executive agencies of the Government of the Commonwealth of Puerto Rico are obligated to render, or hinder the efficient operation of the Executive Branch.

(c) No public official or employee shall use the duties and powers of his office, or public property or funds directly or indirectly, to obtain advantages, benefits or privileges not permitted by law, for himself, any member of his family unit, or for any other person, business or entity.

(d) No public official or employee shall request or accept any asset whatsoever of monetary value as payment for carrying out the duties and responsibilities of his employment other than the salary, wage or compensation to which he is entitled because of his public duties or employment.

(e) No public official or employee shall accept or solicit from any person whatsoever, directly or indirectly, either for himself, for any member of his family unit or for any other person, business or entity, any asset whatsoever of monetary value, including gifts, loans, promises, favors or services, in exchange for the actions of said public official or employee being of influence in behalf of that person or any other.

(f) No public official or employee who is a regular employee of the Government shall receive additional pay or special compensation of any nature from the Government of Puerto Rico or from any municipality, board, commission or body which in no way depends on the Government for personal services or official services of any nature, even though they are rendered in addition to the regular functions of the official or employee, unless said special pay or compensation is expressly authorized by § 551 of this title, or any other legal provision.

(g) No public official or employee shall reveal or use confidential information acquired as a result of his/her employment, to obtain, directly or indirectly, any economic advantage or benefit for him/her, a member of his/her family unit or for any other person, business or entity.

(h) No public official shall intervene, in any way, in any matter in which he/she or any member of his/her family unit has a conflict of interest.

(i) No public official or employee may appoint or promote to a position as a public official or employee or to contract, whether per se or through another natural or juridical person, business or entity with an interest in the executive agency in which the latter works or has the power to decide or influence, to any person who is a relative of said public official or employee within the fourth degree of consanguinity or the second degree of affinity. When the public official or employee with power to decide or influence believes that it is utterly necessary for the good of public service and the sound operation of the agency, to contract, appoint or promote a relative of his/her[s] within the degree of kinship mentioned above, in a position as public official or employee, [he/she] shall be bound to request a written authorization from the Executive Director of the Government Ethics Office in which he or she states the specific reasons that justify such a contract, appointment or promotion in that specific case, before carrying out such an action, pursuant to the regulations adopted by the Government Ethics Office.

The Government Ethics Office shall, within the directive term of thirty (30) days from the date of having filed the request for dispensation, authorize or deny the same. The Government Ethics Office shall notify the person making the request of the approval or denial of the dispensation. In the event the request for dispensation is denied, it shall show the grounds for such a decision by presenting a written report.

The prohibition established herein shall not apply in cases in which a public official or employee that appoints or promotes in a career position in the agency in which he/she works or over which he/she exerts jurisdiction, a public official or employee that is his/her relative within the abovementioned degrees, when the appointed or promoted public employee has had the opportunity of competing on an equal footing with other candidates through a selection process based on education and experience tests or evaluations, and it has been objectively determined that he or she is a suitable or the best qualified candidate in the register of eligibles for the position in question and the relative with power has not intervened in the process. Likewise, the prohibitions described above, with the exception of that on appointments, shall apply to those public employees or officials that acquire such a relationship of kinship degree provided for in this act after their appointment or designation.

(j) No public official or employee of the Executive Branch may use any representative motifs, emblems, logos, buttons, transfers, stickers, signs, or insignias of any political party or candidate, or identify or promote, directly or indirectly, the electoral interests of any political party or candidate while in the performance of their duties, regardless of the location in which same are rendering their services.

TITLE 3. EXECUTIVE; CHAPTER 65. ETHICS IN GOVERNMENT ACT; SUBCHAPTER III. CODE OF

ETHICS FOR THE EXECUTIVE, LEGISLATIVE AND JUDICIAL BRANCHES; RESTRICTIONS ON FORMER PUBLIC SERVANTS

§ 1823. Prohibitions--Relative to other employment, contracts or business

(a) No public official or employee shall accept an employment or maintain contractual or business relationships or responsibilities in addition to those of his public office or employment, whether it is in the Government or in the private sector, which, although legally permitted, has the effect of undermining his freedom of judgment in the performance of his official functions.

(b) No public official or employee shall accept employment or maintain contractual business relationships, with a person, business or entity which is regulated by, or does business with the government agency for which he/she works, when the public official or employee participates in institutional decisions of the agency or is empowered to decide or influence the official actions of the agency related to said person, business or entity.

(c) No public official or employee who is authorized to contract in the name of the executive agency for which he/she works, shall execute a contract between his agency and an entity or business in which he/she, or any member of his/her family unit, has, or has had, during the last four (4) years before taking office, a direct or indirect pecuniary interest.

(d) No executive agency may execute a contract in which any of its officials or employees, or any member of their family units, has or has had, during the last (4) years before taking office, a direct or indirect pecuniary interest, unless the Governor authorizes it, subject to the recommendations of the Secretary of the Treasury and the Secretary of Justice.

(e) No public official or employee shall be a part of, or have any interest in, the profits or benefits resulting from a contract with any other executive agency or government dependency, unless the Governor expressly authorizes it, subject to the prior recommendation of the Secretary of the Treasury and the Secretary of Justice. The contracting may only be executed in a case foreseen by this paragraph, without requesting and obtaining the authorization of the Governor, in the case of:

(1) Contracts whose value is not greater than three thousand (3,000) dollars and [which] occur only once in any fiscal year.

(2) Lease, exchange, purchase and sale, loan, mortgage insurance or contracts of any other nature that refer to housing and/or a lot provided or to be financed, or whose financing is secured or guaranteed by a government agency.

(3) Service, loan, guarantee and incentive programs sponsored by government agencies.

In the cases specified in clauses (2) and (3) of this subsection the contracting agency shall authorize the transactions provided the following requirements concur:

(A) The contracts, loans, insurance, guarantees or transactions are accessible to any citizen who qualifies therefore.

(B) Eligibility requirements are of general application.

(C) The public official or employee meets all the eligibility standards and is not granted treatment which is preferential or different from that of the public in general.

(f) No public official or employee who is empowered to approve or authorize contracts, shall evaluate, consider, approve or authorize a contract between an executive agency and entity or business in which he/she or any member of his/her family unit has or has had, during the last four (4) years before taking office, a direct or indirect pecuniary interest.

(g) No public official or employee shall execute or authorize a contract with a private person knowing that this person, in turn, is representing personal interests in cases or matters which involve a conflict of interest or public policy between the contracting government agency and the personal interests said private person is representing. To those effects, all government agencies shall require all private persons with whom it executes a contract, to include a contractual clause in which said private person certifies that he/she is not involved in a conflict of interest or public policy pursuant to the provisions of this subsection.

(h) In every case in which a contract has been executed in violation of the provisions of this section, and once said violations have been indicated by the Director of the Ethics in Government Office, [if] steps have not been taken to obtain a dispensation within ten (10) days following the notice, the contract shall be annullable and the Office of Ethics in Government and the Secretary of Justice are authorized to petition the courts of justice, in representation of the Commonwealth, for said contract [to] be declared null. When a contract is granted without obtaining the dispensation referred to in subsections (d) and (e), or when the same is obtained after the contract is granted, the Director of the Ethics in Government Office may impose a fine on the officials responsible for failing to obtain the dispensation, pursuant to the provisions of §§ 2201 et seq. of this title, part of the Commonwealth of Puerto Rico Uniform Administrative Procedures Act. The efforts to obtain the dispensation within the ten (10) days following the notification by the Director of a violation to subsections (d) and (e) shall be considered as extenuating circumstances but shall not exempt the officials subject of the deficiency, from liability.

(i) The prohibitions set forth in this section shall not apply to contracts executed by any executive agency for the acquisition of literary or artistic property rights, letters or patent to its officers and public employees.

TITLE 3. EXECUTIVE; CHAPTER 65. ETHICS IN GOVERNMENT ACT; SUBCHAPTER III. CODE OF ETHICS FOR THE EXECUTIVE, LEGISLATIVE AND JUDICIAL BRANCHES; RESTRICTIONS ON FORMER PUBLIC SERVANTS

§ 1824. Prohibitions--Related to the representation of private interests in conflict with official functions

(a) No public official or employee may represent any private person, whatsoever directly or indirectly, to obtain the approval of an act or ordinance, to obtain a contract, the payment of a claim, a permit, license or authorization, or any other matter, transaction or proposal, if he or any member of his family unit has participated or will participate, or will probably participate in his official capacity in the disposition of the matter. This prohibition shall not apply when dealing with official acts of the public officials or employee within the limits of his authority.

(b) No public official or employee shall represent any private person whatsoever, directly or indirectly, before an executive agency, with regard to any claim, permit, license, authorization, matter, transaction or proposal that involves official action on the part of the agency, if he/she, or any member of his/her family unit, possesses executive authority over the agency.

(c) No public official or employee shall represent, or otherwise counsel any private person whatsoever, directly or indirectly, before any executive agency, court or other government dependency, in cases and matters related to the Government of Puerto Rico, or in cases or matters that involve conflicts of interest or public policy, between the Government and the interests of said private person.

(d) No full-time public official or employee shall, during working hours, represent, counsel or serve as an expert for private entities or persons in litigation, trials, public hearings or in any other matter before the courts of justice, quasi judicial bodies and administrative agencies.

(e) For the purposes of this section and § 1827 of this title, the term "matter" means those in which the official or employee has participated personally and substantially, and which occurred through a decision, approval or disapproval, recommendation or advice, or a special investigation involving specific parties. It does not include the participation or intervention of the official or the employee in the promulgation of standards or regulations of general application, or abstract directives and instructions that do not allude to special situations or specific cases.

Rhode Island: § 36-14-7. Interest in conflict with discharge of duties.

(a) A person subject to this code of ethics has an interest which is in substantial conflict with the proper discharge of his or her duties or employment in the public interest and of his or her responsibilities as prescribed in the laws of this state, if he or she has reason to believe or expect that he or she or any person within his or her family or any business associate, or any business by which the person is employed or which the person represents will derive a direct monetary gain or suffer a direct monetary loss, as the case may be, by reason of his or her official activity.

(b) A person subject to this code of ethics does not have an interest which is in substantial conflict with the proper discharge of his or her duties in the public interest and of his or her responsibilities as prescribed by the laws of this state, if any benefit or detriment accrues to him or her or any person within his or her family or any business associate, or any business by which the person is employed or which the person represents, as a member of a business, profession, occupation, or group, or of any significant and definable class of persons within the business, profession, occupation, or group, to no greater extent than any other similarly situated member of the business, profession, occupation, or group, or of the significant and definable class of persons within the business, profession, occupation or group.

§ 36-14-6. Statement of conflict of interest.

Any person subject to this code of ethics who, in the discharge of his or her official duties, is or may be required to take an action, make a decision, or refrain there from that will or can reasonably be expected to directly result in an economic benefit to the person, or spouse (if not estranged), or any dependent child of the person, or business associate or any business by which the person is employed or which the person represents, shall, before taking any such action or refraining there from:

(1) Prepare a written statement sworn to under the penalties for perjury describing the matter requiring action and the nature of the potential conflict; if he or she is a member of a legislative body and he or she does not request that he or she be excused from voting, deliberating, or taking action on the matter, the statement shall state why, despite the potential conflict, he or she is able to vote and otherwise participate fairly, objectively, and in the public interest; and

(2) Deliver a copy of the statement to the commission, and:

(i) If he or she is a member of the general assembly or of any city or town legislative body, he or she shall deliver a copy of the statement to the presiding officer of the body, who shall cause the statement to be recorded in the journal of the body and, upon request of the member, may excuse the member from votes, deliberations, or any other action on the matter on which a potential conflict exists; or;

(ii) If the person is not a legislator, his or her superior, if any, shall, if reasonably possible, assign the matter to another person who does not have a conflict of interest. If he or she has no immediate superior, he or she shall take such steps as the commission shall prescribe through rules or regulations to remove him or herself from influence over any action on the matter on which the conflict of interest exists.

South Carolina: § 8-13-100. Definitions

(11) (a) "Economic interest" means an interest distinct from that of the general public in a purchase, sale, lease, contract, option, or other transaction or arrangement involving property or services in which a public official, public member, or public employee may gain an economic benefit of fifty dollars or more.

(b) This definition does not prohibit a public official, public member, or public employee from participating in, voting on, or influencing or attempting to influence an official decision if the only economic interest or reasonably foreseeable benefit that may accrue to the public official, public member, or public employee is incidental to the public official's, public member's, or public employee's position or which accrues to the public official, public member, or public employee as a member of a profession, occupation, or large class to no greater extent than the economic interest or potential benefit could reasonably be foreseen to accrue to all other members of the profession, occupation, or large class.

§ 8-13-700. Use of official position or office for financial gain; disclosure of potential conflict of interest.

(A) No public official, public member, or public employee may knowingly use his official office, membership, or employment to obtain an economic interest for himself, a member of his immediate family, an individual with whom he is associated, or a business with which he is associated. This prohibition does not extend to the incidental use of public materials, personnel, or equipment, subject to or available for a public official's, public member's, or public employee's use which does not result in additional public expense.

(B) No public official, public member, or public employee may make, participate in making, or in any way attempt to use his office, membership, or employment to influence a governmental decision in which he, a member of his immediate family, an individual with whom he is associated, or a business with which he is associated has an economic interest. A public official, public member, or public employee who, in the discharge of his official responsibilities, is required to take an action or make a decision which affects an economic interest of himself, a member of his immediate family, an individual with whom he is associated, or a business with which he is associated shall:

(1) prepare a written statement describing the matter requiring action or decisions and the nature of his potential conflict of interest with respect to the action or decision;

(2) if the public official is a member of the General Assembly, he shall deliver a copy of the statement to the presiding officer of the appropriate house. The presiding officer shall have the statement printed in the appropriate journal and require that the member of the General Assembly he excused from votes, deliberations, and other action on the matter on which a potential

conflict exists;

(3) if he is a public employee, he shall furnish a copy of the statement to his superior, if any, who shall assign the matter to another employee who does not have a potential conflict of interest. If he has no immediate superior, he shall take the action prescribed by the State Ethics Commission;

(4) if he is a public official, other than a member of the General Assembly, he shall furnish a copy of the statement to the presiding officer of the governing body of any agency, commission, board, or of any county, municipality, or a political subdivision thereof, on which he serves, who shall cause the statement to be printed in the minutes and require that the member be excused from any votes, deliberations, and other actions on the matter on which the potential conflict of interest exists and shall cause the disqualification and the reasons for it to be noted in the minutes;

(5) if he is a public member, he shall furnish a copy to the presiding officer of any agency, commission, board, or of any county, municipality, or a political subdivision thereof, on which he serves, who shall cause the statement to be printed in the minutes and shall require that the member be excused from any votes, deliberations, and other actions on the matter on which the potential conflict of interest exists and shall cause such disqualification and the reasons for it to be noted in the minutes.

(C) Where a public official, public member, or public employee or a member of his immediate family holds an economic interest in a blind trust, he is not considered to have a conflict of interest with regard to matters pertaining to that economic interest, if the existence of the blind trust has been disclosed to the appropriate supervisory office.

(D) The provisions of this section do not apply to any court in the unified judicial system.

(E) When a member of the General Assembly is required by law to appear because of his business interest as an owner or officer of the business or in his official capacity as a member of the General Assembly, this section does not apply.

South Dakota: South Dakota Constitution, Art. III, § 12....

[N]or shall any member of the Legislature during the term for which he shall have been elected, or within one year thereafter, be interested, directly or indirectly, in any contract with the state or any county thereof, authorized by any law passed during the term for which he shall have been elected.

Tennessee: § **8-50-502.** Disclosure statements -- Contents.

Legislators must file a Conflict of Interest Disclosure statement that meets the following requirements:

Disclosure shall be made of:

(1) The major source or sources of private income of more than one thousand dollars ($1,000), including, but not limited to, offices, directorships, and salaried employments of the person making disclosure, the spouse, or minor children residing with such person, but no dollar amounts need be stated. This subdivision (1) shall not be construed to require the disclosure of any client list or customer list;

(2) Any investment which the person making disclosure, that person's spouse, or minor children residing with that person has in any corporation or other business organization in excess of ten thousand dollars ($10,000) or five percent (5%) of the total capital; however, it shall not be necessary to state specific dollar

amounts or percentages of such investments;

(3) Any person, firm, or organization for whom compensated lobbying is done by any associate of the person making disclosure, that person's spouse, or minor children residing with the person making disclosure, or any firm in which the person making disclosure or they hold any interest, complete to include the terms of any such employment and the measure or measures to be supported or opposed;

(4) In general terms by areas of the client's interest, the entities to which professional services, such as those of an attorney, accountant, or architect, are furnished by the person making disclosure or that person's spouse;

(5) By any member of the general assembly, the amount and source, by name, or any contributions from private sources for use in defraying the expenses necessarily related to the adequate performance of that member's legislative duties. The expenditure of campaign funds by an officeholder for the furtherance of the office of the officeholder shall be considered as an expenditure under title 2, chapter 10, and such expenditures need not be reported under the provisions of this chapter;

(6) Any retainer fee which the person making the disclosure receives from any person, firm, or organization who is in the practice of promoting or opposing, influencing or attempting to influence, directly or indirectly, the passage or defeat of any legislation before the general assembly, the legislative committees, or the members to such entities;

(7) Any adjudication of bankruptcy or discharge received in any United States district court within five (5) years of the date of the disclosure;

(8) Any loan or combination of loans of more than one thousand

dollars ($1,000) from the same source made in the previous calendar year to the person making disclosure or to the spouse or minor children unless:

(A) The loan is from an immediate family member;

(B) The loan is from a financial institution whose deposits are insured by an entity of the federal government, or such loan is made in accordance with existing law and is made in the ordinary course of business. A loan is made in the ordinary course of business if the lender is in the business of making loans, and the loan bears the usual and customary interest rate of the lender for the category of loan involved, is made on a basis which assures repayment, is evidenced by a written instrument, and is subject to a due date or amortization schedule;

(C) The loan is secured by a recorded security interest in collateral, bears the usual and customary interest rate of the lender for the category of loan involved, is made on a basis which assures repayment, is evidenced by a written instrument, and is subject to a due date or amortization schedule;

(D) The loan is from a partnership in which the legislator has at least ten percent (10%) partnership interest; or

(E) The loan is from a corporation in which more than fifty percent (50%) of the outstanding voting shares are owned by the person making disclosure or by a member of such person's immediate family.

As used in this subdivision (8), "immediate family member" means a spouse, parent, sibling or child; and (9) Such additional information as the person making disclosure might desire.

Senate Code of Ethics, Article 2

Section 1. A Senator has a personal interest that conflicts with the proper discharge of the Senator's duties if:

(a) The Senator has reason to believe or expect that he or she will derive a direct monetary gain or any other advantage or suffer a direct monetary loss by reason of his or her official activity;

(b) The Senator is employed by a business entity that employs a lobbyist who seeks to influence legislative action regarding a matter before the Senate or any committee thereof; or (c) The immediate family, as defined in T.C.A. Section 3-6-301(12), of the Senator is a lobbyist employed to influence legislative action regarding a matter before the Senate or any committee thereof.

Section 2: ...(b) No Senator shall violate the provisions of T.C.A. Sections 2-10-123, 3-6-304, 3-6-305, or 39-16-102, nor shall any Senator otherwise misuse the Senator's office for personal financial gain.

(i) No Senator shall use the Senator's office either to grant or to obtain special privilege, exemption, or preferential treatment to or for him or herself.

Texas: GOVERNMENT CODE; CHAPTER 572. PERSONAL FINANCIAL DISCLOSURE, STANDARDS OF CONDUCT, AND CONFLICT OF INTEREST

§ 572.005. Determination of Substantial Interest.

An individual has a substantial interest in a business entity if the individual:

(1) has a controlling interest in the business entity;

(2) owns more than 10 percent of the voting interest in the business entity;

(3) owns more than $25,000 of the fair market value of the business entity;

(4) has a direct or indirect participating interest by shares, stock, or otherwise, regardless of whether voting rights are included, in more than 10 percent of the profits, proceeds, or capital gains of the business entity;

(5) is a member of the board of directors or other governing board of the business entity;

(6) serves as an elected officer of the business entity; or

(7) is an employee of the business entity.

Utah: § 76-8-109. Failure of member of Legislature to disclose interest in measure or bill.

(a) "Conflict of interest" means an action that is taken by a regulated officeholder that the officeholder reasonably believes may cause direct financial benefit or detriment to the officeholder, a member of the officeholder's immediate family, or an entity that the officeholder is required to disclose under the provisions of this section, and that benefit or detriment is distinguishable from the effects of that action on the public or on the officeholder's profession, occupation, or association generally.

Vermont: Senate Rule 71.

No senator shall be permitted to vote upon any question in which he or she is directly or immediately interested.

House Rule 75.

Members shall not be permitted to vote upon any question in which they are immediately or directly interested.

Virginia: General Assembly. § 30-101. Definitions.

"Personal interest" means a financial benefit or liability accruing to a legislator or to a member of his immediate family. Such interest shall exist by reason of (i) ownership in a business if the ownership interest exceeds three percent of the total equity of the business; (ii) annual income that exceeds, or may reasonably be anticipated to exceed, $ 10,000 from ownership in real or personal property or a business; (iii) salary, other compensation, fringe benefits, or benefits from the use of property, or any combination thereof, paid or provided by a business that exceeds, or may reasonably be anticipated to exceed, $ 10,000 annually; (iv) ownership of real or personal property if the interest exceeds $ 10,000 in value and excluding ownership in a business, income, or salary, other compensation, fringe benefits or benefits from the use of property; or (v) personal liability incurred or assumed on behalf of a business if the liability exceeds three percent of the asset value of the business.

"Personal interest in a contract" means a personal interest which a legislator has in a contract with a governmental agency, whether due to his being a party to the contract or due to a personal interest in a business which is a party to the contract.

"Contract" means any agreement to which a governmental agency is a party, or any agreement on behalf of a governmental agency which involves the payment of money appropriated by the General Assembly or a political subdivision, whether or not such agreement is executed in the name of the Commonwealth of Virginia, or some political subdivision thereof. "Contract" includes a subcontract only when the contract of which it is a part is with the legislator's own governmental agency.

"Personal interest in a transaction" means a personal interest of a legislator in any matter considered by the General Assembly.

Such personal interest exists when an officer or employee or a member of his immediate family has a personal interest in property or a business, or represents any individual or business and such property, business or represented individual or business (i) is the subject of the transaction or (ii) may realize a reasonably foreseeable direct or indirect benefit or detriment as a result of the action of the agency considering the transaction. A "personal interest in a transaction" exists only if the legislator or member of his immediate family or an individual or business represented by the legislator is affected in a way that is substantially different from the general public or from persons comprising a profession, occupation, trade, business or other comparable and generally recognizable class or group of which he or the individual or business he represents is a member.

"Transaction" means any matter considered by the General Assembly, whether in a committee, subcommittee, or other entity of the General Assembly or before the General Assembly itself, on which official action is taken or contemplated.

Senate Rule 36.

Every Senator present in the Chamber, when any question is put or vote taken, shall vote or be counted as voting on one side or the other, except in the case of pairs, as hereinafter provided. A Senator who has a personal interest in the transaction, as defined in § 30-101 of the Code of Virginia, shall neither vote nor be counted upon it, and he shall withdraw, or invoke this rule not to be counted, prior to the division and the fact shall be recorded on the voting machine. If a Senator invokes this rule, the Senator shall not participate, directly or indirectly, in the matter wherein the rule is invoked.

House Rule 69.

Upon a division of the House on any question, a member who is present and fails to vote shall on the demand of any member be counted on the negative of the question and when the yeas and nays are taken shall, in addition, be entered on the Journal as present and not voting. However, no member who has an immediate and personal interest in the result of the question shall either vote or be counted upon it…

Virgin Islands: TITLE THREE Executive; Chapter 37. Conflicts of Interest §1103. Substantial conflict of interest.

A person subject to this chapter has an interest which is in substantial conflict with the proper discharge of his duties in the public interest and of his responsibilities as prescribed in the laws of the Virgin Islands or a personal interest, arising from any situation, within the scope of this chapter, if he will derive a direct monetary gain or suffer a direct monetary loss, as the case may be, by reason of his official activity. He does not have an interest which is in substantial conflict with the proper discharge of his duties in the public interest and of his responsibilities as prescribed by the laws of the Virgin Islands or a personal interest, arising from any situation, within the scope of this chapter, if any benefit or detriment accrues to him as a member of an industry, profession, occupation, or group to no greater extent than any other member of such business, profession, occupation, or group.

TITLE THREE Executive; Chapter 37. Conflicts of Interest § 1104. Remote interest

(a) A territorial officer or employee shall not be deemed to be interested in a contract entered into by a public agency of which he is a member within the meaning of this chapter if he has only a remote interest in the contract and if he fact of such interest is disclosed to the public agency of which he is a member and noted in its official records, and thereafter the public agency authorizes, approves, or ratifies the contract in good faith.

(b) As used in this chapter "remote interest" means:

(1) that of a non-salaried officer or a nonprofit organization;

(2) that of a former employee or agency of a party contracting with the government, if the territorial officer or employee was an employee or agent of said contracting party for at least three (3) years prior to his initially becoming a territorial officer or employee. Time of employment with the contracting party shall be counted in computing the three (3) year period even though such contracting party has been converted from one form of business organization to a different form of business organization within the three (3) years of the initial taking of office by such territorial officer or employee. Time of employment in such case shall be counted only if, after the transfer or change in organization, the real or ultimate ownership of the contracting party is the same or substantially similar to that which existed before such transfer or change in organization. Stock holders, bond holders, partners, or other persons holding an interest in the contracting party are regarded as having the "real or ultimate ownership" of such contracting party.

(3) that of a parent in the earnings of his minor child for personal services.

(4) that of a landlord or tenant of the party contracting with the government.

(5) that of an attorney of the party contracting with the government but not representing the contracting party in negotiating with the government.

(6) that of a former supplier of goods or services to a party contracting with the government when such goods or services

were supplied to the contracting party by the territorial officer or employee for at least five (5) years prior to his election or appointment to a territorial office or employment.

(c) The provisions of this section shall not be applicable to any territorial officer or employee interested in a contract who influences or attempts to influence another member of a public agency of which he is a member to enter into the contract.

(d) The willful failure of a territorial officer or employee to disclose the fact of his interest in a contract pursuant to this section shall be punishable as provided in this chapter. Such violation shall not void the contract, however, unless the contracting party had knowledge of the fact of the remote interest of the officer at the time the contract was executed.

(e) A territorial officer or employee shall not be deemed to be interested in a contract made pursuant to competitive bidding under a procedure established by law if his sole interest is that of an officer, director, or employee or a bank or financial institution with which a party to the contract has the relationship of borrower or depositor or creditor.

Washington: § 42.52.020. Activities incompatible with public duties.

No state officer or state employee may have an interest, financial or otherwise, direct or indirect, or engage in a business or transaction or professional activity, or incur an obligation of any nature, that is in conflict with the proper discharge of the state officer's or state employee's official duties.

§ 42.52.030.

(1) No state officer or state employee, except as provided in subsection (2) of this section, may be beneficially interested,

directly or indirectly, in a contract, sale, lease, purchase, or grant that may be made by, through, or is under the supervision of the officer or employee, in whole or in part, or accept, directly or indirectly, any compensation, gratuity, or reward from any other person beneficially interested in the contract, sale, lease, purchase, or grant.

(2) No state officer or state employee may participate in a transaction involving the state in his or her official capacity with a person of which the officer or employee is an officer, agent, employee, or member, or in which the officer or employee owns a beneficial interest, except that an officer or employee of an institution of higher education or the *Spokane intercollegiate research and technology institute may serve as an officer, agent, employee, or member, or on the board of directors, board of trustees, advisory board, or committee or review panel for any nonprofit institute, foundation, or fund-raising entity; and may serve as a member of an advisory board, committee, or review panel for a governmental or other nonprofit entity.

West Virginia: 6B-2-5 (d). Interests in public contracts. --

(1) In addition to the provisions of section fifteen, article ten, chapter sixty-one of this code, no elected or appointed public official or public employee or member of his or her immediate family or business with which he or she is associated may be a party to or have an interest in the profits or benefits of a contract which the official or employee may have direct authority to enter into, or over which he or she may have control: Provided, That nothing herein shall be construed to prevent or make unlawful the employment of any person with any governmental body: Provided, however, That nothing herein shall be construed to prohibit a member of the Legislature from entering into a contract with any governmental body, or prohibit a part-time appointed public official from entering into a contract which the

part-time appointed public official may have direct authority to enter into or over which he or she may have control when the official has not participated in the review or evaluation thereof, has been rescued from deciding or evaluating and has been excused from voting on the contract and has fully disclosed the extent of his or her interest in the contract.

(2) In the absence of bribery or a purpose to defraud, an elected or appointed public official or public employee or a member of his or her immediate family or a business with which he or she is associated shall not be considered as having a prohibited financial interest in a public contract when such a person has a limited interest as an owner, shareholder or creditor of the business which is awarded a public contract. A limited interest for the purposes of this subsection is:

(A) An interest which does not exceed one thousand dollars in the profits or benefits of the public contract or contracts in a calendar year;

(B) An interest as a creditor of a public employee or official who exercises control over the contract, or a member of his or her immediate family, if the amount is less than five thousand dollars.

(3) If a public official or employee has an interest in the profits or benefits of a contract, then he or she may not make, participate in making, or in any way attempt to use his office or employment to influence a government decision affecting his or her financial or limited financial interest. Public officials shall also comply with the voting rules prescribed in subsection (j) of this section.

(4) Where the provisions of subdivisions (1) and (2) of this subsection would result in the loss of a quorum in a public body or agency, in excessive cost, undue hardship, or other substantial

interference with the operation of a state, county, municipality, county school board or other governmental agency, the affected governmental body or agency may make written application to the Ethics Commission for an exemption from subdivisions (1) and (2) of this subsection.

6B-2-5. (j) Limitations on Voting.

(1) Public officials, excluding members of the Legislature who are governed by subsection (i) of this section, may not vote on a matter:

(A) In which they, an immediate family member, or a business with which they or an immediate family member is associated have a financial interest. Business with which they are associated means a business of which the person or an immediate family member is a director, officer, owner, employee, compensated agent, or holder of stock which constitutes five percent or more of the total outstanding stocks of any class.

(B) If a public official is employed by a financial institution and his or her primary responsibilities include consumer and commercial lending, the public official may not vote on a matter which directly affects the financial interests of a customer of the financial institution if the public official is directly involved in approving a loan request from the person or business appearing before the governmental body or if the public official has been directly involved in approving a loan for that person or business within the past 12 months: Provided, That this limitation only applies if the total amount of the loan or loans exceeds fifteen thousand dollars.

(C) A personnel matter involving the public official's spouse or relative;

(D) The appropriations of public moneys or the awarding of a contract to a nonprofit corporation if the public official or an immediate family member is employed by the nonprofit. (II) A public official may vote:

(A) If the public official, his or her spouse, immediate family members or relatives or business with which they are associated are affected as a member of, and to no greater extent than any other member of a profession, occupation, class of persons or class of businesses. A class shall consist of not fewer than five similarly situated persons or businesses; or;

(B) If the matter affects a publicly traded company when: (i) The public official, or dependent family members individually or jointly own less than five percent of the issued stock in the publicly traded company and the value of the stocks individually or jointly owned is less than ten thousand dollars; and (ii) Prior to casting a vote the public official discloses his or her interest in the publicly traded company.

(3) For a public official's recusal to be effective, it is necessary to excuse him or herself from participating in the discussion and decision-making process by physically removing him or herself from the room during the period, fully disclosing his or her interests, and recusing him or herself from voting on the issue.

See also Title 58, Legislative Rule of the Ethics Commission, Series 8, Interest in Public Contracts.

Wisconsin: § 19.45. Standards of conduct; state public officials.

The legislature hereby reaffirms that a state public official holds his or her position as a public trust, and any effort to realize substantial personal gain through official conduct is a violation of that trust...The legislature further recognizes that in a representative democracy, the representatives are drawn from society and, therefore, cannot and should not be without all personal and economic interest in the decisions and policies of government; that citizens who serve as state public officials retain their rights as citizens to interests of a personal or economic nature; that standards of ethical conduct for state public officials need to distinguish between those minor and inconsequential conflicts that are unavoidable in a free society, and those conflicts which are substantial and material; and that state public officials may need to engage in employment, professional or business activities, other than official duties, in order to support themselves or their families and to maintain a continuity of professional or business activity, or may need to maintain investments, which activities or investments do not conflict with the specific provisions of this subchapter.

(1) No state public official may use his or her public position or office to obtain financial gain or anything of substantial value for the private benefit of himself or herself or his or her immediate family, or for an organization with which he or she is associated. This subsection does not prohibit a state public official from using the title or prestige of his or her office to obtain contributions permitted and reported as required by ch. 11.

(5)No state public official may use or attempt to use the public position held by the public official to influence or gain unlawful benefits, advantages or privileges personally or for others.... (13) No state public official or candidate for state public office may, directly or by means of an agent, give, or offer or promise to give, or withhold, or offer or promise to withhold, his or her vote or influence, or promise to take or refrain from taking official action with respect to any proposed or pending matter in consideration of, or upon condition that, any other person make or refrain from making a political contribution, or provide or refrain from providing any service or other thing of value, to or for the benefit of a candidate, a political party, any person who is subject to a registration requirement under s. 11.05, or any person making a communication that contains a reference to a clearly identified state public official holding an elective office or to a candidate for state public office.

§ 19.46. Conflict of interest prohibited; exception.

(1) Except in accordance with the boards advice under s. 5.05 (6a) and except as otherwise provided in sub. (3), no state public official may:

(a) Take any official action substantially affecting a matter in which the official, a member of his or her immediate family, or an organization with which the official is associated has a substantial financial interest.

(b) Use his or her office or position in a way that produces or assists in the production of a substantial benefit, direct or indirect, for the official, one or more members of the officials immediate family either separately or together, or an organization with which the official is associated.

§ 19.42

(2)"Associated", when used with reference to an organization, includes any organization in which an individual or a member of his or her immediate family is a director, officer or trustee, or owns or controls, directly or indirectly, and severally or in the aggregate, at least 10% of the outstanding equity or of which an individual or a member of his or her immediate family is an authorized representative or agent.

Wyoming: § 6-5-101.

"Pecuniary benefit" is benefit in the form of property, but does not include: Property with a value of less than twenty dollars

($20.00); Food or drink or entertainment authorized as a proper deductible expense for income tax purposes under the United States Internal Revenue Code up to an amount of one hundred dollars ($100.00) per year; or Contributions to a political campaign of a public servant as provided in W.S. 22-25-102.

§ 6-5-103. Compensation for past official behavior; penalties. A person commits an offense if he solicits, accepts or agrees to accept any pecuniary benefit as compensation for having, as a public servant, given a decision or vote favorable to another, or for having otherwise exercised a discretion in his favor, or for having violated his statutory duties. For purposes of this section, "compensation" does not include mere acceptance of an offer of employment.

§ 6-5-106. Conflict of interest; penalties; disclosure of interest and withdrawal from participation.

(a) Except as provided by subsection (b) of this section, a public servant commits an offense if he requests or receives any pecuniary benefit, other than lawful compensation, on any contract, or for the letting of any contract, or making any appointment where the government employing or subject to the discretion or decisions of the public servant is concerned.

(b) If any public servant discloses the nature and extent of his pecuniary interest to all parties concerned therewith and does not participate during the considerations and vote thereon and does not attempt to influence any of the parties and does not act for the governing body with respect to the contracts or appointments, then the acts are not unlawful under subsection (a) of this section. Subsection (a) of this section does not apply to the operation, administration, inspection or performance of banking and deposit contracts or relationships after the selection of a depository.

(c) Violation of subsection (a) of this section is a misdemeanor punishable by a fine of not more than five thousand dollars ($5,000.00).

Well that was a lot to digest but without that information you can't even begin to be vigilant let alone fight the internal corruption from deliberate conflicts of interest.

Chapter Five
The Government Agenda

Freedom had been under attack for a long time before the culling of American freedom in the early 2000s. Social Engineers had been conditioning the American people's minds for years, dumbing them down to suggestions that government was the answer to all their problems. The term, "dumbing down", was thought up in 1933 as a slang word used by motion picture screenplay writers to mean: *"To revise so as to appeal to those of little education or intelligence."* It was quickly adopted by the government as a PR tool, and later used to take further control over the American people.

The dumbing down of America has been a success that is second to no other movement in our history. It has indeed made the citizens stupid. Here is an example of the brain dead people now infesting our once free nation; There is a video on You Tube that shows a man with a SOLID GOLD one ounce Canadian coin, The real Deal, who was trying to sell it for $100 DOLLARS and the people in Southern California in the LA area along the Beach, didn't want to buy this solid gold coin because Canadian money was no good in California. They actually said that solid gold Canadian money had no value in California. He then asked people if they would pay $50 for the solid gold coin and the people still said Canadian money was worthless in California. This is beyond stupid and its proof that many of the people have the brains God gave an ice cube. The people/sheeple have been dumbed down in public schools and universities for over 30 years and it sure shows! Jonathan Gruber who was the architect of Obama Demo Care has stated in several videos that the American People are not just stupid, some are beyond stupid.

Since the government has its hands in every aspect of our

lives, people are afraid if they speak out against the government, they will be targeted and maybe even fired from their job. America is fast becoming a closed society and bogus arrests are now common and they will start escalating very soon. FEMA camps are very real and will soon be filled up with American Citizens who question the government's authority. If you are unluckily put on the government's Four SSSS list, (Major Security Risk) you will be searched at airports and check points across the nation. And No this isn't a joke, if you see four SSSS on your flight ticket that means you are considered a threat to the government's supreme authority. Finding a job will become harder, especially if you need a background check. You may even be black listed from online sales sites and not allowed to sell on those sites, furthering your inability to make money! The government will do whatever it has to do to frighten you into submission or to ruin you financially so you can't cause them any problems. Then the bogus arrests will begin and the media discrediting you will then start to make you look guilty in the eyes of the people. Since you have no money to fight the government... they win and you lose, rotting in some federal dungeon.

I know this sounds a lot like a nightmare out of some story about Nazi Germany, China or the Soviet Union, but it is happening now as you read this. You can now be arrested in America for being a terrorist and jailed for 10 years for merely protesting, and if you resist, you can be charged with treason and possibly put to death! This is NO JOKE! Any use of force against the government is a crime punishable by death without even a trial if the government deems it necessary.

America has slowly become a prison, and for those who see through the illusion of freedom and try to inform the people of the truth, it will become a nightmare. The First Amendment of the Bill of Rights had finally been abridged when Socialist

President Obama sign bill HR 347 into law in 2013, which makes it a felony to protest if the government says you can't because they don't like what you have to say! Corporations now have total control over the media, the press and the people's government. Insurance corporations ruled the day and also rule the American people and Politicians. The people's elected leaders have passed laws that forced Americans to buy health insurance from private corporations. The once free people of America had become subjects over night and the property of a tyrannical Government.

Like livestock on a gigantic ranch, the majority of the people whinnied and bayed in apathetic complacency like the sheep they once herded, stripped of their will to be free. They had allowed themselves to be owned by a master that saw them as nothing more than revenue generating animals. Those who spoke out against the tyranny were labeled crazy people that should not be listened to. Most of the people knew those who spoke out were doing it because they knew allowing the government the power to force people to buy anything was a direct violation of the Constitution... and they were right. But the US Supreme Court had been infiltrated, poisoned and corrupted by the corporate government shills and they ruled that the government now had the power to command the people to obey and buy insurance, or whatever the government deemed was in the best interest of the Country. The Supreme Court Justices Rulings were merely Political Opinions and Political Opinions are like a Fart in a wind storm, they blow the same direction as the political wind blows! Resistance was futile, the citizens were to be assimilated, like taking a page out of George Orwell's 1984 novel... the people had become the property of the Federal Government.

For years the government had been disarming the public in anticipation of taking total control with no regard or threat from the Second Amendment, so the people could not resist the enslavement that was coming. Police were turned into military killing machines, killing anyone who refused to obey the government. They killed citizens without question if their government master ordered it, destroying anyone who witnessed it or spoke out against their murderous Gestapo tyranny. America had become a prison camp to those who could not afford the tens of thousands of dollars a person needed to flee to a free country. Citizen's hatred of the country they once loved was growing every time they were subjected to the tyranny of the new American Gestapo. The corporate government controlled media would quickly create propaganda to convince the apathetic complacent masses that the new American military police were heroes. Even when they were caught on video recordings kicking in the doors of innocent men, women, children and killing the family pet and anyone who moved to protect their family members including children... the complacently apathetic people would not do anything to stop the tyranny. But not everyone believed the corporate government controlled media's lies. More and more people were waking up to see the nightmare they helped create by their silence.

The Government and their Police knew the people were starting to fight back. Citizens were posting videos on the internet that showed Police tyranny, so the government started to seize the people and their recorders, destroying the evidence that clearly showed the treasonous tyrannical crimes the police perpetrated against the people. Then the police would lie and the controlled Media would tell the masses it never happened, and sadly, many of the American Sheeple believed those lies without question, even after seeing proof to the contrary.

The government had also installed an "Internet Kill Switch" that could be used to stop the spread of information the government didn't want people to know. All forms of communication had been taken over by the government and they were listening to everyone, everywhere! The citizens, sadly enough, would be the very reason the government would take total control over the Internet. The Government had a plan to pretend they are backing away from controlling the Internet and spying on everyone, and if they already haven't said anything about it by the time you read this, they soon will. They will publicly announce they are no longer going to allow agencies to spy on Americans and the people will be safe from government eyes on the internet. Then just like so many other staged catastrophic attacks on the people, the country will be attacked by some "Terrorist" threat to your safety. Of course the sheeple will cry "Help Me Master Government" and the government will jump in and tell the mindless dumbed down masses they will be saved. But only at the price of total control over the Internet and their privacy, and sadly most won't mind, because they will be saved by the government!

The government knows that one day the people will rise up against their tyranny. They know all too well that the endless lies they told to take your freedom will one day come back to haunt them. They're not too worried though, because they are working on armored suits that would make the police supermen, impervious to small arms weapons fire. Basically being able to walk up to you under fire and kill you without worrying about getting hurt. Without these super suits, smart people know if they are going to get in a gun fight with Gestapo, they need to aim for the head preferably the face or neck area because that is the least protected and best chance of getting a kill shot. But once these suits get perfected, the citizens won't stand a chance against the government and their enslavement will be sealed. The media will tout these supermen suits as great for our military because our brave men and women will be protected from the "Terrorist's" small weapons fire, and most of the mindless masses will say hurrah to the new super-police/military, never thinking beyond the media hype that those suits will be used against them one day.

'Iron Man suit'

Concept suit from the animated video produced by the Army's Research, Development and Engineering Command

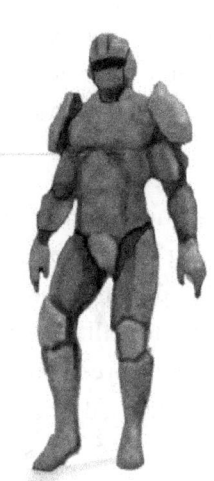

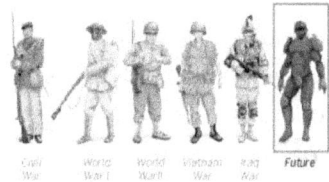

Head gear:
Live data feed projected on a see-through display inside the helmet.

Uniform:
Head-to-toe armor would protect the soldier from bullets and sharpnel.

Pack essentials:
The prototype should be able to cure minor wounds with inflatable tourniquets. It would also carry an oxygen supply, cooling system and vital-signs sensors.

The suit would be connected with drones and satellite systems.

Pack weight:
Motors in the exoskeleton would allow a soldier to jump and run carrying 100 pounds or more.

It is called the *"Iron Man Tactical Assault Suit"* and the United States military/police will be wearing these in a town near you as soon as the government perfects them. Once they get these gems perfected it will provide the wearer with superhuman abilities like night vision, enhanced strength, and protection from gunfire... and you can kiss any resistance against your government goodbye, because resistance will indeed be futile. Unless of course, you can get one for yourself, but I wouldn't bet on that, but I would however bet the proverbial farm it will be illegal for citizens to own... any takers?

The government defiantly has a plan in place to disarm America and damn the Constitution and your Rights, and they have several scenarios where the police will bang on the door then bust in telling residents they have to search for weapons. If too much resistance is seen and cops are being shot at or killed the second scenario will be to go house to house with an armored tank or gun truck and demand over a loud speaker that all residents come outside their homes with their hands on their head. Any home that does not comply would be attacked with tear gas, grenades and bullets before Gestapo, Police, Military entered. This would put a scare into the people's resistance in that area and send a message to others by destroy dwellings and hopefully any weapons and supplies of those resisting might have had.

Now if you don't think this is going to happen you are a fool. The training of the troops is being done subtly and most people never see it happening. But it is happening and it is happening in a major way. Only those willing to kill on demand are to be trained for the American occupation force. Troops from all over the world are being stationed and trained on American soil and taught to wage urban warfare on Americans. They are being trained to *"Take them out when in doubt"* which means if you are a suspected threat, you will be killed without warning.

I was over at an apartment building in Yuba City, California in the summer of 2014 and was witness to a police raid on a fellow who was reported to have a shotgun and apparently threatening to kill himself. I watched as the police came storm trooping in and blocked off all access, which also blocked me from leaving, which I was about to do. Cops came from all sides and told us to get back as they took out their full auto AR15s. There must have been 20 or more of them there for a supposed man with a gun. I had just been over by this apartment and saw kids in the pool and all seemed calm. The parents who had their kids in the pool were told to stay back, and that had some extremely worried. Finally they got the kids out of the pool and a short time later we heard a flash bang grenade go off and several minutes later they came out with the guy in cuffs. What was the most disgusting to me, was when I saw two cops high-fiving each other with their AR15s held high and one said; "This has been a GREAT DAY!"

I couldn't help but think to myself "Gestapo" when I heard that.

I know that you Law Enforcers will try and spin what that cop said as meaning it was a great day because no one got hurt....but that is WRONG! All of those people who witnessed it were hurt and worried mentally, and that display of jack booted storm troopers attacking was not the face of a friendly peace officer. I have known and respect Peace Officers, but have nothing but contempt for Law Enforcing Gestapo. A friend of mine was a Peace Officer before the militarization of the police, and do you know what a Great Day for a Peace Officer is? A day when he didn't have to write any tickets or warnings and he didn't have to use his gun, let alone a machine gun and grenades, because that was a day he knew he had been doing his job, keeping the peace. Merely by his presences, walking his beat, meeting and greeting friends, neighbors, business owners and strangers alike, everyone had a peaceful day. Now that is a GOOD DAY for a Peace Officer!

Ever since the Supreme Court in 2005 ruled that police are not Peace Officers and do not have to keep the peace, they are now Law Enforcers who are there to "Enforce the Law!" They have been turned into storm trooper Gestapo, and you can expect and bet your life raids will take place against all citizens who refuse to obey. It will only be a matter of time before those who are believers in the US Constitution and Freedom will be targeted. The raids will come early in the morning, and the government attackers will even bring their own film crews dressed in body armor and cameras to video the government rounding up the scourge terrorist patriots who would not denounce the Constitution and the Bill of Rights. Acres of bodies will pile up in government dead zones.

The government has places that now store coffin liners and body bags waiting to be used against you. Your Federal

Government has ordered one billion dollars worth of these coffin liners and body bags and that amounts to about 5 million each of them. Who do you think these are for, some invading army, or for us?

How can you survive an attack by government forces? Well You may not, but here are some things you can do...The first thing you need to know about a raid on your home is that they will either come in early in the morning guns waving and screaming at you, in hopes you are woken up confused... Or they will come in force wearing body armor and carrying AR15s or M16s full auto, with stun grenades ready to kill. Then they will secure your block and remove your neighbors, then shut of all your utilities and jam your cell reception and then give you a call and either try and talk you out or wait you out, or just storm the building after using their grenades. Odds are they will either kill you or capture you unless you have a small army helping out.

But it is always a good idea to have either battery back up or a generator that is secured like a generator in your garage you can use. Have water storage and food storage. Have a 2-way radio like a CB or ham radio you can use. Then try and get as much media attention as possible, especially if you are being attacked for publicly denouncing the government for their violations against our Rights. If you do have Cell phone usage, uplink video of the attackers to your Face Book, Twitter or YouTube site and try and get as much public support as you can. Then pray others will come and help you.

A neighborhood militia would be an ideal idea to create. Training yourselves in attack scenarios is also a good idea. Attacking an attacking force from behind or flanking them always scares the hell out of them. Just remember once you head down this road there is no going back, it is full steam ahead and damn the torpedoes. Once you hear the enemy being attacked by your allies from behind, or ahead of you, if you happen to be the back up force, you have to hit them with everything you have and you will either win the battle or die fighting tyranny like a free human. Now remember this is a worse case scenario, when and if, the government declares war on those people that not only believe in the Constitution, but those of us who have swore an oath to uphold and defend the Constitution.

If or when that dreadful day comes, those too cowardly to fight and are lucky enough to escape the mass culling of Constitutionalists, but not able to escape America, will hide like scared mice in dark dirty places, many to slowly die of hunger and illness. Only those smart enough to escape America before the government stops the exodus will have a chance of surviving. Those who do not, will be rounded up and will be forced to work as they are herded into cities and camps made to toil from dawn to dusk. If you refuse to work you will not be fed, and anyone caught giving you food will be executed for treason! Only the controlling elite will be allowed the pleasures once known to all Americans, food, clean water and drink, comfort, and only those loyalists will be allowed to freely move about. All the rest will be told what to wear, what to eat, what to drink, where they can live, what they can own, and who they can talk to. Any violation of the rules will bring swift painful punishment! America will become a nightmare prison for those who remembered the freedoms they once had.

Does this sound like an over exaggerated nightmare that can never ever happen in America?

Well much of it already has!

In 2114 this was a News Headline; *{ALBUQUERQUE, NM — Outrage has ignited over a helmet-cam video of officers fatally confronting a homeless man, James Boyd at his primitive campsite in the foothills. Video shows the man standing by his meager possessions, surrounded by rifle-toting officers who were citing him for illegally camping without government permission. Officers ultimately tossed a concussion grenade in his face,*

attacked him with an attack dog, and shot him to death in a flurry of gunfire.}

Countless recorded video of cops/Gestapo murdering citizens are out on the internet and have been reported in the news for all to see, yet most of the people never bother to view them, or they say to themselves it can never happen to me. Apathetically complacent towards the video and audio evidence that proves beyond any doubt that the person murdered was murdered without any justified reason, people keep standing aside, looking the other way. Most never realize or even think that if you look the other way, without saying a thing against it…you are in a sense, aiding and abetting the police/Gestapo in the senseless murders of your fellow Americans!

Did you know that over 15% of the police are indeed sociopaths and hope they get the chance to kill someone? A study was done and never released to the public that stated;

"Most people who are attracted to law enforcement careers are sociopaths. Completely lacking in conscience, and unable to feel any empathy for fellow human beings, these monsters are given a badge and gun, and the government backing to impose their will on society. For many years we had intensive psychological tests in place to weed-out these undesirables but in the past two decades these tests have largely been replaced with less intensive ones that don't really predict future behavior problems.

One psychologist that developed new tests for the state of Indiana's law enforcement has stated that conventional tests such as the Minnesota Multiphasic Personality Inventory and Millon Clinical Multiaxial Inventory-III that are routinely given to prospective applicants at Fortune 500 companies cannot be given to applicants of law enforcement agencies because too many subjects would register as psychopaths and thus be ineligible for employment.

What we are now seeing appears to indicate that psychological testing is being used to locate and hire sociopathic deviants rather than a tool to screen them out."

The person who wrote this didn't want their name attached in fear of retaliation.

The rest of those hired as cops are bullies who enjoy harming people and being in total command. If you don't believe this you are indeed a fool, because you have bought into the "police are your friend" propaganda, just as countless other enslaved people have throughout history. Those who are hired as Law Enforcers are chosen because they are willing to shoot to kill and many of them enjoy it! You Don't believe that? Just try and disarm the police through legislation and see how much resistance, hate and threats you get from them. Now I realize not all cops are psycho, but the ones who are normally caring people are just as much as fault, and maybe even more at fault for the crazy cops, because they refuse to say or do anything to stop the carnage.

Did you know that there are more sociopathic personalities in government and law enforcement than there are diabetics in America?

Source: http://wearerespectablenegroes.blogspot.com/2013/05/is -united-states-of-america-sociopathic.html

Another alarming figure is that from January 1st to April 1st 2015 over 368 people have been killed by police in America. In 2014 over 1000 people were killed by police in the USA. These statistics are from killedbypolice.net which started in 2013 because no one was keeping track of how many citizens get killed each year. Not even the FBI had an accurate number and 2013 proves that fact because according to the FBI 461 people were killed by police. Killedbypolice.net started collecting data in May of 2013 from news reports and police reports from all over the country, and the number they came up with from May through December was 748 killed by police. Many States like New York don't report citizens killed by police only police killed by citizens. So the total numbers killed by police maybe even higher. In the last ten years over 5000 people have been reportedly killed by police, actual number is probably much higher. That is far more than were killed in the Iraq war which was 4489 and only a small number of Cops have been charged with a homicide or negligent homicide out of that 5000 murder death toll.

Now there is no doubt we need policing for thieves and thugs. There is a need for peace officers and neighborhood police. But we have to be in control over how they conduct themselves when interacting with citizens.

Chapter Six
Destroying the Constitution with Demo-Obama-Care

Demo-Obama-Care or the socialist Affordable Health Care Act, which was un-constitutionally imposed no matter what the Supreme Court tells the public, was the biggest lie the American people ever had to swallow. It really had nothing to do with making people healthy; it had to do with totally destroying the Constitution and Seizing total control over the American People.

I know the medical industry has its problems and has had problems for a long time. I know from first hand experience that it has gotten as corrupt as the government because of the government involvement. I also know that the medical industry is as full of liars as our government. I refuse to go to any doctor that lies to me and I have caught several liars. My philosophy is real simple; If a Doctor, namely Your Doctor lies to you about any of your medical care, how the hell can you trust your health with them? When I catch a healthcare individual bold faced lying to me, I will call them on that lie, and if they persist, I normally just put on my hat and walk out. Unless I am in an exceptionally aggravated state, then I will put on my hat and tell them they are fired, and then walk out never to return.

Years ago when I was a kid you could call a doctor and they would make a house call. Now you can't get a doctor to return your phone call. Years ago the doctor or nurse or their staff never lied to you by telling you that because you take this or that medication you have to come in every 30 days, and I am not just talking about class 2 drugs. Now doctors and staff routinely lie out their pie-holes to people and I have caught them at it. It is all revenue generation, and if lying gets the job done, then they are going to lie to you! They are now just as bad, and even worse, than the Politicians and Gestapo because your life and general health is in their hands. That is a sad epitaph for medical in the USA, and it is getting harder and harder to find a good old country doctor. Because they are being replaced with government taught brown-nose medical lackeys that could care less about your health only about the bottom financial line and pleasing their government masters.

I am often asked; "Well what can you do?" and the answer is simple, don't do business with manipulating liars! Shun them and tell people who they are and refuse to accept the excuses they use to explain their lies! Especially, if you catch them in a bold faced lie that was aimed at you to control you! Stop financing them!

Now with Demo/Obama-Care law, which was sold to the American people by lies, and now to be enforced by the IRS, which is run by Bold Faced Liars, you can pretty much expect to be lied to about the real agenda of the government. And that is total control over you, their slave property!

This is a letter from a former Constitutional Lawyer that was posted on the internet that tells the real truth:

"The Truth About the Health Care Act" - Michael Connelly, Ret. Constitutional Attorney

"Well, I have done it! I have read the entire text of proposed House Bill 3200: The Affordable Health Care Choices Act of 2009. I studied it with particular emphasis from my area of expertise, constitutional law. I was frankly concerned that parts of the proposed law that were being discussed might be unconstitutional.

What I found was far worse than what I had heard or expected.

227

To begin with, much of what has been said about the law and its implications is in fact true, despite what the Democrats and the media are saying. The law does provide for rationing of health care, particularly where senior citizens and other classes of citizens are involved, free health care for illegal immigrants, free abortion services, and probably forced participation in abortions by members of the medical profession.

The Bill will also eventually force private insurance companies out of business, and put everyone into a government run system. All decisions about personal health care will ultimately be made by federal bureaucrats, and most of them will not be health care professionals. Hospital admissions, payments to physicians, and allocations of necessary medical devices will be strictly controlled by the government.

However, as scary as all of that is, it just scratches the surface. In fact, I have concluded that this legislation really has no intention of providing affordable health care choices. Instead it is a convenient cover for the most massive transfer of power to the Executive Branch of government that has ever occurred, or even been contemplated. If this law or a similar one is adopted, major portions of the Constitution of the United States will effectively have been destroyed.

The first thing to go will be the masterfully crafted balance of power between the Executive, Legislative, and Judicial branches of the U.S. Government. The Congress will be transferring to the Obama Administration authority in a number of different areas over the lives of the American people, and the businesses they own.

The irony is that the Congress doesn't have any authority to legislate in most of those areas to begin with! I defy anyone to read the text of the U.S. Constitution and find any authority granted to the members of Congress to regulate health care.

This legislation also provides for access, by the appointees of the Obama administration, all of your personal healthcare information, a direct violation of the specific provisions of the 4th Amendment to the Constitution, information, your personal financial information, and the information of your employer, physician, and hospital. All of this is a protecting against unreasonable searches and seizures. You can also forget about the right to privacy. That will have been legislated into oblivion regardless of what the 3rd and 4th Amendments may provide.

If you decide not to have healthcare insurance, or if you have private insurance that is not deemed acceptable to the Health Choices Administrator appointed by Obama, there will be a tax imposed on you. It is called a tax instead of a fine because of the intent to avoid application of the due process clause of the 5th Amendment. However, that doesn't work because since there is nothing in the law that allows you to contest or appeal the imposition of the tax, it is definitely depriving someone of property without the due process of law.

So, there are three of those pesky Amendments that the far left hate so much, out of the original ten in the Bill of Rights, that are effectively nullified by this law. It doesn't stop there though.

The 9th Amendment that provides: The enumeration in the Constitution, of certain rights, shall not be construed to deny or disparage others retained by the people; The 10th Amendment states: The powers not delegated to the United States by the Constitution, nor prohibited by it to the States, are preserved to the States respectively, or to the people. Under the provisions of this piece of Congressional handiwork neither the people nor the states are going to have any rights or powers at all in many areas that once were theirs to control.

I could write many more pages about this legislation, but I think you get the idea. This is not about health care; it is about seizing power and limiting rights. Article 6 of the Constitution requires the members of both houses of Congress to "be bound by oath or affirmation to support the Constitution." If I was a member of Congress I would not be able to vote for this legislation or anything like it, without feeling I was violating that sacred oath or affirmation. If I voted for it anyway, I would hope the American people would hold me accountable.

For those who might doubt the nature of this threat, I suggest they consult the source, the U.S. Constitution, and Bill of Rights. There you can see exactly what we are about to have taken from us."

Here are some points to consider that Doctor Ron Paul had written that are right on target:

"No one has a right to medical care. If one assumes such a right, it endorses the notion that some individuals have a right to someone else's life and property. This totally contradicts the principles of liberty.

If medical care is provided by government, this can only be achieved by an authoritarian government unconcerned about the rights of the individual.

Economic fallacies accepted for more than 100 years in the United States has deceived policy makers into believing that quality medical care can only be achieved by government force, taxation, regulations, and bowing to a system of special interests that creates a system of corporatism.

More dollars into any monopoly run by government never increases quality but it always results in higher costs and prices.

Government does have an important role to play in facilitating the delivery of all goods and services in an ethical and efficient manner.

First, government should do no harm. It should get out of the way and repeal all the laws that have contributed to the mess we have.

The costs are obviously too high but in solving this problem one cannot ignore the debasement of the currency as a major factor.

Bureaucrats and other third parties must never be allowed to interfere in the doctor/patient relationship.

The tax code, including the ERISA laws, must be changed to give everyone equal treatment by allowing a 100% tax credit for all medical expenses.

Laws dealing with bad outcomes and prohibiting doctors from entering into voluntary agreements with their patients must be repealed. Tort laws play a significant role in pushing costs higher, prompting unnecessary treatment and excessive testing. Patients deserve the compensation; the attorneys do not.

Insurance sales should be legalized nationally across state lines to increase competition among insurance companies.

Long-term insurance policies should be available to young people similar to term-life insurances that offer fixed prices for long periods of time.

The principle of insurance should be remembered. Its purpose in a free market is to measure risk, not to be used synonymously with social welfare programs. Any program that provides for first-dollar payment is no longer insurance. This would be similar to giving coverage for gasoline and repair bills to those who buy car insurance or providing food insurance for people to go to the grocery store. Obviously, that could not work. The cozy relationship between organized medicine and government must be reversed.

Early on medical insurance was promoted by the medical community in order to boost re-imbursements to doctors and hospitals. That partnership has morphed into the government/insurance industry still being promoted by the current administration.

Threatening individuals with huge fines by forcing them to buy insurance is a boon to the insurance companies. There must be more competition for individuals entering into the medical field. Licensing strictly limits the number of individuals who can provide patient care. A lot of problems were created in 20th century as a consequence the Flexner Report (1910), which was financed by the Carnegie Foundation and strongly supported by the AMA. Many medical schools were closed and the number of doctors was drastically reduced. The motivation was to close down medical schools that catered to women, minorities and especially homeopathy. We continue to suffer from these changes which were designed to protect physician's income and promote allopathic medicine over the more natural cures and prevention of homeopathic medicine.

We must remove any obstacles for people seeking holistic and nutritional alternatives to current medical care. We must remove the threat of further regulations pushed by the drug companies now working worldwide to limit these alternatives." – Doctor Ron Paul

Those who think DemoCare/Obamacare is a good thing never considered the 3,000 to 5,000 dollar deductible that you have to pay before you get any benefit, and if you can't afford the 3,000 to 5,000 deductible and do get sick, you go bankrupt anyway. This healthcare nightmare and cost problem never existed before 1965 when the government signed into law Medicare and took control and dictated how and what hospitals and doctors could

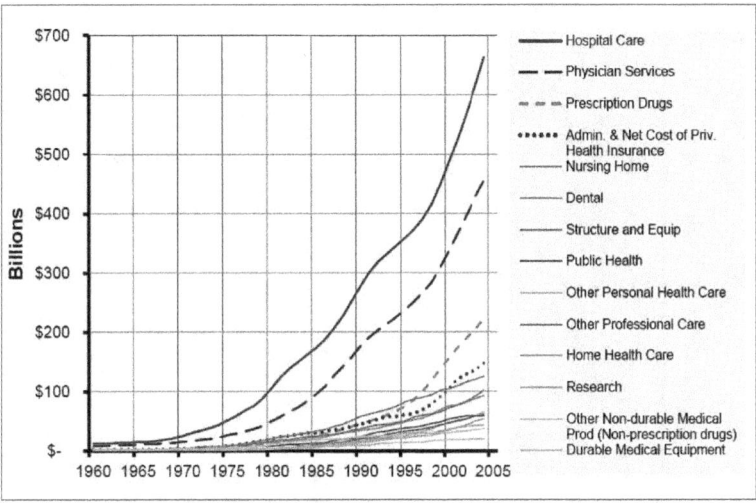

do. The moment President Johnson signed the Medicare law costs started to skyrocket! The following chart is an indexed comparison of inflation of Total Medical Prices (-) and Physician Services (- – -) from 1950 to 1993 with Base Year 1950. As you can see, prices didn't start to spike until after 1965. (Source: US Census 2013) If you listen to those who blame the doctors, you'll hear them spew that the doctors and hospitals have created the problem by creating the demand and that is not totally true. Yes, there were doctors and hospitals that were creating problems and inflating prices to profit from, but nothing like we are seeing today. Since 1965 doctors and hospitals have been too busy meeting the demands created by the government, and complying with government regulations has become an enslaving daily nightmare. So costs have skyrocketed and will continue to do so, as quantity replaces medical quality.

Below is a chart that shows the rise after 1965 that proves when government gets control you pay more! Costs have skyrocketed since the Government has gotten involve in your healthcare.

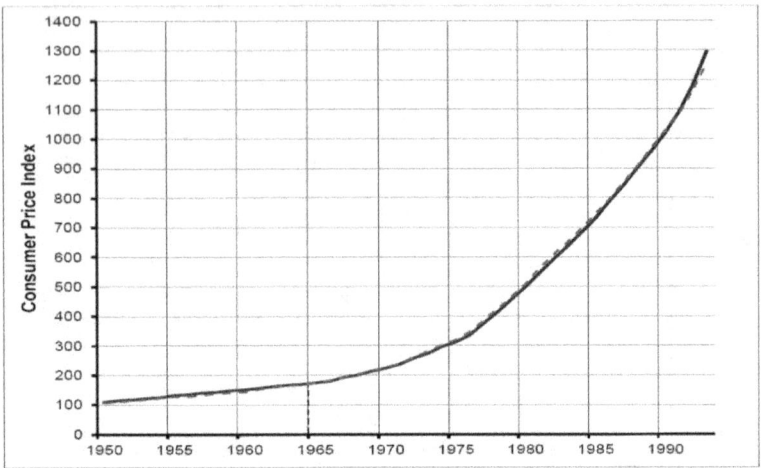

Welcome to the new Fast Food approach to medical care! But with one gigantic difference, they are charging you Bentley prices as they move you as quickly as they can through the chopped meat grinder!

Insurance and its involvement:

In a free competitive insurance market consumers want the most benefits for the lowest health care premiums. So would the Insurance companies, and self-insured employers, want to pay the lowest amount possible to the physicians and hospitals. If the health care industry was competitive at all supply levels, and not regulated by government mandate, suppliers would aggressively offer insurers competitive prices for high quality services. Insurance companies would have no problem selecting health care policies for their policyholders that encouraged them to obtain the best service they could for the lowest cost.

Consumers would protect themselves from unethical providers by taking their business to those who had a good reputation and did quality work at reasonable prices without unnecessary services. In a free competitive market, providers are forced to obtain this reputation or they go out of business.

It has been proven over and over again that government is bad for consumers and bad for business once they take control, and the reason for that is because once the government takes control you lose control. There is a good article by Mike Holly that goes into detail on this subject, and that is where I got a lot of this information.

Since the healthcare take over started we have seen a steady decline in service and a steady increase in cost. Before the big takeover of healthcare in the mid 60s costs were relatively low and doctors even made house calls. Now you are treated like you are when you go to a government agency like the DMV or Court House... "What are you here for, fill out this form and go to window 6, then take a number and wait until it is called." It's really sad when you are made to feel like you are being pushed through the system like going through a fast food line. And good luck in finding a good doctor if you lose the one you have, especially if you have a regiment of medications you are taking. You will go through them screwing everything up and possibly not getting your meds refilled at all. Getting a good doctor or a good healthcare provider has become a real nightmare in America...Why?... because most of the new doctors have their head stuck so far up the government's ass their shoulders don't even show. Healthcare is now just like all other government agencies, inept, incompetent, suspicious of you, and downright rude in many cases.

The following are major laws and other policies implemented by the Federal and state governments over the years that have interfered with the health care marketplace.

In 1910, the physician oligopoly was started during the Republican administration of William Taft after the American Medical Association lobbied the states to strengthen the regulation of medical licensure and allow their state AMA offices to oversee the closure or merger of nearly half of medical schools and also the reduction of class sizes. The states have been subsidizing the education of the number of doctors recommended by the AMA.

In 1925, prescription drug monopolies begun after the federal government led by Republican President Calvin Coolidge started allowing the patenting of drugs. (Drug monopolies have also been promoted by government research and development subsidies targeted to favored pharmaceutical companies.)

In 1945, buyer monopolization begun after the McCarran-Ferguson Act led by the Democrat President Roosevelt's Administration exempted the business of medical insurance from most federal regulation, including antitrust laws. (States have also more recently contributed to the monopolization by requiring health care plans to meet standards for coverage.)

In 1946, institutional provider monopolization begun after favored hospitals received federal subsidies (matching grants and loans) provided under the Hospital Survey and Construction Act passed during the Democrat President Truman's Administration. (States have also been exempting non-profit hospitals from antitrust laws.)

In 1951, employers started to become the dominant third-party insurance buyer during the Truman Administration after the Internal Revenue Service declared group premiums tax-deductible.

In 1965, nationalization was started with a government buyer monopoly after the Democrat President Johnson's Administration led passage of Medicare and Medicaid which provided health insurance for the elderly and poor, respectively.

In 1972, institutional provider monopolization was strengthened after the Nixon Administration started restricting the supply of hospitals by requiring federal certificate-of-need for the construction of medical facilities.

In 1974, buyer monopolization was strengthened during the Nixon Administration after the Employee Retirement Income Security Act exempted employee health benefit plans offered by large employers (e.g., HMOs) from state regulations and lawsuits (e.g., brought by people denied coverage).

In 1984, prescription drug monopolies were strengthened during the Reagan Administration after the Drug Price Competition and Patent Term Restoration Act permitted the extension of patents beyond 20 years. (The government has also allowed pharmaceuticals companies to bribe physicians to prescribe more expensive drugs.)

In 2003, prescription drug monopolies were strengthened during the Bush Administration after the Medicare Prescription Drug, Improvement, and Modernization Act provided subsidies to the elderly for drugs.

In 2014, nationalization is strengthened after the Patient Protection and Affordable Care Act of 2010 ("Obamacare") forces people to have Insurance and provided mandates, subsidies and insurance exchanges, and the expansion of Medicaid.

The Government is now also working on forcing employers who reduce their employees to under the number that exempts them from providing healthcare, to prove they have to downsize their labor force or prove they have to cut hours to fewer than 30, or they will not be excluded from providing healthcare insurance. The government is also working on signing laws that would make business give more people overtime. This is a major takeover of American Business just as the government took over healthcare and energy. The Fascists and Communists have done this throughout time around the world and now are doing it in America.

The Government is also working on forcing employers who are exempt from providing healthcare insurance, to request and prove their employees carry healthcare insurance before they can hire anyone. The Government is also working on making it mandatory to show proof of not only car insurance but also health insurance before you can get a drivers license or register your vehicle. You can bet this will evolve into showing proof of healthcare insurance before you get a loan or bank account or credit card, unless the American people wake up and put a stop to this anti-American tyranny.

Here is a letter that was intended to make people aware of the Real Omamcare or DemoCare:

"My name is Ashley and I'm a 26-year-old recent graduate from Michigan.

The phony Obamacare signup poster boy made me want to send a message about how Obamacare is really affecting people.

I graduated from The University of Michigan in 2009. In my state, this used to mean something, but even with a bachelor's I was told I was too educated and wouldn't stay. I watched as kids with GEDs and high school diplomas took the low-paying jobs for which I applied.

I went back to school and got a second degree and finally found work at a gym. I work nights and only get 32 hours a week for eight dollars an hour. I'm unable to find a second job at this time.

I have asthma, ulcers, and mild cerebral palsy. Obamacare takes my monthly rate from $75 a month for full coverage on my "Young Adult Plan," to $319 a month. After $6,000 in deductibles, of course.

Liberals claimed this law would help the poor. I am the poor, the working poor, and I can't afford to support myself, let alone older generations and people not willing to work at all.

This law has raped my future.

It will keep me and kids my age from having a future at all.

This is the real face of Obamacare and it isn't pretty."

I realize at present the USA has some of, if not the best medical care in the world, but give this Obama/Demo Care a few years and you'll see that healthcare will become a lot worse, and other countries will have just as good healthcare and even better than the USA. Still blows me away that this draconian law was forced on over 315,000,000 supposed free American citizens, so it could provide health insurances to 7,000,000 uninsured. Talk about a major scam on a supposed smart, free nation, this is the biggest of any I've seen. What makes this look even more pathetic is those responsible are not only still in office, but were re-elected to stay in office! Then Americans wonder why the rest of the world is laughing at America as a joke full of fools.

I have an idea that could work to the benefit of not only Doctors and the un-insured but the benefit of the heath care in America. It is really simple to. I know, you're thinking; not another idea, and it maybe un-doable but without ideas we get no solutions, so here is my idea; All of those who go to college on a student loan or grant for a medical degrees, would have to spend time for FREE in a Government Clinic to pay off the loan. Let's say they would have to work 5 to 8 hours a week at a Free Clinic and they would reduce the amount owed by whatever the going rate is for their experience level for those 5 to 8 hours. Now since the government has numerous building all across the nation that are sitting vacant, we the locations and for areas that don't the government could give a Tax Instinctive to the building owner(s) for leasing it to the government for a reasonably low amount.

The government could also give drug and lab equipment companies tax breaks for donation supplies and equipment to the Free Clinics. These Free Clinics would also be a great training ground for medical students, thus helping create more sorely needed medical personnel. This is a win win for the Medical Students who would otherwise have to pay back a government insured loan which many never get paid back. It also creates a way for those who want to be in the medical field a way to get into it without having to weigh into their decision the cost of paying back a medial student loan.

Now these Free Clinics could give just about all the basic care needed for most people and could for sure let them know if they had a serious problem. Now if a person had a serious problem that required a top notch surgeon, the government has salaried government surgeons already that could assist or they could give a private surgeon a tax break for donating his time to do the surgery. Since these clinics would be basically a None-Profit they could also accept donations that could be written off as a tax deductible charity.

Now here is the best part of this. I realize these places will need janitors and office staff and other folks like grounds keepers and all of that could be supplied by local people on welfare as training them for a job or to work for their welfare. They too would have to donate several hours a week to qualify for their free taxpayers hand up and not a free handout. I say hand up because they would be learning a job and hopefully get off the public dole one day.

I know the emergency issues will come up and how do we pay for those. Well nothing would change because many places don't take Obama/Demo Care now so if someone couldn't make it to the Free Clinic ER and had to go to another hospital the same thing that happens now will still happen then. The Big Difference in my plan is NO ONE is forced to buy something or be labeled a uninsured criminal in American! That is Un-Constitutional no matter what the Supreme Court of Criminals have Ruled! Their Unconstitutional rulings on this is another good reason Supreme Court Justices need term limits!

This may have been thought of before, and it may not be as great as having a great insurance plan, but it would be a far sight better than destroying health care like Obama/Demo-Care is doing... unless of course, the government is just looking for another way to bleed more Tax/Fine money out of the American people? It maybe since Obama-Demo-Care was also created to prop-up the insurance industry. Note: Health Insurance Stocks have gone up since the Supreme Court ruled twice in favor of it.

So can you trust your Doctor? Probably Not, they now work for the government, not for you or your health. How can you tell? Well if the doctor's staff starts asking questions like what religion are you. Or demand you take random drug tests just because you look like you could be an Illegal drug user, get up and walk out. Because that is prison camp medicine... So much for Constitutional Rights and freedom in America anymore.

Chapter Seven
Jury Nullification to protect Freedom
&
The Too Big To Fail Conundrum

One very important Constitutional Right that we the people have is "Jury Nullification." What is Jury Nullification? Well, it is a tool you have as a juror that you can use if you find the charge against someone is just plain wrong! So you refuse to convict that person and you vote Not Guilty.

Jury nullification was debated in a 1895 Supreme Court decision, Sparf vs. U.S. But as we see today, the Supreme Court played political power games and ruled that judges were not required to tell jurors about jury nullification. The ruling didn't say that jurors didn't have the power or Right to nullify. Nor did it say that judges couldn't tell the jury about nullification; it simply said that the court didn't have to tell the jury they had that power.

This decision has led to the common practice by U.S. judges

of penalizing criminal defense lawyers who try to present a nullification argument in front of the jury. Consequently, jury nullification is seen as a de facto power of juries' and judges across the country get really pissed off if it is mentioned. So unless you're a citizen of New Hampshire, where they still inform the jury of this Right, most jurors cannot rely on judges to inform them of this "secret" Constitutional power.

If you believe in the Constitution and believe a law like gun control should never be allowed, becoming a stealth juror to get on a jury in order to nullify the law can be beneficial to American Freedom. A smart lawyer will also use a shadow defense to get information entered into the record that would otherwise be inadmissible, hoping that evidence will trigger a jury to nullification. An example of this tactic was the claim by the defense in the Roger Clemens perjury trial to have the charges against Clemens dismissed due to "prosecutorial misconduct", i.e. that the prosecution intentionally introduced video evidence which Judge Reggie Walton had ruled inadmissible, for the purposes of getting, in the words of the defense, "a second bite at the apple", to the jury because of the prosecution's poor performance. The introduction of the tainted evidence caused a mistrial after only two days. The judge denied the defense's motion to dismiss but noted his strong displeasure with the prosecution.

The Government however had fear that nullification could be used to permit violence against socially unpopular factions so they have checks in place. They point to the danger that a jury may choose to convict a defendant who has not broken the letter of the law. However, judges retain the rights both to decide sentences and to disregard juries' guilty verdicts, acting as a check against malicious juries. Jury nullification may also occur in civil suits, in which the verdict is generally a finding of liability or lack of liability (rather than a finding of guilty or not guilty).

But the government is working on a way to avoid possible jury nullifying their wish to convict someone...Trial by judge or arbitrator. If they can push the idea for a long enough time, the citizens or sheeple will accept it as law and your chances of winning against the government will be slim and none.

Only Thee Elite Will Be Free

Corporations have become too big to fail because they were created like a pyramid scheme backed up by the governments they controlled. Because the corporations need people to buy what they create, and they employ millions of people, and move billions of dollars, they have become like a standing domino in a long line. If one falls, many more will follow along that line, and the government and its leaders would also be at risk of falling, and they aren't going to jeopardize losing the gravy train they control. The Government knows the people are the real corporate assets, so the government treats them like cash-cows or livestock. People are told through media and social engineering what to think, what to eat, what to wear, where to live, what to buy and how to live. The Corporations now own the world and the people in it. The only thing stopping them from totally enslaving the American people, are those pesky people with the freedom of the human spirit and the belief in the Constitution and the Bill of Rights. Those people who know things are very wrong in the once free country called America are the real threat to those who want total control. The corporate globalists are working hard to control any resistance caused by those constitutional minded free spirits, with constant corporate media messaging telling the people to obey. Because if the people ever woke up and realized their financial system was just an illusion and merely a tool to control, the government and the corporations which controlled them would collapse. When, or if, the corporate controlled government does ever collapse, the people will once again have their freedom back, at least for a time. Of course the people will have to work hard to survive because those who were in control will fight and kill to try and regain control, and you can count on invasion from the UN forces to try and regain that control. But the real threat to them is what George Orwell coined "The tom-tom beat of tribal emotions." That mob mentality that causes people to revolt. They have to control that and have done a pretty good job so far. But as population explodes, the greater is the threat of mass revolt. That is when the tanks will roll in and tactical nukes will be diploid.

America is the only thing standing in the way of a global government and the elite globalists hate it. They literally hate the Constitution and try to destroy is daily. They have attorneys and their paid politicians and judges working on ways to strip Americans of their Civil Rights. Unfortunately, most Americans just stand aside and watch their Rights slip away.

Did you know that the elite globalist are so well insulated from the commoners that the really important elitists bring their own private toilet with them that is installed where ever they are staying? Yes it is true! For instance, The White House is so concerned about the President's security that the veil of secrecy extends over the president's bodily excretions. The special port-a-john captures feces and urine and is flown back to the United States in the event some enterprising foreign intelligence agency conducted a sewage pipe operation designed to trap and examine waste material of our leaders.

Why does the government take such precautions? Because our government conducts operations collecting urine and feces from foreign leaders and the elite to determine their medical conditions and we don't want them checking on our government elite. Intelligence waste collecting operations have been directed against dictators, dignitaries and political leaders in countries where medical conditions of the top political leaders and elite are considered "State Secrets."

The Israeli Mossad has admitted conducted waste collecting operations against Syrian President Hafez Assad when he visited Amman, Jordan in February of 1999 for the funeral of King Hussein. The Mossad and its Jordanian counterparts installed a special toilet in Assad's hotel room that rerouted the waste to a specimen canister. Assad had diabetes and cancer and the waste spying operation was to discover the actual medical condition of Assad so they could plan future events.

Even Soviet President Mikhail Gorbachev's waste was collected when he visited Washington in 1987. The CIA placed a special trap under a sewage tank to collect the Soviet Union leader's bodily waste for analysis. The CIA has even collected waste samples from Ugandan President-dictator Yoweri Museveni's toilet when he visited Washington.

Now that the elite leaders know this crap, (pun intended) has been going on, many now take along their own pooper scoopers with them when they travel.

Just think what personal virus' could be created to attack an individual without infecting anyone else if the government has your DNA and Medical information to work with. That's why the Affordable Healthcare law is so scary. Everything about you is shared with the government, and even if you don't believe you are important enough for them to worry about, you just might be too insignificant and consider a disposable liability!

The elite also have underground cities waiting for the uprising of the surfs, or you commoners. Some have underground farms, opulent rooms, swimming pools, restaurants, places for the humble help and of course their personal security. There is a major underground city in the Ozarks that stretches for miles waiting for the political elite.

Control by Edict

Laws in the early 2000s were being enacted at an all time high, and the citizens had no say in the making of those laws. Most of the people were oblivious to the slow but steady tightening of the chains of bondage. The corporate social engineers knew it was easier to control the minds of people if they were in a large herd. So they started corralling them in cities where they could be conditioned to think and act like the masses living along side of them. Without ever really knowing any of their neighbors, they were conditioned through mass media messaging. The people were being programmed like mindless robotic automatons. They had become so stupid many of them didn't even know what the Bill of Rights was! The city dweller had become unlike those people who lived in small communities. Those who live in small towns know their neighbors for miles around. But in the city people don't really know the people who live next door, and could care less about anyone but themselves.

People in small towns banned together to protect one and other from threats like thieves and thugs, and talk to each other to find solutions to problems that might arise. People in the city only looked out for themselves and hardly ever looked out for anyone else or talked to their neighbors. The city dwellers are not allowed to find solutions because that is the job of the government, so most don't bother and eventually given up hope that things will change.

The corporate government knows a divided people are much easier to control than a united people, so Agenda 21 was implemented to herd people into cities where they will be disarmed and reduced to living in a small space. Their own personal space or cage, free but not really free, because cities have many rules and regulation you have to follow. But this was not enough; they had to control the people's life and needed the ability to control their lives. So they devised a plan to take over the people's healthcare, essentially controlling life, and in the process totally destroy the Constitution so they could take total control over all human life in America!

The thing corporate government hates the most is independence, because they need all humans working to support the government in corporate jobs that pay a wage they can control and tax. Only then can the corporate government know how much money the people make, and how much they can take, and only then would they be able to force them to pay for living in America. In the Cities, people not allowed to own livestock or grow their food. They have to buy everything to survive and that makes the corporate government rich. Every time you buy anything, what extra charge is added into the price? Taxes! Whether it be sales tax or income tax, property tax, there is a tax imposed by the government on what you buy, make, create, consume, even the water you drink and the air you breath is taxed in some way. So the corporate government started passing laws, regulation and taxes, making it hard for people to live in the country and produce their own necessities. The counties, states and federal governments passed restrictive laws and charged excessive fees and taxes on those who wanted to live away from the masses. The government charges outrageous taxes for fire protection and policing protection that is non-existent in many rural areas. Only if the local town's people put together a volunteer fire department or petitioned their state or county to allow the people to elect one of their own as local sheriff or patrolmen, can they get the protection they are forced by law to pay for.

Living in America has become like living under the thumb of the government masters of old in the former Soviet Union, Nazi Germany, and China. Only if your master government gives you permission, are you able to do what you want with your own land, property and life. This is a sad epitaph for a once freer Country, because free men and women shouldn't have to ask for permission from their masters, and free men and women aren't forced by their government to buy anything! Any people who think they are free living in any country that forces the people to obey without question and are forced by their government to buy anything, is a country of enslaved fools!

The people now work for the government and those in power have an iron hold on every aspect of human life. They control just about everything, and they are even trying to control the most important thing of all, Water! They can never totally control all the water because of rain and natural streams and rivers, but they are trying, and have a hold on man made lakes and reservoirs and charge for the water they control. The government is even passing laws to control the ground water and the wells that people own. The President of the United States, Barack Obama, even tried to close the oceans at one point so no citizen could use them. Californians have just lost their water Rights in 2015 by emergency drought decree signed by governor Jerry Brown who is directly responsible for the lack of water storage to begin with. Under his first term as governor in the 70s he and his leftwing cohorts stopped the building of reservoirs.

History seems to repeat itself over an over again, and people never seem to learn from it. Doubt many of you can remember the drought in the 70s in California, but some of us can still remember "If it is brown flush it down and if it is yellow it is still mellow" slogan then Governor Jerry "Moonbeam" Brown and his cohorts came up with to persuade people to conserve water. Yes the same Governor Jerry "Moonbeam" Brown

Californians elected governor again! You would think the leftist media would be screaming at the tops of their lungs or their collective grasp of historic mentality, (Very Doubtful), like they do about racial equality, {since running out of water is a tad more important} over the FACT that Moonbeam and his cohorts are directly responsible for this drought California is in!

Jerry "Moonbeam" Brown and cohorts on the left, legislated the slowdown of Dam building in the mid 70s and the last major dams built were Pyramid, Castaic and before that Oroville.

In 1959 California leaders knew the state needed more water storage and from 1959 to 1969, added a whopping 21 million acre-feet of storage, including some of the largest reservoirs in the State. Then in 1969, the peace, love, tree hugging nature freaks started jumping up and down over damming up the water and the State only added over 8,600,000 AF of storage which included the massive New Melones Dam which accounted for most of the water storage. Then in 1979, when even more leftist freaks infested California's government, they only added over 1,600,000 acre-feet including New Spicer Meadows Dam and Warm Springs Dam. From 1989 to date, when the socialist/communist had totally taken over the State, they have only added over a million acre-feet of water reserve including Diamond Valley and Los Vaquero. Now here is the irony of these water facts. Since 1959 the State of California's population has more than doubled from 15,288,000 to almost 40 million and in the last 26 years only a little more than one million acre feet of water storage has been created! The dry southern portion of the state has taken water from the northern part of the state that has plenty of water and now the northern Californians are also in a drought! All because the south refuses to create water storage. Why? Because of rich developers that want to build more homes, and dams take up a lot of valuable land.

The people are to be fined up to 1,000 dollars a day for using over their limit of water allowed them, yet corporate government/industries of California are exempt from water rationing. Now you the people no longer own Water Rights in California...Just imagine what the property will be worth in a year or two without water? I guess cutting off the water is one way to deflate the state population though?

In Oregon a man was arrested and convicted of collecting rain and snow water to use on his property. Yes... arrested and convicted and jailed! Oregon now says the government owns the water, not the citizens. Gary Harrington was convicted of nine misdemeanors and sentenced to 30 days in prison, as well as slapped with a $1,500 fine, for diverting snow runoff and rainwater into three reservoirs on his property.

Once the people allowed the corporate government control over all water, all freedom will be controlled and there won't be any freedom at all... America's enslavement will be total and final!

Chapter Eight
The Tightening of Control with Lies!
Inch by Inch it is a Synch!

Just as I foretold to a group of my friends back in 1973, when a group of friends and I were stopped in one of the first CHP Supposed Head-Light Check Points in California and asked just about every question about who we were, where we were going, and nothing about the headlights on the car...I told my friends that this was just the beginning and I foreseen the Gestapo would have armed road block check points and would forcibly be able to drag you out of your car and throw you to the ground, and search you and your car for no real reason, and you wouldn't be able to do a thing about it. They Laughed at me and said the people would riot! I also told people that one day the Jack Boots would be able to kick in your door without a warrant and kill your dog, beat your family to the ground and you wouldn't be able to do a thing about it... I was also laughed at and told it would never happen! Well I never saw one protest, let alone a riot, and everything I predicted has happened. Now the government controls every aspect of your lives, from the food and water you drink, the air you breathe, the home you can live in, the medical care you can have, and each and every one of you who were complacent and apathetic when this was happening is directly responsible.

The Government's Talking Points on this tyrannical healthcare act was that getting people health insurance would stop the emergency room defaults and bring down the costs, yea right that hasn't worked. So now you force Millions of Americans to buy something they can't afford who are just paying the minimum payments on their bills, so they will have to go bankrupt anyway! Those who think people can just go on

Medical or Medicaid are crazy… if you make over 15,000 a year OR YOU OWN TOO MUCH you don't qualify!

I don't know about any of you, but to have to sell off what little you own to afford health care isn't freedom…. Might as well go bankrupt, and quit working in America, and get all the free-bees…but then who is going to pay for it? On the flip-side, that would bleed the proverbially beast to death and it would die of lack of funding. So maybe sucking the system dry might be an effective way to destroy it?

Once they have control over your body and organs and you can't do anything about it, you might as well consider yourselves spare parts slaves, and that day is coming! What I foresee would rival George Orwell's darkest nightmare and be the Borg's brightest Epiphany! I no doubt will be laughed at once again, but once again I will warn you of things to come! Welcome to the New Orwellian America, once you check in You Won't Be able to Check Out!

"First they came for the kids to teach them the government way was the only way, and none of you people said anything… Then they demanded you buy health Insurance and most of you just obeyed… Then they came for the guns and none of you did anything… Then they came to put chains on you and there was no one around to say anything and it was far too late for you to do anything to stop it!" A prediction of mine.

I say once again; "Any Country that demands their citizens obey and force the citizens to buy anything, is a Country Enslaved! And any people who believe they are free in any Country that demands they obey and force the citizens to buy anything, is a Country full of Fools!"

I have a bad feeling that one day all of us Constitutionalist Patriots will be attacked by the Jackboots. Our homes will be raided, our pets and families murdered, because we refuse to answer questions and do not submit to warrant-less searches from any government employees. Of course that will be a good day to die fighting tyranny, but sadly the government controlled media will spew bogus lies and make people like us look like crazy people. They will report that the police had to kill terrorist patriots who refused to submit to a warrant-less search. When asked by the media; what evidence they had against those they murdered? The Police/Gestapo will claim they had reasonable cause to search the house because the resident refused to allow them to search the home without a Search Warrant!

I know, this sounds absurd but it is already happening now! Yes this is already become a popular ploy used by Gestapo when people refuse to allow the Gestapo to violate the people's Constitutional Rights! The sickening part is that the dumbed down brain dead sheeple believe the lies the government controlled media spew, and it is becoming another precedent that the government can use to take away more of your Constitutional Rights. Yes, "We The People" have become a threat to the government leaders. Because we believe in the Constitution and in many of our cases, we have sworn an oath to uphold and defend the Constitution against all who attack it, both foreign and domestic, and by God there are a lot of domestics in the government attacking the Constitution these days!

Did you know that the Sheriff is considered the top law enforcement official of a county? Why? Because he or she is elected directly by the people and not appointed or hired, and only the people can remove a sheriff by either recall or voting them out of office.. All other supposed law officials have been created by edict or special order from the President, or governor and by city leaders. And did you know that the Sheriff and States can refuse to obey the Federal Government? Mack/Printz v USA, the U S Supreme Court declared that the states or their political subdivisions "are not subject to federal direction." What this means is the Sheriff or any other "Subdivisions" i.e. judges, district attorneys, police, etc, do not have to obey the Federal Government when they come into a State like Storm Troopers and demand cooperation.

James Madison had stated that; "The local or municipal authorities form distinct and independent portions of the supremacy, no more subject, within their respective spheres, to the general authority [federal government] than the general authority is subject to them, within its own sphere."

So we the people were supposed to have had our own States Rights under the Tenth Amendment, but inch by inch that was handed over to the Federal Government. How did this happen? That is an easy question to answer, we allowed it to happen. The question should be; who is in the control of the Federal Government now since obviously we the people aren't?

Chapter Nine
Who is Really in command?

If you want to know who is controlling the government all you need to do is follow the money. The America Government is always using war to defuse the people, and get their attention off their agenda to totally control them, and controlling the government is the corporations. In the 50s and 60s you used to see Gas Wars that were attempts by oil companies to get your business. Then in the 70s the oil corporations started warring with each other and the Great Oil Company Mergers started. Many of the Mobil Gas Stations became Enco then Exxon in the Mobil/Exxon pre-merger. Then in 1999 when the merger was official it created the biggest corporation in the world. But what is the most interesting thing about the Great Oil Company Mergers is that all the American Oil Corporations were all originally Standard Oil owned up until 1911, which was the largest corporation in the world at the time.

In 1911 Standard Oil was broken up because it was rule an illegal monopoly. So along with other world oil barons it just recreated its self and has once again became the largest corporation.

So who is controlling our governments? Yep....the corporations and many of the wars are being created by large corporation who couldn't convince the leaders of those countries to work with them. Syria is a classic example of the corporate power that controlled America. The Oil Corporations wanted to build a pipeline through Syria and the Syrian President wouldn't work with them, so they convinced their dupes in the American Government to somehow threaten Syria into submission. Yea, I know, that hasn't worked well for them yet.

Do you remember these gas stations? Well, if you do you lived in a freer and friendlier America when America owned them.

Most of the Left and Right elected people in Washington have been paid off directly or through a straw donation by the Saudi

Prince Bandar bin Sultan one of the richest oil barrens in the world. Senators like Harry Reid, John McCain, Lindsey Graham, Dianne Feinstein, Barbara Boxer, Robert Menendez and House Speaker John Boehner, Minority Leader Nancy Pelosi, House Intelligence Committee Chair Mike Rogers, New York's Peter King, Minority Whip Steny Hoyer, and many others have been paid in campaign contribution through Bandar according to several reports available on the internet.

The henchmen of the corporate government control are the judges; they are the real traitors of freedom. It amazes me when I see blame going to the wrong group when the real blame needs to be aimed at the courts who rule against the constitution and freedom.

It is a sad fact that most have no conception of what it takes to be free. The Libertarians, Democrats and Republicans speak of peaceful rebellion to change government and that is the biggest smoke up your backside lie any enslaved group could ever spew! Those who have too much cowardice to fight for their freedom are bound to enslavement! Freedom is worth dying for and those who aren't willing to die to be free aren't worth listening to. If you really want to be free, you must be willing to die for it. Otherwise you might as well just shut up and cower in your illusionary safe corner, in the cage your master, the government has created for you, and hope a peaceful rally will free you one day, and you see how that works for you. Those in power got there by fighting to get there, and they did it by force, and no other way will get them out. We have to take to the streets to stop the culling of freedom. You can't just bitch at your TV as you sit in your easy chair and expect things to get better, it aint gonna happen! Now when I say take to the Streets, I mean get up and out and convince people that there is a pending doom and rally the masses to throw the bums out before it comes to war!

We The People should have the same power as the Government and we should have the same exemption if we defend ourselves against tyrannical Government/Gestapo! If attacked by a tyrant we should defend ourselves with any force necessary to protect ourselves and the lives of our families! But unfortunately we allowed the Right we had under the Bill of Right, Second Amendment, to be eroded away and now we will be killed by the government if we defend ourselves against their tyranny. Can you say Police State?

Now I hear tell, not that I would know, that there are insurance plans you can get in South America that start out at $500,000 and up as high as you can afford that stipulates that if you are killed/murdered, to anyone who makes sure all involved are brought to "Justice" they will receive the money. Note: "Justice" is loosely defined! And they must show proof! i.e. those responsible in jail or a death certificate and you are the one who avenged the insured. This will ensure you are not murdered in vain and anyone who kills you "period" including Gestapo will be dealt with accordingly, and hopefully have no place on the face of planet they can hide! Now if this is true, then that is true international post mortem health insurance.

It is amazing to think this all started 100 years ago, before most people were alive. What is the amazing part is that while the communist movement was growing in Russia and China, the people oppressed over there were coming to America to be freer. Now Russia and China are moving away from communism and into a more capitalist society and America is moving into a Communist society. It is like the American people have been asleep for the last 100 years and hadn't been watching the demise of Communism in Europe and how it hadn't worked. Or Americans are all junkies who just don't care as long as they get their government fix of free-bees... At any cost, freedom, health, self worth, pride, life and happiness, none of that matters as long as they get their government free-bee dope that they have become addicted to! I guess I have to consider that "Just Say No To Drugs" didn't work and can only be as naive to think "Just Say No To Total Government Control" will work? Dependency is a very hard Drug Habit to get over and the Government knows this too well. They have had centuries perfecting and domesticating the citizens into dependent farm animals with little or no will to be free again. Luckily there are still those of us with the wild animal still in us that will never ever be truly domesticated.

We have to fight to get our freedom back, and there is no doubt in my mind that many of us who believe in freedom will be killed and murdered by the new American Gestapo when they are ordered to round up the Constitutionalists. Just remember it is better to die fighting tyranny than to live enslaved under it! If that day comes, don't die cowering like a beaten enslaved dog, die fighting standing up for freedom and taking as many of the enemy as you can with you! The American People are being targeted by the government, and it is a War as far as they are concerned, so you better except the fact that we are under siege and prepare!

Chapter Ten
Escape from behind the American Iron Curtain?

There are still free places to go in the early 2000s, but the American government makes it very hard to escape America. If you attempt to leave America and take your money with you, beware, because the Government frowns on their property (YOU) trying to escape! They will tax away your money and hound you for more tax if you escape to a country America has control over. So you need to find a country that doesn't allow America to control it. People fleeing America had already overwhelmed Canadian Authorities in the early 2000s. Americans were Illegally Immigrating to Canada because it was easier to take their money there, and leave from there to other freer destinations. There were many also leaving to Mexico and South America as well. So the American government made it mandatory to have a passport to visit Canada and Mexico. Years ago you didn't need a passport to go into Mexico or into Canada, but that had to be changed to stop the exodus of Americans and the influx of illegal aliens who don't pay any taxes.

The government also charges you to renounce your citizenship and that has gone up 500% in the last few years because so many people are fleeing.

The Government did a study on Americas living outside the USA and found that 6.4 million people were no longer living and working in America. Almost all of them had moved to countries that had far more personal freedom than America and many of those people would become citizens of their new country. The numbers of American people living abroad had skyrocketed in a 2 year period from 1% to well over 5% and the trend was also skyrocketing with American from ages 25 to 35 thinking of leaving the country. Ages 18 to 40 had shown a major increase in a 4 year period from 15% to 40% that would like to have another home in a different country. This was a valid study and not fiction folks. Needless to say, it was a scary trend for the government and they had to figure out a way to put a stop to it.

So the Federal Government is working on passing laws that would forbid any American Citizen from fleeing the country if they owe taxes, fines, student loans or have any American debt at all. Passports will be revoked, and if caught trying to escape America, you will be arrested and convicted then sent to a FEMA detention/re-education center forced to work off your debt to the corporate government. If you are lucky enough to be able to escape from behind the American Iron Curtain, countries like Uruguay, Brazil, Costa Rica, New Zealand, Iceland and Argentina are safe havens and many Americans are moving to these countries.

Many of the countries in South America are also freer than America in many ways and could be a safe place but you need to check out their laws and if they cooperate with American demands. Brazil is one of those Country the American Corporate Government does not want the American people to know about because Brazilians cannot be extradited to any country period, it is in their Constitution, and you can become a Brazilian Citizen in as little as 12 months. Brazil also does not allow America's rogue agencies like the IRS to seize the assets of Americans, or former Americans, who move there to escape the American tyranny. Brazil also voted into their Constitution in 2005 that they have the Right to own guns. Best choice is Uruguay if you are looking for a new country with a large population of former Americans. But they have heavy gun control in Uruguay, so if you are a gun advocate Brazil might be a better choice, but they have more control in other areas, like free speech and mandatory voting. You have to research what country you go to, because some of the American controlled South American countries will likely kick out American patriots, if the American Government demands those countries return former American citizens for almost any reason. So you have to choose carefully and make sure you can survive wherever you go. Most all countries require you have at least a $500 dollar per month, per person income before they will give you a resident visa. Most will give you a 90 day visa but you will have to get a Work Visa if you plan on making some kind of a living working, if you don't have enough money to live on and plan on staying. Sadly the American media propaganda machine keeps most Americans obvious to freer countries because they don't want you cash-cows escaping. Also because most other countries will not extradite you or your assets you've earned, just because the American government wants your assets.

Now the freest Nation according to many studies, and the only other country that believes you have the Right to Bear Arms other than America, Brazil and Switzerland, is New Zealand, but they have pre-70s American laws on abortion. But according to those people who study over all freedom, New Zealand is the number one freest nation on the planet according to them, with the exception of minimum wage laws that equal America's. But they don't just let in anyone. You have to be either a professional or well off money wise, $1000 per month income to get into New Zealand with a permanent residence. Cost of living in New Zealand is equal to America. Switzerland is also a gun friendly country but has mandatory health insurance similar to the USA so it too has anti-freedom elements. Sadly, just about anywhere you go you'll find something you don't like. So you have to carefully weigh your options and weigh out what you can tolerate. You may find that you are no better off anywhere else and decide to stay and fight it out here. But if you can afford another place in another free country, can't hurt to own one just incase it gets real bad in America like some sociopolitical economists are predicting.

America has fallen well below the top ten in over all freedom and it was rated 47th when it comes to freedom of speech. The Netherlands, Hong Kong, Australia, Canada, Ireland, and even Cambodia, yes Cambodia, finished above the U.S. in over all freedom other then the right to bear arms.

Now you're going to hear the ludicrous sheeple tell you that if you leave America and give up your citizenship you can never come back, and to those who tell that to you.... you have to laugh. Because thousands of illegal aliens enter the USA every day and most are never caught or deported! So once you leave to find a country you like, if it doesn't work out, well hell, while you are looking for a new one you can come back to the USA and live without having to pay taxes or worry about money because the government will give you Alien Assistance Welfare and you'll never have to worry about being deported as long as you move around.... Hell you'll have all the free-bees and none of the enslaving payments and taxes American citizens have to pay. Yes, LOL = (Laugh Out Loud) I know, you never though about that before now, have you?

Constitutional Free Zones

America's new Social Fascist government has moved quickly to strip the citizens of freedom. They are trying to imposed a Constitution Free Zone 100 miles wide around the country. This would give them the ability to use whatever tactics needed to stop people from leaving or entering the USA.

There is now an increased presence of armed government

agents at check points where you can be searched and detained without a warrant in these zones. If we allow the government to get away with this for much longer, soon there will be no Constution at all!

It is only a matter of time before all the freedom Americans had, will be gone forever, and most of the people are oblivious to the enslavement they are under. What makes this even more unbelievable is that most Americans are apathetically complacent about it! The word "Sheeple" is right on, because it is like looking into the eyes and face of a Sheep. I don't know if any of you have ever done it, but to me and many people who have, the blank look that a sheep has, makes it look like one of the stupidest creatures there is. Then again maybe the Sheep are thinking the same thing about Humans?

The Government had been dumbing down children for so long, decades in their schools, and the government is never going to educate the people on how to stop the tyranny the government is committing against them. Only those older Americans who knew that the Constitution and Bill of Rights was once the law of the land, have a chance of educating the young, but it is going to be hard to convince those who have been brainwashed that the Constitution and Bill of Rights are worth saving. Most of the citizens have no conception of their granted freedom and the controlling elitist government isn't going to tell them about it.

It never ceases to amaze me when I read that someone in government has an intellectual solution to the haves and have-nots. They guarantee if they pass a law the people will see miraculous results, but first they have to pass it. My amazement is the fact that their vanity assumes their solution is backed up by some study or statistics gleaned from questions created by themselves, when in reality it is to control the people.

One very important fact is always missing in their divine revelations. We live in a parasitic universe, and everything feeds off of something else, thus survival of the fittest. Therefore there is always going to be the haves and have-nots. The best thing we can do is just make sure no one is being physically hurt or threaten and let people have the freedom to choose their own destiny.

There are only 2 constants in our dimensional universe; #1: Nothing lasts or lives forever. And therefore #2 Everything dies. I have had some people try and inject a 3rd "Being Created" but that is an irrelevant since we are here and if we were not here, nothing would be a constant or matter period. So to think man can ever achieve some utopian Shangri-La of equality is merely an illusion. Man is a parasitic animal whether it wants to believe that or not, and therefore there will always be those who succeed and those who do not. You can take as much as you want from those who have and give it to those who have not, but those who have will eventually find a way to stop that. That is just how it is, so educating the down trodden, not conditioning them to expect a free ride, is the answer to helping them achieve at least a livable existence.

The Game Plan

It is ironic that the majority will never understand human nature and will most likely become one of the majority of the have-nots. Why? Well let me explain it like this; Lets say you put 100 people in a room and gave them equal amounts of cash...lets say 500 bucks, and they had to conduct business amongst themselves only. They only have 30 days to see who came out with the most cash at the end of that time. You can bet that there would be one maybe 2 with all the cash or most of it... You could repeat the test as many times as you want and you'd get the same results. 90% of those in the test would have nothing left at the end of the test. 5% would have some cash left but not much. 3% would have the original 500 and 1 or 2% would have all the rest of the cash.

Same goes in life, and the greatest fear of the top 10% of the population is when it all comes crashing down and that 90% start demanding from the 10%...the blood hits the fan...Yep, the blood of the 90% because the 90% want to tear the 10% apart to get what they have. It will not happen all at once... inch by inch those on the bottom will start hitting the streets and little by little they will be rounded up. That "Tom-tom beat of tribal emotions" will take over and the protests and riots will get larger and larger all across the Country until those in power respond. If a mass culling is in order, there will be a staged calamity that rallies thousands. They will be taunted to get out of control, then the tanks will roll in and bullets will start flying and people will die and be arrested never to be seen again. Yep...the culling of man will begin, which is a planned agenda to decrease the surplus population. The powers that be want only around 500,000,000 people on earth in the future, because the resources on Earth will only accommodate that many until the planet can revive from all the depletion the billions of people have consumed and depleted. Human reproduction has now entered into the times to the tenth power scenario. Count Billions of people overall, then divided by two, (since it takes two to create a baby) times by two and add the half that were originally divided and do the math...then factor in a 20 or 25 year cycle, and consider people have more than one child in most cases, and over population of this planet is eminent! Isn't going to happen in my time, but it is eventually going to happen if humans keep multiplying at the current rate.

Chapter Eleven
Awakening the Dumbed Down Masses

I don't know what it's going to take to get people to understand that our freedom is in major jeopardy, if we all don't demand that the government comply with the Constitution. But I do know if we can't get people to realize that, and they don't take a stand, then the loss of all freedom in this country is imminent. America has already lost its status as being the freest nation, and very soon might become one of the least free places to live, if it isn't already!

I know, some of you just can believe America isn't the freest country, but you have to understand you are given so much propaganda to make you believe it is, that you just take it for granted. Just about everyone takes it for granted! If you are talking to a group of people you don't really know, and mention America isn't really the freest county, I'll bet you'll get the classic rebut; "If you don't think you're free here, why don't you leave!" There is always some totally brainwashed automaton that will spew that garb without listening to anything else you have to say. They have been programmed to shut down all reason and turn on a defensive posture and consider you the enemy. So most people don't dare say the obvious in fear of condemnation and peer pressure. Those of us, who know we aren't free anymore, are up against a major propaganda machine. With a media that has become nothing more than a stenographer for corporate government propaganda, automatons coming out of the government controlled schools, and the apathetic and complacent masses that just don't give a damn as long as they get their free-bees. People have been bred like government owned livestock and domesticated to obey. So most people don't want to hear that their freedom is slipping away. I see people who just refuse to believe the government would deliberately do anything against the people. Even after seeing the NDAA passed by the federal government, Wikileaks, and the information Edward Snowden released that prove beyond a shadow of doubt that our government has been unconstitutionally spying, arresting, killing and bold faced lying to us! Through all of these blatant attacks on our freedom, the majority of the populace still stands by apathetic and complacent. It reminds me of the HG Wells "Time Machine" movie version, with Rod Taylor, where the people of the future watch a girl "Weena" I believe her name was, fall into a river and start to drown, and no one lifts a hand to help. No one but Rod Taylor even cared or showed any emotional response. Have we as a Nation really become so cold and uncaring about our future and freedom? Or have we just become too afraid to say or do anything about it? Our Government is threatening Reporters, Elected Officials, Military Personnel, Public Employees, and even Us, if we expose their illegal actions against our Rights, and our Constitution, and most of the people don't seem to realize how serious this really is… It's absolutely amazing to me!

The Militarization of the Police

America is beginning to see its police force turned into a military force right in front of their eyes. Military Armored vehicles, military uniforms and military weapons are replacing the men in blue, and it's transforming our country into a national army at an alarming rate. Anyone who can say with a straight face, that this is a great model for a Free Country needs to have their head examined or needs to be deprogrammed. What this should tell the American people is that our government is preparing for the use of deadly force against us. The people in power know we are waking up and we realize that they are way out of control. They know once we decide to stand up for ourselves and attempt to put that evil government genie back into its proverbial bottle, they will have to unleash the dogs of war against the people.

Why aren't we hearing our elected officials denounce this national build up of military troops in our country? Could they be a part of this, or could they be too scared and threatened by a government machine that they can't even control? Why are they going along with recommendations by police chiefs and sheriffs to buy military equipment like armored trucks and gun tanks? Do you know how easy it would be to install a chain gun or a 50 or 75 caliber rapid fire weapon to the tanks? Pretty easy since everything is there but the guns. These tanks and armored gun trucks can blow through block walls and go through your homes and cars like they are tissue paper.

DHS BUYS 2500 ARMORED FIGHTING VEHICLES
Government Plans For War With American Citizens

We really need to ask our elected leaders a couple questions, like: How much does the government really know about the pending financial collapse that many of our financial advisors are predicting? Do they have any intention of telling us about it, or when they expect it to happen? From the military build up in our communities it would seem they expect this to happen soon. We have to look at this from a financial perspective, because if this country was in the black and everyone was working and making money, there wouldn't be any need for Tanks and Machine Guns in the hands of the Police. So things must be coming to a head pretty soon, as many financial pundits are predicting. This Country can not keep shelling out billions a day it doesn't have to pay its bills without either having a plan to deal with it the day it all comes crashing down, or foreseeing a turn-around coming in the very near future. I for one don't see that turn around happening anytime soon, but one can always hope I guess.

One of the most concerning parts of this military build-up of our police is the cost. Maybe not the cost of the donated obsolete military equipment but the cost to maintain it. If the government just stopped spending money we don't have, we could avoid a financial collapse; but since our government is the largest employer in the country, cutting spending would also cut jobs which would add to civil unrest and the government might need the military to crush any civil unrest. A very real conundrum indeed. Crimes like theft and robbery are on the rise because of the unemployment problem in America, so they don't want to make it worse. Yet we see and allow our government officials to side with the socialists, fascist, tree-huggers and climate doomsayers and regulate business out of this country. They full well know it is only a matter of time before it all comes crashing down and people hit the streets in protest. So they also have to know the people will be gunned down by the very people who are supposed to protect and serve.

Are we feeling overwhelmed and overcome by our government? Well, we can do something by starting with our local government. This all starts at the local level, because we have control over our City Councils and County Supervisors. If we complain about the Militarizing of our police and sheriff, or some state or federal law that we want them to publicly denounce and they ignore us, then recall is in order, where recall is allowed, or we can wait and vote them out when they come up for re-election. We should and can make it clear to who ever we elect that we want to get rid of the military police force and return to community policing where they have cops that walk a beat. This is good healthy policing literally!

"Those who would give up essential Liberty, to purchase a little temporary Safety, deserve neither Liberty nor Safety." - Benjamin Franklin

Jade Helm 15 a 2015 Military Training Drill on US Soil

Jade Helm 15 is or was by the time many of you read this, a supposed "Soft Opts" major massive military training drill that happened across nine states from July through September. It was supposedly to train troops to infiltrate a community and assess friend and foe. The very notion that the military was training in America had people very disturbed. In a video the government created for city, county and state leaders, it states the training drill is to assess who will be friendly toward a military take over and who will not. The commentator tells the audience that his people will come in and work with police, sheriffs and community leaders to gain information about possible threats and gain support from citizens who will give them information about people they believe to be a possible threat. They also want to find places they can hide ordinances and troops, like barns and homes and will ask the citizens to help hide and transport troops covertly at night. He also says if the people become alarmed his people will be doing something wrong. Yet many of the troops will be in full military uniforms with loaded weapons, military vehicles as well as aircraft. Others will be dressed like normal civilians but they will be asking a lot of personal questions about people. It was supposedly for use in foreign countries but normally the military trains in the environment they will be fighting in.

Army Regulation 210–35 the Civilian Inmate Labor Program

There are a lot of government documents available that tell us the government is planning on thinning out the herd. Army Regulation 210–35 the Civilian Inmate Labor Program will scary the crap out of you, once you read how this is being planned. This is a really long document and this book is getting long winded enough, so I will high light some of it and if you want to look it up on the internet and download a copy you can read through the whole thing.

This document explains how the government is going to process entire families by SSI numbers and flight risk and it basically lays out how we are to be rounded up and placed into labor concentration camps. I probably should print the entire document because I can foresee one day someone quoting part of this book to some government official that questions how they know about Army Regulation 210-35 and once they see this book, having the book confiscated as subversive material or classified information. Of course it isn't now, but the Gestapo lies out their pie hole when it suits them and tells people something is illegal when it isn't. So I can see information like this becoming a threat to them and their authority in the very near future, and I wouldn't be the least bit surprised if they re-classify it so the general public can't see their enslavement coming.

1–6. The process

Figure 1–1 diagrams the Army Civilian Inmate Labor Program process. The flowchart reads top down and left to right, starting with the decision to establish both a prison camp and an inmate labor program (the diamond–shaped box in the upper left corner of the diagram labeled "prison camp inmate labor?"). The diamond–shaped boxes are decision nodes; the rectangular boxes are steps in the process to establish a civilian inmate labor program, establish a civilian inmate prison camp on post, or do both. Follow the arrows through the flowchart. Chapters 2 and 3 address procedures for establishing a civilian inmate labor program and/or on–post civilian inmate prison camp.

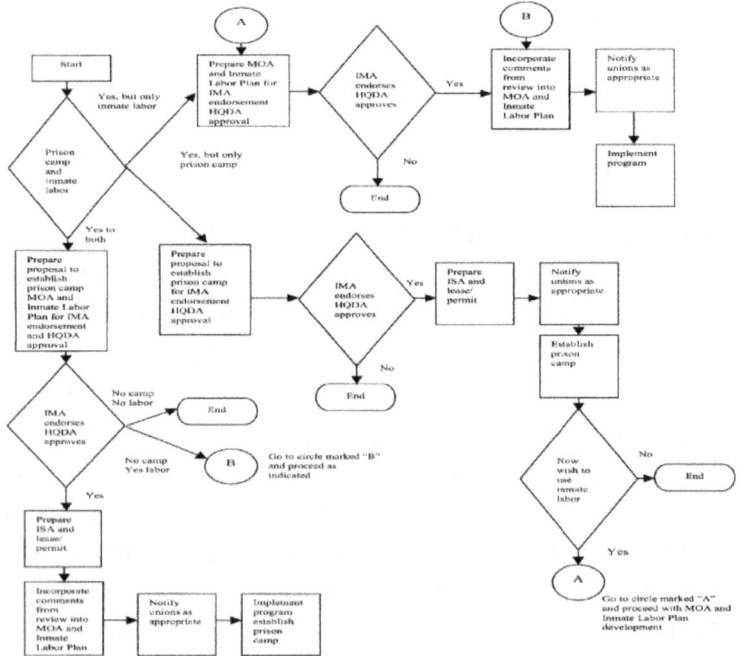

Environmental Scares

Water has become a controlling factor. Our government knows fresh water is something the people can't live without, so we are starting to see them use this valuable resource as another way to control us. They know when they have control of our water, they have control our life! We are hearing the media tell us we have a water crisis and we must conserve water. Don't believe it for a moment, it is just the beginning of their brainwash propaganda. Think for yourselves when you see all these Hollywood stars and commentators tell us there is a water shortage across the planet, and then look at all the flooding that has happened that year. They will show a drought in places in America that didn't have water problems years ago. But what they won't tell us, is that area is having a drought because the environmentalists had the dams removed to protect a tiny guppy that they thought was impacted by those dams that had been there for 75 years saving people from drought in dry times. If America is having a water shortage it's because we aren't building enough dams and canals for storing the abundant amount of water that flood and destroys communities each year. It is all about who controls the water, plain and simple. Once we get duped into believing the lies that those in power feed us about an illusionary water problem, and we don't challenge them, we all lose. Because once they get total control of the water, game over, and they almost have total control now!

It all comes down to dollars and cents, and that means controlling us. Most every new law the government creates that is supposed to protect us, cost us more of our freedom. It is merely an illusion to make us feel protected, when all the while they have an agenda, controlling us completely. Just as if we are a pet or farm animal, because we are a Cash-Cow to our government and just like any farm animal, we are expected to earn our keep or off to the chopping block we go! This is NOT what our Founding Fathers had in mind when they created this country, they expected us to manage the government and control it, not the other way around!

Years ago people who were self-sufficient and grew their own food, raised their own livestock, created their own energy and didn't need to buy much from anyone, were people we admired. Now they are hated and called isolationists and un-American and even tax evaders because they don't make an income and they don't need to. They grow, raise, or make most everything they need and try to stockpile whatever they can't use right away. The only thing self-sufficient folks can't get around is property tax. Property tax was put in place for the reason stated above. The government has a hard time getting any revenue out of people who are self-sufficient.

The government relies on our need to buy new cars, homes, computers, health insurance, car insurance, home owners insurance, DMV fees and many other government revenue generating things that they can collect tax on, so they can stay in power. Every time you buy something other than most food, what do you have to pay extra? Tax! If you are in the business of selling things, what do you have to pay on the money you make? Tax! What do you get taken out of your hard earned 40 hour paycheck? Tax! Even if you are on unemployment or disability you are Taxed. The government pretty much has their hand in everything!

It's only a matter of time before all food items will have some kind of tax or environmental fee attached to it. And I doubt anyone will say or do anything about it, because at first it will be associated with an environmental problem and only be a cent or two on the dollar. Then inch by inch and year by year the need to increase the tax and or fee will rise. It's the classic frog in the pot syndrome, where you place a frog in a pot of cold water and slowly turn up the heat. The frog does not realize what is happening until it is too late, and unfortunately if we keep going at the rate we've been going for the last 30 years or so, and we don't put a stop to this; It won't be too long before we can't jump out of that pot of boiling water and our future and the future of our children is cooked.

Global Anomalies & Other Diversions

You are probably wondering what global anomalies have to do with the American enslavement. Well, a lot! Government has been boring tunnels underneath our feet for years, literally, and playing with our atmosphere, our food and our genetic make-up, and more importantly, our minds. We are all just a cash cow labor force for government revenue generation, and they need a way to keep us enslaved. What better way to do this than to create and control mini-disasters and make you believe that the only help for these mini-disasters is the government?

Sink-holes, floods, storms, disease are increasing in severity and frequency, and you could chalk it up to natural anomalies, and in many cases you'd be right. But not all cases are naturally occurring. Many are indeed man made and not from the bogus global warming either. Just as finances and the Stock Market are rigged, so are many of the global crisis and global anomalies, and wars. It's all about control folks, plain and simple, your control and obedience. Yet most Americans keep believing the lies that their "Con-members and Thief's" continue to spew!

Let's look at the conflicts that the American government gets into in the Middle East. None have been anything but a nightmare and failure. You hear the excuses by military leaders and elected officials alike. But no one ever seems to notice the time the media and the people spend talking about it and the massive resources the government spends on it. Could it be that these crises are deliberately created and not the result of bungling fools in power as we are lead to think? It would benefit those in power to keep the American people's mind off the out of control government corruption, and benefit those who build and create weapons of war, now wouldn't it?

Your government also has frequency weapons that can create havoc on you and your surroundings. These frequency weapons are both audio and electrical. Sometimes they are combined, sometimes they aren't. Audio weapons are different than electrical weapons, audio weapons are like those uses by police and military which send out a low or high frequency to disperse protester. Electrical frequency weapons use high or low voltage frequencies at different amps to disable not only the living, but also just about anything, machines, homes, water, air, you name it! With an electrically charged frequency weapon, that combines audio and electrical frequency, that has enough amperage and concentration, you can bring down a mountain or create a title wave capable of wiping out anything along a coast line.

When I was heavily into the electronics business in the 80s and early 90s, we experimented with frequency. We were heavily into audio and speaker design as well as radio frequency stuff. I was also interested in ion power and created a little ion generator that would float a paper straw craft around the table. That is when I got interested in what frequency could do.

One day an older gentleman had come in to talk with me about an invention he was working on and ask if I would be interested in teaming up with him to develop it. I was intrigued when he told me about his ideas, so I was in. His name was Cliff and he had created a frequency boring tool, or I should say he was in the process of modifying a dental frequency drill that was able to bore a 15 thousand perfect round hole in selenium substrate material. It was basically a transducer and a hollow surgical needle that was tuned to a specified frequency that equaled the resonating frequency of whatever we wanted to bore a hole in. There was a slurry abrasive that was used also, and we were able to bore a hole through a quarter inch in less than three minutes.

Now for those of you who don't know what selenium substrate is? It is a condensed rock like material that can withstand high heat used in electronic applications and other industrial applications. So creating a way to machine it was a big deal in the late 80s and early 90s, back when we were experimenting with it.

Now the reason I bring this up is because the engineer that I was working with was one of the engineers that helped create cold rolled steel, and he was in his late 70s at the time. He had me designing the electronics and he would do most of the testing. I knew the frequencies we were dealing with, at the power levels coupled with the transducer should be shielded, or whom-ever used it should be shielded, but engineer Cliff scoffed it off saying I was too paranoid. But I can tell you this, that darn thing made my skin crawl when ever I was with in a foot or so of it, and I knew we needed to shield the transducer at least. But since we were in the R&D stages and testing several different transducers that we made on site with a lathe, and Cliff was in a hurry to get it perfected because he had a potential investor in Florida.

He didn't believe there was any problem or harm it could do and disregarded my safety concerns regarding the resonate frequencies. After months of testing Cliff came into the shop and said he wasn't feeling well and was going to the doctor to get some tests done. He was in his 80s after all, so I figured that at his age the doctor would probably tell him to start taking it easy. About a week later he came in and told me he had developed cancer. He had it everywhere even in his brain. I immediately, said I knew that he should have shielded himself around that damn thing, but he scoffed it off and said it wasn't from the machine, he thought it was from the work he did in WWII developing cold rolled steel and the exposure to toxins they had worked with including asbestos. I however believed otherwise, and still do! He had been working on that boring machine several years before we teamed up, so his exposure to it had lasted years.

Even though it was low voltage and a low amperage table-top boring unit, and we never got any microwave radiation detected off the unit, I would always use the table-top windowed lead shield after realizing its potentially damaging resonating frequency radiation. When the unit was on not boring into anything, it didn't bother me, but once it started boring a hole I could feel the frequency it resonated.

I am telling you this story so you can get an idea of the potential power of Frequency and what it can do, and what it has done! Ironically years later I too developed cancer but luckily it was cut out and so far no more has been detected.

Now imagine what the government and military have been playing with over the years. They have basically an unlimited budget if they see a potential weapon or tool they can use, and there is no doubt that they have play-toys that would pop your mind like a champagne cork.

Earthquakes and Volcanoes

You're going to see a lot more Earthquakes and Volcanoes in places that never had any, and in places that have never had any. And the information that we the people used to be able to get to detect the possibility of them, are now being hidden or not subject to public information anymore. We are seeing activity in the west and east, in American, that never been recorded before, and your government is making less and less of the information available. Why? Because they want to stop the reality of a major earth shaking volcanic problems from the public so they can use it to the government's advantage! How? To control you!

Some say a lot of these anomalies are caused by our government. Our government is building deep under ground bases that go for miles, and some of those subterranean facilities maybe right under your feet!

Open Your Mind and Stop Falling Prey to Diversions

Stop buying into the news diversions that divert your attention from the real problem of government abuse. You have to be aware of the diversion that crop up every time a government problem or embarrassment becomes daily conversation on the internet or in the media. Planes missing, weather anomalies, or Putin and Russian issues that have absolutely nothing to do with you, or absolutely will do nothing to you or for you! Oh and the ever increasing Race Baiting and working up the people into a riot so the government can move the military in and declare Marshal Law. Then they can go door to door and take all weapons from us.

All the media outlets play the diversion game and sadly people keep buying into it and taking their eye off the real enemy and real disaster that will and does directly affect them... The Government's seizing of your freedom and financing! It has become pathetic to the point that it is hard to believe people are thinking for themselves at all! Like automatons marching in a lock step goose march without the slightest idea of what is going on.

I am laughing at the once free Country called America crying over the Russians taking charge of their own destiny, and I have to say I think Putin is a far better President than America has seen in their own Country in years. The guy doesn't mess around and takes care of business...Maybe he should fake a U.S. birth certificate and run for President in the U.S?...He'd probably get elected, and maybe then we would secure our borders and stop the criminals flooding into the U.S.

America as a free nation is over anyway because the brain dead keep voting in mentally handicapped people like Pelosi and Reid who are so out of touch with reality they should be in a home for the mentally handicapped. Or that dummy senator from Texas of all places that think the constitution is not valid because it is over 400 years old.

America has become a laughing stock, and a lot of people think of Americans as morons across the world, and the funniest part is the dopy people in this country don't care how stupid other people think they are or how owned they are... But I guess that is pretty obvious since they keep voting in idiots that should be mentally evaluated or at least have to prove they done grad-gee-ated the 6 grade like Jethro Bodine.... It is so pathetic it is sickening and just adds to the destruction of our freedom and our enslavement.

So...Who really owns you? Well the protectioneers ... yep just like the gangsters who offer protection, only they are now your corporations and the insurance companies who own the government. Think about it... you have to have insurance for everything, and now the government is forcing and demanding you pay for insurance by threat of fines and in some instances imprisonment. So you are basically being strong-armed by the very government that you are supposed to control. Even with headlines of corrupt officials like San Francisco's State Assemblyman Leland Lee. Who spews the gun control that all the other leftist spew... "No citizen should own guns!", who is now under arrested for setting up a gun and weapons buy to an under cover FBI agent for rocket launchers and machine guns. Some of you still vote these crooks into office This Democrat poster child, Leland Lee, was also demanding pay-offs for political favors and protection according to what he was charged with. Want to bet real money this will be silently reported by the fascist/leftist media? No...didn't think so.

Social Economic Engineering

We have been herded into a consumption society expected to buy, buy, buy and spend, spend, spend, so the government can Tax, Tax, Tax, us to support them. It isn't working though, because it can't ever keep up with the spending promises the government has made. And like any pyramid scheme, it one day will come crashing down and only those at the top of the pyramid are the winners because they got theirs already.

Social Economic Engineering has been around since the government has been taxing, but it really took center stage in the 1970s. The new version relies on fast moving technology to provide the public stimulus to work now. Social Economic Engineering is the art of manipulating people into performing actions, i.e. buying or spending or believing something. It's a type of confidence trick for the purpose of information gathering, fraud, or manipulating people to buy into a scheme. It differs a little from traditional Social Engineering cons, that often is a mere step in a more complex fraud scheme, by using statistics to brainwash people into believing there is no scheme, and their skewed statistics prove their weak or totally bogus claims.

Wikipeda.org sums up "Social engineering" as "An act of psychological manipulation, that had previously been associated with the social sciences, but its usage has caught on among computer and information security professionals." This includes the State and Federal Governments. What this does is utilize information gathered to be used to manipulate people into believing some issue or some product is either good or bad. The Government controls the Media and has been using this technique for a long time to make us believe something, by using supposed factual information gathered by social engineers...it's even been used in Hollywood programs and movies to control how we think. Yes, I know this is a little hard to wrap your head around, but I guess the easiest way to explain this is, Subliminal Perception Messaging, anything that sends you a message without your Conscious Knowledge of it, usually picked up by your subconscious mind, or in short; Mind Control normally using an emotional stimuli. We have been, and still are, being mentally conditioned to believe whatever those in control want us to believe, and unless we can see through the manipulation, or know what is being told to us is a bold faced lie, we don't have a clue to what is really going on and will tend to believe it.

Unfortunately too many people are way too gullible and believe many of the untrue stories they are told. If we are told a lie over and over again we start to believe it. There is a saying that if you tell a lie three or more times in the media people will tend to believe it, even the people in the media who are telling the lie start to believe it themselves. Social Economic Engineering is not much different with the exception that it uses supposed data and statistics to back up weak claims or down right untrue claims. Mark Twain pretty much hit the nail on the head when he said; "There are three kinds of lies...Lies, damned lies, and statistics".

The US Department of Commerce has even gotten into the act and in 2013 started using the US Census Bureau to knock on doors and ask residents if they were victims of crime. Although this letter states in the third paragraph it is voluntary now, you can bet it will become mandatory in the future. Notice how official it looks and if you merely glance over it like most people will do, or you don't even bother to read it, you can get the impression that it's mandatory that you answer the questions when the census worker comes to your door. Once people except this it will become mandatory, and you can bet your life and carve it in stone that they will in the future be asking each house member if they have guns in the home. The reason I know it is only a matter of time before they make this a mandatory compliance is because I never responded to the first letter. Then the next year they sent another letter stating that since I never responded to the first Question Asker that came to my door, they were sending another Question Asker. Well I didn't answer the door for that one either and guess what I got the following year? Yep...another letter saying they were sending another Question Asker since I never answered any of the questions from the first two question askers. The data gathered clearly states in these letters that it is "Voluntary" and will be used by legislators and policy makers... So watch out America! Get ready for more laws backed up by statistics that the government has setup to skew a subject like gun control, because these clever deceptions are just another form of Social Engineering. Social Security and especially Obama/Demo/Care is another example of agencies that uses social engineering and deception to gain information from those who collect it, basically it's a tool to use to create a Ponzi Scheme for revenue generation.

UNITED STATES DEPARTMENT OF COMMERCE
Economics and Statistics Administration
U.S. Census Bureau
Washington, DC 20233-0001
OFFICE OF THE DIRECTOR

FROM THE DIRECTOR
U.S. CENSUS BUREAU

The U.S. Census Bureau is conducting a survey for the U.S. Department of Justice to obtain information on the type and amount of crime committed against households and individuals throughout the country. A Census Bureau representative will be contacting you soon. Our representative will show an official identification card and ask for some important information on this subject from you and your household.

The information you provide our representative will help inform the country about how much crime there is, where it occurs, when it occurs, what crime costs victims, and which segments of the population are most frequently victimized. Since many crimes are never reported to the police, information from this survey will show a more complete picture of the amount and types of crime occurring in the United States. The survey results are used in many ways, including by citizens to evaluate their vulnerabilities, by legislators and policymakers to develop programs to aid crime victims and prevent crime, and by researchers to understand various aspects of crime victimization.

Your address is part of a scientifically selected sample of addresses chosen throughout the country for participation in this survey. Because this is a sample survey, your answers represent not only you and your household, but also hundreds of other households like yours. For this reason, your voluntary cooperation is very important. I hope you will answer all the survey questions as completely and accurately as possible. Although there are no penalties for failure to answer any questions, each unanswered question substantially lessens the accuracy of the final data. Your answers will be used only to prepare statistical summaries, and no information about your household or you as an individual can be identified from these statistics. The law completely protects your confidential answers from disclosure.

Answers to the most frequently asked survey questions are on the reverse side of this letter. If you would like further information, contact the Census Bureau by writing or calling the following office:

REGIONAL DIRECTOR
US CENSUS BUREAU
15350 SHERMAN WAY STE 400
VAN NUYS CA   91406-4203

Telephone: 1-800-992-3530

Thank you for your cooperation. The Census Bureau appreciates your help.

A Message From the Director

Chapter Twelve
America's Food Poisoning from Corporate Greed and the Government it Owns

The Government control over food is just as bad as their attempt to control all the water. Regulation after regulation and law after law are heaped on to, not only the farm and ranch industry, but also the individual citizen who wants to eat Fresh Foods. Police and FDA agents have raided small farms and families for selling milk, cheese, garden vegetables, lemonade and meat, to neighbors who want untainted fresh food, and even arrested and jailed a man in Oregon for collecting rain water on his property! The totally unconstitutional raids were for no other reason than they didn't have government approval, and didn't raise, grow or collect rain water or what they sold according to government regulations. The people who were raided weren't alone, no sir, the people who bought from the farmers were also arrested! The farmers had grown and raised their vegetables and animals naturally without any preservatives like most farmers and ranchers used to raise and grow the food that we ate years ago. But because the farmers would dare sell fresh untainted food to their neighbors who had asked them if they could buy it, the government attacks them. I can sight several headline cases such as: "Wisconsin Farmer to Stand Trial for Selling Raw Milk", another "Feds sting Amish farmer selling raw milk" and on Aug 3, 2011 – "Police Seize Cash, Produce, Dump Raw Milk .... Government arrest and persecute individuals merely for buying and selling raw milk and cheese ... Healthy Family Farms is a sustainable, pasture-based farming operation" ... even children have been arrested for selling Lemonade: Aug 20, 2011 ... Children Arrested for Selling Lemonade at Capitol... The children were selling lemonade on the Capitol lawn. The list of attacks by the government on farmers and people who just want to raise, grow and eat fresh natural food goes on and on.

I don't know about some of you younger readers, but I think many of you people 50 and over would agree with me when I say that meat, fish, bird, and vegetables you buy in the supermarket today taste different than it used to taste when you were a kid. I can remember sitting down at the table to a great tasting hamburger, and T-bone steaks, and the roasts my mom used to bake in the 60s were out of this world. Even chicken, turkey and fish just does not taste the same. Food used to taste so much fresher years ago. Back as early as the 1980's you could still get a pretty good piece of beef. Now it seems that you really have to shop around to find any type of food that even comes close to the taste of food years ago. Unless it's from a family farm, now that I have had and it tastes pretty close to what I remember good beef tasted like 40, 50 years ago!

I asked a butcher a while back, why our food doesn't taste as good as it use to years ago? He told me that most of the farmers today feed and fertilize with so many chemicals that it's a wonder people are not dropping dead in droves. He told me he was lucky to have a small farm where he could grow and raise his own food like most of the commercial farmers and ranchers used to do back in the 50s and 60s. Food was natural and full of flavor back then, the way it was suppose to be! I recently found out first hand what the butcher told me was true. My daughter and Son-in-law who live on a ranch, butchered one of their cattle and gave my wife and I some of the meat. There was that taste I had been missing! It was the flavor that I remembered years ago that use to make me run to the dinner table. The flavor that I once took for granted. They allow their cattle to graze in the spring through fall and feed them grain and cattle feed in the winter. No anti-bodies or other chemicals are ingested by their cattle. They do not use chemical fertilizers on the pasture, just good old natural horse manure and boy does it show by the taste of the beef! Grass and other grain really grow good with just plain old natural fertilizer, no pesticides or chemicals just manure. But that wasn't the only surprise I had. Several weeks before my daughter had bestowed that prized beef on me, my young grandson had gone fishing in Alaska with his other grandpa and brought back some fresh Ocean Halibut and Salmon that they had caught. Once again I tasted fish like it used to taste, fresh! Not "Farm Raised" or whatever they sell in the supermarkets today.

Sadly, since the government regulations have become so expensive for farmers and ranchers, many of them have just quit. Now only the large corporate government controlled farmers and ranchers are supplying the stores with chemically enriched produce, poultry, Sea food and beef; which the large chemical corporations with government contracts control. If the little farmers attempts to sell, or even in some cases, give what they grow and raise to anyone even their family, without all the permits, licenses and regulations required…off to jail they go… Another freedom lost…I don't believe for a moment this is good for America's Health, do you?

Let's look at America's health from the late 1960s to today, and the government regulations the FDA passed on farming and ranching from the same time. This information is readily available to anyone on the internet. The chemicals listed below have been introduced in our food for about 40 years now.

Bovine Growth Hormone (rBGH)

This genetically modified hormone was developed to be injected into dairy cows to produce more milk. Cows subjected to rBGH suffer excruciating pain due to swollen udders and mastitis, and the pus from the resulting infection enters the milk supply requiring the use of additional antibiotics. rBGH milk has been linked to breast cancer, colon cancer, and prostate cancer in humans. Bovine somatotropin or bovine somatotrophin (abbreviated bST and BST), or BGH, is a peptide hormone produced by a cow's pituitary gland. Like other hormones, it is produced in small quantities and is used in regulating metabolic processes. After the biotech company Genentech discovered and patented the gene for BST in the 1970s, it became possible to synthesize the hormone using recombinant DNA technology to create recombinant bovine somatotropin (rBST), recombinant bovine growth hormone (rBGH), or artificial growth hormone. Four large pharmaceutical companies, Monsanto, American Cyanamid, Eli Lilly, and Upjohn, developed commercial rBST products and submitted them to the US Food and Drug Administration (FDA) for approval and rBST was approved for use.

Genetically Modified Crops, (GMOs)

In the 1980s and early 1990s, began gene-splicing corn, cotton, soy, and canola with DNA from a foreign source to achieve a couple of traits; an internally generated pesticide and an internal resistance to the weed killers like Round-Up or "glyphosate" so farmers could control weeds without hurting the crop. Despite decades of promises that genetically engineered crops would feed the world with more nutrients, that were drought resistant and had greater yield, the GMO crops haven't lived up to the promise. They have however, caused health problems, according to the Organic Consumers Association, "There is a direct correlation between our genetically engineered food supply and the $2 trillion the U.S. spends annually on medical care, namely an epidemic of diet-related chronic diseases."

The U.S. government subsidizes corporate farms and food processors that produce genetically engineered junk food that has increased heart disease, stroke, diabetes and cancers. You would think the US Government would be supporting naturally grown healthy fruits, vegetables, grains, and range and pasture fed animals, but most organic farmers receive no such subsidies and are often targeted by the FDA. Why? Could it be that naturally grown food means no money for the government and the chemical corporations who support the government with taxes and their contribution/pay-offs?

Unfortunately most of the land we grow food on has already been chemically altered and it can take years for some of the chemicals to degrade. Take the Rice Growing industry for instance. Before 2000 most Rice Farmers would burn their fields to control pests and disease, but after 2000 regulations were put on burning, chemicals were used instead. A lot of old style ways of farming have been forgotten or made illegal and farmers are left with little choice but to use chemicals. One drawback to all this chemical use is human occupational exposure to pesticides and chemicals that has become a significant cause of death.

Ask yourself is the government mandates on food and their seemingly deliberate attacks on people who wish to eat naturally good for America's Health and our Freedom? Or is this just another illusion of control. I think another question should be asked; who is profiting from these mandates and laws? Remember, everything you buy has a tax attached to it somewhere down the line, either a sales tax or an income tax or both.

Corporate Government

It's hard for most people to believe or except they have no control over their lives and very little control over their government. Hopefully some of the things you have just read in the previous chapters are starting to tie things altogether. The real controllers of the government today are corporations and money. Our founding fathers knew this all too well and attempted to put checks and balances in the Constitution to protect the citizens from a corporate take over of the government. They had seen corporations take over governments, like the East Indies Company that traded mainly in cotton, silk, indigo dye, salt, saltpeter, tea and opium. The Company was granted a Royal Charter by Queen Elizabeth in 1600, making it the oldest among several similarly formed European East India Companies. Shares of the company were owned by wealthy merchants and aristocrats, many of whom had ties to the government or were in the government. The government itself didn't own any shares and had only indirect control, but that was because the corporation was controlling what the government was doing. The Company eventually came to rule large areas of India with its own private armies, exercising military power and assuming administrative functions. It had a major influence on the British Government, just as many corporations today have major influence on the government.

Most media is corporate driven, meaning the corporation controls most of what you see and how you see it. Corporations are great users of social engineering, and even the supposed honest fair and balanced news media is controlling what you see and read. So the Corporations control the media, and the government, and you are merely a resource to them. Yet, most people seem content with this, and don't really care as long as they have some creature comforts. The mass feed their children poison and teach the children to obey the corporate government, and they do it without thinking of the future consequence, as if they are zombified. Is this what man has to look forward to, mindless compulsion? We should not comply with bad laws and regulations created by ruthless tyrants! Our Constitution and Founding Fathers pretty much demanded it, if we were to remain a Free Nation, we must rise up against tyranny, because it is our duty.

Sadly we have to realize some hard cold facts. One is that we live in a parasitic universe and everything feeds off of something. We also have to understand the two constants in this dimensional universe; nothing lives or lasts forever and everything must come to an end and die one day. So for us to believe that freedom in the USA will last, is a fallacy... but to believe there is nothing you can do to change the speed at which it ends is also a fallacy. We have the power, and the corporate government not only knows it, but is terrified that we may one day wake up and use that power. This is why we are seeing the build up of military police and the confiscation of weapons and freedom. People like you and I are waking up and saying NO to the powers that be that have been herding us like sheep to the slaughter house. The government and their corporate bosses are preparing for that day when everything comes crashing down and the people decide to band together and march on them, for all the crimes they have committed against humanity and our Constitution. So we must be prepared or we will be caught like a deer in the headlights of an oncoming tank or armored truck, with a driver that knows they have to speed up to avoid major damage!

Chapter Thirteen
Being Prepared for the Worst &
Expressing Yourselves

We don't have much time left to effectively stop this total takeover of all freedom in America. We have to get all the people to realize they are being manipulated into the classic divide and conquer approach to totally conquering them. We have a major divide in this country which is purposely being fueled to create the Illusion that you need more rules and laws to protect you from the other side. This is going to be the hardest thing to overcome. Hate runs long and deep, and the left vs. right has been played for a long, long time.

Both sides point the finger at each other and say we don't own, watch, read or eat the same thing! So because of this we try and pass a law to stop the other side from owning, watching, reading or eating something different then us. We do this in a fueled anger created by our government even if we have to cut off our own nose to spite our face! All the while, our controllers sit back calm and collect, as they manipulate our feelings and point us in the direction they want us to go.

Who are the controllers you ask? They are a rogue government shadow corporation that have far more power than the President will ever have! They are comprised of people that we will never know or see to our knowledge. They have been in the shadow for as long as time and are the reason and the start of government control. They are very powerful individuals and have been controlling and manipulating us and our government like farm animals for centuries all for revenue generation!

There are two very effective ways to get a person to do or believe something: One is to tell them the truth and hope they believe it and do the right thing. The other is to get them angry or sad at the truth and then point that anger or sadness in the direction you want it to go. This is called control by using an emotional stimuli and it works really well; especially if the person you are using it on has no idea what you are up to. This is also used openly by Military Law Enforcers who are trained to deliberately push your buttons and get you mad at them or sad over something, so you will do or say something that they can arrest you for, or get information out of you. Watch out for the direct and indirect use of this technique. We have to remember to try and stay in control and not allow ourselves to be controlled or manipulated or we will lose! I know it is hard not to get mad at views you strongly disagree with, and God knows I lose my temper when I am confronted with a person I know is trying to push my buttons. It is really hard not to blow up, especially when you have those people who deliberately try and push you to the breaking point just so they can say; "What's the matter with you, why are you freaking out, you are crazy or are you insane!" This way they can try and destroy any credibility you had and make you out to look like a nut.

Express Yourself

We need to express our likes and dislikes to our elected representatives. I hear time after time from people that it does not matter what they say, and it does not do any good to call their elected officials because they do not listen. This is another fallacy! They must be listening to someone or they wouldn't vote the way they do on issues that directly affect you. What you have to do to be effective, is talk with your neighbors and friends and see if they feel the same way you do. If they do, write up a letter of approval or disapproval on the subject and have them sign it, get as many signatures as you can and send it in to your local elected official. Then call them after you know they have had time to read it, like three days to a week later.

(You will need to wait a couple of weeks for State and Federal representatives to get around to reading it.) Believe me they'll be more inclined to listen to you then!

Another very effective way is to get people who feel the same way as you do on an issue, and go to the Government meetings. City Council, County Supervisors, School Boards as well as other local agencies have regular monthly and weekly meetings that the public can attend. You can speak your concerns at the meetings when they ask if there are any public comments. It is best to call ahead and make it known that you will be there and what the topic is. Then you will be put on the agenda for that meeting and who ever you are going in front of will call you up and make it known to the people what you are there for. You usually will have a time limit to get your point across. They will expect you to adhere to that set that time limit, especially if you are going against their authority or some new law they want to pass. Of course it is best to have everything you want to say written down so you can make sure that you get your point across and or get all your questions answered. Being a former elected official, I can assure you this will get their attention, and if it doesn't, and they basically ignore you and your group, all you need to do is mention the word, "Recall" and that will get their attention for sure.

Get to know your State Reps. I know my assemblyman and have his personal cell phone number. You may not be able to get your State Reps cell number but you sure can speak with their office staff and complain or let them know how you feel. Now if you really get involved as I have, you can help get your people elected to office and then the odds are that you too might have a personal cell phone number or direct line you can call when you want to express yourself. But if you stand on the sidelines and never get involved, you won't have anyone to call and you will surely lose what little freedom you have left!

Civil Disobedience

We are going to see a lot more regulations and laws passed to control us. You may have to break those regulations and laws to regain your freedom. Civil Disobedience has been the most used way to affect change. Wikipedia, the free encyclopedia, describes this as the active, professed refusal to obey certain laws, demands, and commands of a government, or of an occupying international power. Civil disobedience is commonly, though not always, defined as being nonviolent resistance. It is one form of civil resistance. In one view (in India, known as ahimsa or satyagraha) it could be said that it is compassion in the form of respectful disagreement.

Thoureau's 1848 essay called; "Civil Disobedience", was originally titled; "Resistance to Civil Government", has had a wide influence on many later practitioners of civil disobedience. The driving idea behind the essay is that citizens are morally responsible for their support of aggressors, even when such support is required by law. In the essay, Thoreau explained his reasons for having refused to pay taxes as an act of protest against slavery and against the Mexican-American War. He writes; "If I devote myself to other pursuits and contemplations, I must first see, at least, that I do not pursue them sitting upon another man's shoulders. I must get off him first, that he may pursue his contemplations too. See what gross inconsistency is tolerated. I have heard some of my townsmen say, 'I should like to have them order me out to help put down an insurrection of the slaves, or to march to Mexico; — see if I would go'; and yet these very men have each, directly by their allegiance, and so indirectly, at least, by their money, furnished a substitute."

Henry David Thoreau's classic essay Civil Disobedience inspired Martin Luther King, Mahatma Gandhi and many other activists.

In seeking an active form of civil disobedience, one may choose to deliberately break certain laws, such as by forming a peaceful blockade or occupying a facility illegally, though sometimes violence has been known to occur, and protesters practice this non-violent form of civil disorder, have to have the expectation that they might or will be arrested. You also have to expect that you might be violently attacked by the authorities and maybe even killed. Protesters often undergo training in advance on how to react to arrest or an attack, so that they will do so in a manner that quietly or limply resists without threatening the authorities, so they can avoid getting hurt.

Mahatma Gandhi outlined several rules for civil resisters at the time when he was leading India in the struggle for Independence from the British Empire. For instance, they were to express no anger, never retaliate, submit to the opponent's orders and assaults, submit to arrest by the authorities, surrender personal property when confiscated by the authorities but refuse to surrender property held in trust, refrain from swearing and insults (which are contrary to ahimsa), refrain from saluting the Union flag, and protect officials from insults and assaults even at the risk of the resister's own life. This worked in India's case but doesn't always work. China is one of those cases where peaceful protest can get you killed.

Now one other effective way of peacefully protesting is to form a general American strike. This has never been effectively accomplished yet, but it would get the attention of the government really fast, especially if it lasted for days or weeks. However, it would take hundreds of millions of people all across the county to be successful. Essentially people would just quit working and quit buying anything so no taxes would be paid which would eventually shut down the country's revenue. We have seen this in mid-eastern countries and it does work, but it takes weeks or even months to bring a country or government to its knees.

Chapter Fourteen
Defense against Abusive Law Enforcers
& The Lack of Law Enforcement
Protecting You From Them

Because we have given way too much power and authority to Law Enforcers they have become a military power that in many cases runs rogue. Abusing their power has become the norm and they don't care if you like it or not. With local district attorneys and the courts backing them up, they can lie, cheat, steal, and murder without fear. Anyone who questions their authority is routinely bullied and arrested, and there is little you can do about it, or is there?

The Police Chief and Sheriff are most often elected or hired by their cities and counties who are controlled by the City Council and the County Board of Supervisors, who are elected by the people. If you see someone being beat and or arrested by the police just for merely questioning their authority, or your city or county has a known reputation for this happening, than you probably have a Gestapo problem. The Police and Sheriff Deputies hate being called Gestapo, but since the advent of being able to directly upload police and sheriff abuse of power on the internet, the word Gestapo fits. The sad thing is "We The People" have allowed it to get this bad, but not because we weren't warned.

"First they came for the Jews, and I didn't speak out because I wasn't a Jew.

Then they came for the communists, and I didn't speak out because I wasn't a communist.

Then they came for the socialists, and I didn't speak out

because I wasn't a socialist.

Then they came for the trade unionists, and I didn't speak out because I wasn't a trade unionist.

Then they came for me, and there was no one left to speak out for me." – Martin Niemöller

An English translation of Niemöller's speech for the Confessing Church in Frankfurt on the 6th of January 1946 states: "When Pastor Niemöller was put in a concentration camp we wrote the year 1937; when the concentration camp was opened we wrote the year 1933, and the people who were put in the camps then were Communists. Who cared about them? We knew it, it was printed in the newspapers.

Who raised their voice, maybe the Confessing Church? We thought: Communists, those opponents of religion, those enemies of Christians - "should I be my brother's keeper?"

Then they got rid of the sick, the so-called incurables. - I remember a conversation I had with a person who claimed to be a Christian, He said: "Perhaps it's right, these incurably sick people just cost the state money, they are just a burden to themselves and to others. Isn't it best for all concerned if they are taken out of the middle [of society]?' -- Only then did the church as such take note. Then we started talking, until our voices were again silenced in public. Can we say, we aren't guilty or responsible? The persecution of the Jews, the way we treated the occupied countries, or the things in Greece, in Poland, in Czechoslovakia or in Holland, that were written in the newspapers. I believe, we Confessing-Church-Christians have every reason to say: mea culpa, mea culpa! We can talk ourselves out of it with the excuse that it would have cost me my head if I had spoken out."

301

If only people now would stand up and speak out on all of the abusive treatment that has been going on with our people and our country, but ironically most people have the same excuse written above by Martin Niemoller, "it might cost me my head". So it seems that history is repeating it self again right here in America. Luckily there are a few of us who are speaking out and denouncing the Gestapo that are infecting our country. But it's going to take a lot more people to change the trend and that means more people speaking out and demanding that this stop.

To do that we have to stand up to our elected officials and demand they put a stop to it, or we will remove them from office, and elect someone else who will put a stop to all the abuse and corruption. Only then will we see these rogue bullies be charged with crimes that they committed against the people and hopefully convicted, never to be able to wear a law enforcement uniform ever again. Many of them should have never been allowed to wear one in the first place, from some of the videos that are posted on the internet, but somehow because of whom they know, they are allowed to continue their abuse against the taxpaying citizens. A good site to visit is: Flexyourrights.org, there is a lot of good information on that site that you can use to defend yourself from some abusive tactics.

Someone needs to also challenge how search warrants are executed in the US Supreme Court. Gestapo like tactics should not go unchallenged. To allow police to break-down your door and destroy your home, shoot and kill your animals and hold you face-down on the floor while ransacking your home and destroying personal property, should not be tolerated in any free society. Since when was it deemed OK to destroy a citizen's personal property just because the government suspects you may have committed a crime? Any law enforcer who tries to lie to you and says they don't destroy personal property needs to be reminded that breaking down a front door is destroying personal property. Police killing a family pet should also be a crime just as killing a police dog is a crime. We the people should never allow ourselves to have less rights than the police, because if we do, we're living in a police state and that is not Freedom.

State Supreme Courts have condoned and allowed police to do whatever they want whether legal or not, and this cannot be tolerated in a free society. One case in point was in Indianapolis where the state supreme court overturned a common law dating back to the English Magna Carta of 1215, the Indiana Supreme Court ruled in May of 2011 that no one has the right to resist unlawful police entry into their homes.

In a 3-2 decision, Justice Steven David writing for the court said, "If a police officer wants to enter a home for any reason or no reason at all, a homeowner cannot do anything to block the officer's entry."

"We believe ... a right to resist an unlawful police entry into a home is against public policy and is incompatible with "modern" Fourth Amendment jurisprudence," David said. "We also find that allowing resistance unnecessarily escalates the level of violence and therefore the risk of injuries to all parties involved without preventing the arrest."

David said a person arrested following an unlawful entry by police still can be released on bail and has plenty of opportunities to protest the illegal entry through the court system.

So what he is saying in short, is we have no Rights against Police/Gestapo no matter what they do to you, even kill you. This is a classic case of rewriting the Constitution by inference. Notice the "modern" Fourth Amendment jurisprudence quote and his attempt to cleverly say that resistance is futile because he wasn't going to allow his Gestapo to be put in harms way. This is only one of many cases where our Rights have been overruled by judges that should have never been allowed to sit on any legal bench.

On the flip side of this Law Enforcement equation is the lack of protection by police from the vandals and thieves in this country anymore. Police seem to do little or nothing when we call in to report a theft or vandalizing of our property. Yet, if we have a taillight out on our car, watch out, they will pull us over and give us the third degree, probably search our car and then ticket us...and if we question their authority, oh boy, we could be in for a beating and a POP (Pissing Off Police) charge.

I have complained several times about the vandalizing of our property and the theft of a number of items, only to get smoke blown up my backside by law enforcers who claim they are too busy and/or understaffed. When I asked if an officer could go out and see the vandalizing that was done, it took them 5 days to respond. The Vandals destroyed a 1,450 square foot mobile home that I was putting together for my wife and I on the property in Butte County, California that we were hoping one day to eventually live in. They broke every window, shower door, light fixture, mirror, bedroom door, cabinet, and fan, in the place. They also shot holes throughout the home making it a total loss. Since I was in the first stage of the building process, there was no insurance company that would insure me unless I paid thousands, or until I had all of the permits signed. You can not get county permits period until you have HUD sign off on a mobile or modular home in California. You have to have it built before they approve it. So my wife and I ate over $35,000 dollars worth of damage which did not even include the total destruction of a 1966 Kaiser jeep that was parked on the property and a Semi Truck that they broke the windshield and windows out of and slashed two of the tires. They also pushed our boat off of its trailer. It all makes me wonder why we have to pay tax on this property at all! It sure is not for police or sheriff protection against vandals and thieves and they don't even maintain our road and our grown children do not go to the schools. We don't even live up there as planned because of all the damage that has been done! As far as paying tax for fire protection goes, well that is a joke because everything on our property has been trashed so if there was a fire we would have nothing to lose except for maybe the beautiful trees and scenery. But since we do not have the money to start over, we will probably never be able to live there and enjoy that beautiful scenery as planned! I realize that the law enforcers can not be there 24/7. But when you call to report a major vandalism and it takes them 5 days to even come up and look at the damage that is outrageous! Of course by then any evidence that they might have found such as finger prints would be gone and the people that did it will be long gone!

I've come to find out that my horrible story of vandalization is not the exception, but more of the rule. It seems that most everyone that I have spoke with since than, that have property around the same vicinity as mine have had damage done to their property too, and have had pretty much the same results with the law enforcers; which is doing little or nothing to stop the problem. Of course California is not the best place to invest in, so it is partly my fault for attempting to develop my property. But you would think that our local officials would want their law enforcers to go out and catch the real criminals, not the poor individual who had no idea that their taillight went out on their car. Instead they seem to go after the easy money, while the real hardcore criminals sit around and laugh while getting high on the drugs they bought with the money they made off the things they just stole from you.

I used to think some of the mid-eastern laws were a bit harsh, like if a thief gets caught they cut off a finger, and if they get caught a second time they cut off their hand; but after becoming a victim of vandalism and theft, I am starting to think that law looks pretty good. This is why people have formed Neighborhood Watch Patrols to protect each other against vandals, thugs and thieves. The police unfortunately do not seem too interested in going after some of these lowlife criminals. Once again the citizens who live by the rules and obey the laws have become the victims!

So the government imposing laws for our safety is another illusion. Laws are arbitrarily enforced and abused, it is imperative that we take control of our government and return policing back to going after the real criminals, and not a tool for revenue generation and public control.

Here is something to also think about; If a thief or vandal takes or destroys something and is never caught, what do you have to do to replace it?........You have to buy a new one and what do you have to pay extra on what you buy? Bingo.......Taxes! Either income tax, sales tax or both, so once again the revenue generation comes into play. It is all a numbers game to get the masses to make more money and spend more money, and pay more taxes to support the pyramid scheme called "The Government"

You Own Nothing in America Anymore!

Under the forfeiture laws you own nothing! And Americans say little or nothing about it... let alone do anything to stop it! What's even worse is the Government can seize anything you own and there is little you can do about it. Police steal billions of dollars of seizes property every year and it can be bank accounts, cars, money, jewelry and even your house! All they have to say is you are suspected of being a criminal, and they don't even have to charge you with a crime! Oh you can try and fight them but once they take everything you own, how are you going to pay an attorney to fight the tyrants?

Americans are suppose to be innocent until proven guilty in a court of law, but we all know that is a joke on us especially under the civil forfeiture laws that make you guilty until proven innocent. Under the Civil Forfeiture Law the police/Gestapo can steal any or all of your personal property merely because they say it may have been obtained through criminal activity. It was originally used by the British in the 1700s to seize ships and their content that didn't fly the British Flag. The British law required any ship transporting goods from a British port had to fly the British flag and of course to do that you had to pay a tax to the crown. Ships that were caught flying any other flag were subject to attack and the ship, crew and cargo seized and forfeit. This was done because the owners of the ships were normally not on the ships used to transport goods and therefore the British couldn't arrest and seize the owner's total wealth, so they would take what they could from them, which was their ship, cargo and crew. This was used as a tool in the Revolutionary War against America, and unfortunately was parroted by the U.S. Congress as a model for the first American Forfeiture Laws aimed at customs revenue which was about 90% of the Government's funding at the time. It was supposed to be used against those braking maritime law and not paying duty tax when it was almost impossible to arrest the owner or kingpin who was breaking the law. Now this "maritime law" tool use to combat crime and tax evasion has been perverted into any illegal or supposed illegal activity, and the police/Gestapo routinely use this to fund their army and buy equipment used against you the common citizens... There is no reasonable cause involved. If the local Gestapo were to take a disliking to you, they could claim you gained your home and cars and other personal property by illegal activity and seize it all. The odds on you being able to get it back is slim and none since they don't actually have to prove you did anything illegal, just claim they believe you had, or plant some incriminating evidence against you.

In 1984 the Department of Justice created the Asset Forfeiture Fund, and in the second year 1986 after its creation Department of Justice took in $93.7 million in proceeds from forfeited assets. After they realized this was a gold mine to collect a fortune without having to justify stealing it, the amount in 2008 skyrocketed to more than $1 billion in forfeited assets. It no doubt has risen since then with more and more agencies taking advantage of these free stolen goods and cash they now can easily take from you without proving you committed any crime. Once again this goes back to your 4th, 5th, 6th and 8th Amendments that have been ignored.

People are waking up and stopping this unconstitutional theft. New Mexico has passed legislature stopping the forfeiture laws. New Mexico is the first State at this time to stop the blatant theft by poling for profit. New Mexico's Governor Susana Martinez has signed into law House Bill 560, the first asset forfeiture reform legislation in the nation. The bill had complete bipartisan approval in the state's House and Senate. Nobody voted against it.

New Mexico's has now eliminated the concept of "civil asset forfeiture", now law enforcers have to actually convict people of crimes to take their assets. It also stops cold their incentive for stealing, or policing for profit, because the new law requires all proceeds from asset forfeitures be put into the state's general fund. They're no longer able to keep what they take from the citizens, period, because the law forbids police from partnering up with the Department of Justice's Equitable Sharing Program to get around the new law. New Mexico's House Bill 560 forbids law enforcement agencies from retaining any forfeited property.

Here is the letter the governor wrote explaining her decision to sigh the bill into law: April 10, 2015 HOUSE EXECUTIVE MESSAGE NO. 25 The Honorable Don L. Tripp, Speaker of the House and Members of the House of Representatives State Capitol Building Santa Fe, NM 87501 Honorable Speaker Tripp and Members of the House: I have this day SIGNED HOUSE BILL 560, as amended, with certification of correction, enacted by the Fifty-Second Legislature, First Session, 2015. House Bill 560 (HB 560) makes numerous changes to the asset forfeiture process used by law enforcement agencies in New Mexico. As an attorney and career prosecutor, I understand how important it is that we ensure safeguards are in place to protect our constitutional rights.

On balance, the changes made by this legislation improve the transparency and accountability of the forfeiture process and provide further protections to innocent property owners. For these reasons, I have signed HB 560.

However, I must make it clear that "policing for profit" is an overused, oversimplified, and cynical term that, in my opinion, disrespects our law enforcement officers. These heroes in our communities take on extraordinary risk, face incredible harm, and operate with tremendous courage, and this catch phrase improperly questions their motives and disregards their desire to serve and protect. It is also dangerous to discount the role that funds acquired through forfeitures have played in keeping our communities safe and in protecting our officers from harm. We cannot allow this new law to undermine our efforts to combat crime throughout this state. With the passage of this legislation, it is more critical than ever before that every county and municipality, as well as the state legislature, makes a stronger commitment to fully fund our law enforcement agencies so that they can continue undertaking complex investigations, protecting the public, and protecting themselves while doing so. New Mexico is a border state. The trafficking of narcotics and the presence of other crimes is a very real threat to the public safety of our communities. We must ensure that HOUSE EXECUTIVE MESSAGE NO. 25

The Honorable Don L. Tripp April 10, 2015 Page 2 our law enforcement officers have the training, protection, and tools necessary to fight crime within our borders. The burden is on public officials at every level to ensure that our law enforcement officers are respected for the work they do and have all the resources they need to protect our families.

Respectfully yours, Susana Martinez Governor

Chapter Fifteen
Some Quotes & Philosophies Of Our Founding Fathers

"The Facts of History, is that History is written by the winners of wars and conquerors of nations. Losers of wars and those conquered lose their history, and are written in to history as their conquerors want them remembered. The Truth and Facts about those conquered have nothing to do with History in the eyes of the winners of wars." – R.W. Gless

Our founding Fathers were wiser than most people today give them credit for. As a matter of fact most of the people have no idea what our Founding Father's philosophies were. Even teachers in your public schools have no idea, nor do they want to know because that would be in direct conflict with their progressive socialist agenda.

It is hard to argue with the facts and the quotes of our Founding Fathers, but sadly many of the teachers and people in charge of your government are trying to teach history by omission and deception. Or they just plain refuse to teach about it if it goes against whatever agenda they worship. So I decided to put together some historic quotes and philosophies of our Founders so you can be better educated about our once much freer nation, and so you can understand the hopes our Founders had for America. I am working on another book which will contain as many of the founders quotes as I can find.

"If the American people ever allow private banks to control the issue of their money, first by inflation and then by deflation, the banks and corporations that will grow up around them (around the banks), will deprive the people of their property until their children will wake up homeless on the continent their fathers conquered."

— Thomas Jefferson, 1802 letter to Secretary of State Albert Gallatin.

Of course the later leaders never listened and later created the Federal Reserve which is controlled by the banks and now we can see Thomas Jefferson's statement has come true.

"I hope that we shall crush in its birth the aristocracy of our moneyed corporations, which dare already to challenge our government to a trial of strength, and bid defiance to the laws of our country."— Thomas Jefferson.

"The power of all corporations ought to be limited in this respect. The growing wealth acquired by them never fails to be a source of abuses." — James Madison.

"If freedom of speech is taken away, then dumb and silent we may be led, like sheep to the slaughter." — George Washington

"A primary object should be the education of our youth in the science of government. In a republic, what species of knowledge can be equally important? And what duty more pressing than communicating it to those who are to be the future guardians of the liberties of the country?" — George Washington

"As Mankind becomes more liberal, they will be more apt to allow that all those who conduct themselves as worthy members of the community are equally entitled to the protections of civil government. I hope ever to see America among the foremost nations of justice and liberality." — George Washington

"A free people ought not only to be armed, but disciplined; to which end a uniform and well-digested plan is requisite; and their safety and interest require that they should promote such manufactories as tend to render them independent of others for essential, particularly military, supplies." — George Washington

"In politics as in philosophy, my tenets are few and simple. The leading one of which, and indeed that which embraces most others, is to be honest and just ourselves and to exact it from others, meddling as little as possible in their affairs where our own are not involved. If this maxim was generally adopted, wars would cease and our swords would soon be converted into reap hooks and our harvests be more peaceful, abundant, and happy." — George Washington

"99% of failures come from people who make excuses." — George Washington

As you can see by the Quotes above, Our Founders knew all too well what atrocities would happen if people became apathetic and complacent and allowed the corporations to control our government. It is almost as if they saw the future and were trying to warn us of things to come.

James Madison's Detached Memoranda, Observations and Warnings

"The danger of silent accumulations & encroachments by Ecclesiastical Bodies have not sufficiently engaged attention in the U.S. They have the noble merit of first unshackling the conscience from persecuting laws, and of establishing among religious Sects a legal equality. If some of the States have not embraced this just and this truly in principle in its proper latitude, all of them present examples by which the most enlightened States of the old world may be instructed; and there is one State at least, Virginia, where religious liberty is placed on its true foundation and is defined in its full latitude. The general principle is contained in her declaration of rights, prefixed to her Constitution: but it is unfolded and defined, in its precise extent, in the act of the Legislature, usually named the Religious Bill, which passed into a law in the year 1786. Here the separation between the authority of human laws, and the natural rights of Man excepted from the grant on which all political authority is founded, is traced as distinctly as words can admit, and the limits to this authority established with as much solemnity as the forms of legislation can express. The law has the further advantage of having been the result of a formal appeal to the sense of the Community and a deliberate sanction of a vast majority, comprising every sect of Christians in the State. This act is a true standard of Religious liberty: its principle the great barrier against usurpations on the rights of conscience. As long as it is respected & no longer, these will be safe. Every provision for them short of this principle, will be found to leave crevices at least thro' which bigotry may introduce persecution; a monster, that feeding & thriving on its own venom, gradually swells to a size and strength overwhelming all laws divine & human.

Ye States of America, which retain in your Constitutions or Codes, any aberration from the sacred principle of religious liberty, by giving to Caesar what belongs to God, or joining together what God has put asunder, hasten to revise & purify your systems, and make the example of your Country as pure & complete, in what relates to the freedom of the mind and its allegiance to its maker, as in what belongs to the legitimate objects of political & civil institutions.

Strongly guarded as is the separation between Religion & Government in the Constitution of the United States the danger of encroachment by Ecclesiastical Bodies, may be illustrated by precedents already furnished in their short history. (See the cases in which negatives were put by J. M. on two bills passed by Congress and his signature withheld from another. See also attempt in Kentucky for example, where it was proposed to exempt Houses of Worship from taxes.

The most notable attempt was that in Virginia to establish a Genl assessment for the support of all Xn sects. This was proposed in the year by P. H. and supported by all his eloquence, aided by the remaining prejudices of the Sect which before the Revolution had been established by law. The progress of the measure was arrested by urging that the respect due to the people required in so extraordinary a case an appeal to their deliberate will. The bill was accordingly printed & published with that view. At the instance of Col: George Nicholas, Col: George Mason & others, the memorial & remonstrance against it was drawn up, (which see) and printed Copies of it circulated thro' the State, to be signed by the people at large. It met with the approbation of the Baptists, the Presbyterians, the Quakers, and the few Roman Catholics, universally; of the Methodists in part; and even of not a few of the Sect formerly established by law. When the Legislature assembled, the number of Copies & signatures prescribed displayed such an overwhelming opposition of the people, that the proposed plan of a genl assessmt was crushed under it; and advantage taken of the crisis to carry thro' the Legisl: the Bill above referred to, establishing religious liberty. In the course of the opposition to the bill in the House of Delegates, which was warm & strenuous from some of the minority, an experiment was made on the reverence entertained for the name & sactity of the Saviour, by proposing to insert the words "Jesus Christ" after the words "our lord" in the preamble, the object of which, would have been, to imply a restriction of the liberty defined in the Bill, to those professing his religion only. The amendment was discussed, and rejected by a vote of   against (See letter of J. M. to Mr Jefferson dated) The opponents of the amendment having turned the feeling as well as judgment of the House against it, by successfully contending that the better proof of reverence for that holy name wd be not to profane it by making it a topic of legist discussion, & particularly by making his religion the means of abridging the natural and equal rights of all men, in defiance of his own declaration that his Kingdom was not of this world. This view of the subject was much enforced by the circumstance that it was espoused by some members who were particularly distinguished by their reputed piety and Christian zeal.

But besides the danger of a direct mixture of Religion & civil Government, there is an evil which ought to be guarded against in the indefinite accumulation of property from the capacity of holding it in perpetuity by ecclesiastical corporations. The power of all corporations, ought to be limited in this respect. The growing wealth acquired by them never fails to be a source of abuses. A warning on this subject is emphatically given in the example of the various Charitable establishments in G. B. the management of which has been lately scrutinized. The excessive wealth of ecclesiastical Corporations and the misuse of it in many Countries of Europe has long been a topic of complaint. In some of them the Church has amassed half perhaps the property of the nation. When the reformation took place, an event promoted if not caused, by that disordered state of things, how enormous were the treasures of religious societies, and how gross the corruptions engendered by them; so enormous & so gross as to produce in the Cabinets & Councils of the Protestant states a disregard, of all the pleas of the interested party drawn from the sanctions of the law, and the sacredness of property held in religious trust. The history of England during the period of the reformation offers a sufficient illustration for the present purpose.

Are the U. S. duly awake to the tendency of the precedents they are establishing, in the multiplied incorporations of Religious Congregations with the faculty of acquiring & holding property real as well as personal? Do not many of these acts give this faculty, without limit either as to time or as to amount? And must not bodies, perpetual in their existence, and which may be always gaining without ever losing, speedily gain more than is useful, and in time more than is safe? Are there not already examples in the U. S. of ecclesiastical wealth equally beyond its object and the foresight of those who laid the foundation of it? In the U. S. there is a double motive for fixing limits in this case, because wealth may increase not only from additional gifts, but from exorbitant advances in the value of the primitive one. In grants of vacant lands, and of lands in the vicinity of growing towns & Cities the increase of value is often such as if foreseen, would essentially control the liberality confirming them. The people of the U. S. owe their Independence & their liberty, to the wisdom of descrying in the minute tax of 3 pence on tea, the magnitude of the evil comprised in the precedent. Let them exert the same wisdom, in watching against every evil lurking under plausible disguises, and growing up from small beginnings. Obsta principiis....see the Treatise of Father Paul on beneficiary matters.

Is the appointment of Chaplains to the two Houses of Congress consistent with the Constitution, and with the pure principle of religious freedom?

In strictness the answer on both points must be in the negative. The Constitution of the U. S. forbids everything like an establishment of a national religion. The law appointing Chaplains establishes a religious worship for the national representatives, to be performed by Ministers of religion, elected by a majority of them; and these are to be paid out of the national taxes. Does not this involve the principle of a national establishment, applicable to a provision for a religious worship for the Constituent as well as of the representative Body, approved by the majority, and conducted by Ministers of religion paid by the entire nation.

The establishment of the chaplainship to Congress is a palpable violation of equal rights, as well as of Constitutional principles: The tenets of the chaplains elected [by the majority] shut the door of worship against the members whose creeds & consciences forbid a participation in that of the majority. To say nothing of other sects, this is the case with that of Roman Catholics & Quakers who have always had members in one or both of the Legislative branches. Could a Catholic clergyman ever hope to be appointed a Chaplain? To say that his religious principles are obnoxious or that his sect is small, is to lift the evil at once and exhibit in its naked deformity the doctrine that religious truth is to be tested by numbers. or that the major sects have a right to govern the minor.

If Religion consist in voluntary acts of individuals, singly, or voluntarily associated, and it be proper that public functionaries, as well as their Constituents should discharge their religious duties, let them like their Constituents, do so at their own expense. How small a contribution from each member of Congress would suffice for the purpose? How just would it be in its principle? How noble in its exemplary sacrifice to the genius of the Constitution; and the divine right of conscience? Why should the expense of a religious worship be allowed for the Legislature, be paid by the public, more than that for the Ex. or Judiciary branch of the Government

Were the establishment to be tried by its fruits, are not the daily devotions conducted by these legal Ecclesiastics, already degenerating into a scanty attendance, and a tiresome formality?

Rather than let this step beyond the landmarks of power have the effect of a legitimate precedent, it will be better to apply to it the legal aphorism de minimis non curat lex: or to class it cum "maculis quas aut incuria fudit, aut humana parum cavit natura."

Better also to disarm in the same way, the precedent of Chaplainships for the army and navy, than erect them into a political authority in matters of religion. The object of this establishment is seducing; the motive to it is laudable. But is it not safer to adhere to a right principle, and trust to its consequences, than confide in the reasoning however specious in favor of a wrong one. Look thro' the armies & navies of the world, and say whether in the appointment of their ministers of religion, the spiritual interest of the flocks or the temporal interest of the Shepherds, be most in view: whether here, as elsewhere the political care of religion is not a nominal more than a real aid. If the spirit of armies be devout, the spirit out of the armies will never be less so; and a failure of religious instruction & exhortation from a voluntary source within or without, will rarely happen: and if such be not the spirit of armies, the official services of their Teachers are not likely to produce it. It is more likely to flow from the labors of a spontaneous zeal. The armies of the Puritans had their appointed Chaplains; but without these there would have been no lack of public devotion in that devout age.

The case of navies with insulated crews may be less within the scope of these reflections. But it is not entirely so. The chance of a devout officer, might be of as much worth to religion, as the service of an ordinary chaplain. (were it admitted that religion has a real interest in the latter.) But we are always to keep in mind that it is safer to trust the consequences of a right principle, than reasoning in support of a bad one.

319

Religious proclamations by the Executive recommending thanksgivings & fasts are shoots from the same root with the legislative acts reviewed.

Altho' recommendations only, they imply a religious agency, making no part of the trust delegated to political rulers.

The objections to them are #1 that Governments ought not to interpose in relation to those subject to their authority but in cases where they can do it with effect.

An advisory Government is a contradiction in terms. 2. The members of a Government as such can in no sense be regarded as possessing an advisory trust from their Constituents in their religious capacities. They cannot form an ecclesiastical Assembly, Convocation, Council, or Synod, and as such issue decrees or injunctions addressed to the faith or the Consciences of the people. In their individual capacities, as distinct from their official station, they might unite in recommendations of any sort whatever, in the same manner as any other individuals might do. But then their recommendations ought to express the true character from which they emanate.

3. They seem to imply and certainly nourish the erroneous idea of a national religion. The idea just as it related to the Jewish nation under a theocracy, having been improperly adopted by so many nations which have embraced Christianity, is too apt to lurk in the bosoms even of Americans, who in general are aware of the distinction between religious & political societies. The idea also of a union of all to form one nation under one Government in acts of devotion to the God of all is an imposing idea."

This is the most complete writing I could find of James Madison's Memoranda that was penned sometime between 1818 and 1820 in several stages and times. This pretty much proves that our Founders believed in a Government that not only believed in God but as is stated One Nation Under One Government in acts of Devotion to the God of All. Of course the anti-religious atheists want you to believe that our Founders wanted no part of religion and as you can see that wasn't the case. They just didn't want religion to rule over the Rights that everyone was given under the Bill of Rights and the Rights in the Constitution. They were all too cognizant of the probability of a zealot religious government becoming a tyranny as they had seen throughout history not only in America in the 1600s but also, and especially in England. "The purpose of separation of church and state is to keep forever from these shores the ceaseless strife that has soaked the soil of Europe in blood for centuries." – James Madison. Many of our Founding Fathers were Free Masons and back in the 15 and 1600s some Free Masons were labeled warlocks and burned at the stake! So they were indeed weary travelers who had been down that road before.

"It may not be easy, in every possible case, to trace the line of separation between the rights of religion and the Civil authority with such distinctness as to avoid collisions and doubts on unessential points. The tendency to usurpation on one side or the other, or to a corrupting coalition or alliance between them, will be best guarded against by an entire abstinence of the Government from interference in any way whatsoever, beyond the necessity of preserving public order, and protecting each sect against trespasses on its legal rights by others. - James Madison. This statement may better explain what James Madison was afraid might happen if there wasn't great vigilance monitoring those zealots that would oppress those they didn't like. Therefore keeping the government out of religion was necessary to avoid governmental religious oppression. He did not want to see this country do what was to come later in history by the socialists and communist when they conquered China, Russia, Germany and now what we are seeing in the Middle East.

"The means of defense against foreign danger, have been always the instruments of tyranny at home." - James Madison A truer statement has never been said. Today we see the government using foreign terrorism as a tool to militarize the police and make them protected against prosecution for the crimes they commit against the people in the war on terror.

"The advancement and diffusion of knowledge is the only guardian of true liberty."— James Madison.

What does this mean you ask? It means informed people are much harder to fool into slavery and government oppression, than uninformed stupid people. Unfortunately, the spin doctors and down right liars within our government and those in league with them, are doing everything they can to keep you as uninformed as they can. This includes most schools and universities the media, and most political organizations today. "Knowledge will forever govern ignorance, and a people who mean to be their own governors, must arm themselves with the power knowledge gives. A popular government without popular information or the means of acquiring it, is but a prologue to a farce or a tragedy or perhaps both" — James Madison

"I believe there are more instances of the abridgment of the freedom of the people by gradual and silent encroachments of those in power than by violent and sudden usurpations." – James Madison. Man oh man isn't that the truth! Inch by inch it is a synch because yard by yard it is too hard to take your freedom from you! And take your freedom they have! Hopefully, once you read this book you will see and understand the wisdom our founders had, and the things they forewarned us would happen if we became apathetic and complacent.

"Wherever the real power in a Government lies, there is the danger of oppression. In our Governments, the real power lies in the majority of the Community, and the invasion of private rights is chiefly to be apprehended, not from the acts of Government contrary to the sense of its constituents, but from acts in which the Government is the mere instrument of the major number of the constituents." – James Madison. Once again we have not taken heed of this warning and we have allowed our leaders to tell us lie after lie after lie and we have now become a nation of lies.

"A well-regulated militia, being necessary to the security of a free state, the right of the people to keep and bear arms shall not be infringed." – James Madison. Many of the socialists and communists have tried to spin this statement which became the Second Amendment. But it seems very clear that freedom depended on the people's Right to defend themselves against tyranny from all enemies both foreign and domestic and that included the government. Unfortunately the "Well-regulated militia" part of this statement has given the government the excuse to infringe on the Right to Bear Arms. Even though other statements by James Madison and other Founding Fathers clarify this Right that clearly states that the people should have ample arms and ammunition to fend off all enemies including the government! "Americans have the right and advantage of being armed - unlike the citizens of other countries whose governments are afraid to trust the people with arms. The Constitution preserves the advantage of being armed which Americans possess over the people of almost every other nation where the governments are afraid to trust the people with arms." – James Madison.

"The accumulation of all powers, legislative, executive, and judiciary, in the same hands, whether of one, a few, or many, and whether hereditary, self-appointed, or elective, may justly be pronounced the very definition of tyranny." – James Madison. What this warning conveys is that once any group has total control over government it becomes tyrannical because those in power make themselves above the law and exempt from prosecution if they commit crimes against the people, and tyranny runs unchecked. We are seeing some of that in government now, and once all the branches of government get on the same page... what little is left of the people's freedom will be over forever!

"It will be of little avail to the people that the laws are made by men of their own choice if the laws be so voluminous that they cannot be read, or so incoherent that they cannot be understood."- James Madison. Needless to say this warning was never taken seriously, and now it is routine to make laws so convoluted and voluminous that the government can tell the citizens that law means whatever the government wants the people to believe.

"I cannot undertake to lay my finger on that article of the Constitution which granted a right to Congress of expending, on objects of benevolence, the money of their constituents." – James Madison. He saw the government's attempt to create entitlements and free-bees for those who supported those in Congress as a benevolent act of a monarchy that was found nowhere in the Constitution, let alone Constitutional. It is one thing to feel charitable with your own money to those with less than you. But it is quite another thing to be charitable with other people's money. Especially when those people expected you to use that money to run the government, not to give it away!

"History records that the money changers have used every form of abuse, intrigue, deceit, and violent means possible to maintain their control over governments by controlling money and it's issuance." — James Madison. Another warning that was never taken seriously and the "Money Changers" took control over America 100 years ago in 1914 with the creation of the Federal Reserve Bank.

Chapter Sixteen
Can America Regain It's Freedom?

I will try and be optimistic, but I have my doubts, so with saying that, I do hope and pray that Americans will one day get back some of the freedom that they have lost. But unless we all get involved, unfortunately more freedom, if not all freedom, will be lost. Too many people just don't seem to care. They go along to get along and most people get real uncomfortable when you tell them that they need to get involved. I've shown you some historic facts and figures and some laws to back up my comments, along with the abuse and crimes the government has commit against us. I hope I was able to show you enough, and you can now see how un-free we really are. We all need to get off the sidelines and fight together, stand up for our rights, and help America restore the freedom that was granted under the greatest documents ever written, our Constitution and our Bill of Rights. You are either for Freedom or you are against it! You have to take a side! I know there will be those who say they aren't taking a side, but they have. They're just playing games trying to remain safely in the middle. But they are more for one side than they are against another, or more against one side than they are for the other. So they lie to you and themselves, thinking that will keep them safe. It won't, sooner or later they will be forced to take a side or forced to leave America. Hell, those of us who believe in Freedom may have to leave too, if we can. Most of the spineless cowards will choose the side that is winning at the time, and they better hope that side wins, because has history has written, turncoats aren't well received. Yes, I predict it is going to come to war in America, if it hasn't already quietly started. I suppose by the raids on citizens reported on the internet it sure looks like it has started. Main stream media will paint anyone who resists as a criminal or terrorist, so you can't believe anything on TV or major newspapers. No you have to go to the Internet and now that the government has taken control over it, expect that to be compromised very soon. It has already started on Face Book, You Tube and Twitter. So it is only a matter of time before the truth is silenced on the Internet.

Recall a very important tool

There are tools at our disposal. One very important tool is Recall, the ability to remove elected officials from office. Most states have provisions for recalling officials, but unfortunately most of the citizens rarely use it because the bureaucrats have made it increasingly difficult to accomplish. Recalling an elected official is a great way to get rid of a tyrant in office, and it sends a crystal clear message to all other elected officials that the people will not tolerate any official that goes against the people. Of course, you have to be successful and ouster the tyrant or tyrants to be effective. So you have to do a lot of door knocking and ear bending to get the signatures and votes to remove someone from office.

Sadly less than half of the States allow the people to remove elected officials before their term ends. This has creates a mess for states that elected incompetent people because they have no way to remove them. Here are 19 States that permit recall of state officials: Alaska, Arizona, California, Colorado, Georgia, Idaho, Illinois, Kansas, Louisiana, Michigan, Minnesota, Montana, Nevada, New Jersey, North Dakota, Oregon, Rhode Island, Washington, and Wisconsin.

Here is a list of elected officials that have been removed from office.

1913: California state senator Marshall Black was recalled.

1914: California state senator Edwin Grant was recalled.

1914: California state senator James Owens survived a recall election.

1921: North Dakota Governor Lynn Joseph Frazier was recalled.

1932: Wisconsin state senator Otto Mueller survived a recall election.

1935: Oregon state representative Harry Merriam was recalled.

1971: Idaho state senator Fisher Ellsworth was recalled.

1971: Idaho state representative Aden Hyde was recalled.

1981: Washington state senator Peter von Reichbauer survived a recall election.

1983: Michigan state senator Phil Mastin was recalled.

1983: Michigan state senator David Serotkin was recalled. (Technically he resigned from office before the results of the recall election were certified, but the results were sufficient to recall him.)

1985: Oregon state representative Pat Gillis was recalled.

1988: Oregon state senator Bill Olson was recalled.

1990: Wisconsin state assembly member Jim Holperin survived a recall election.

1994: California state senator David Roberti survived a recall election.

1995: California assembly member Paul Horcher was recalled.

1995: California assembly member Michael Machado survived a recall election.

1995: California assembly member Doris Allen was recalled.

1996: Wisconsin state senator George Petak was recalled.

2003: California Governor Grey Davis was recalled.

2003: Wisconsin state senator Gary George was recalled.

2008: California state senator Jeff Denham survived a recall election.

2008: Michigan house speaker Andy Dillon survived a recall election.

2011: Wisconsin state senators Robert Cowles, Alberta Darling, Dave Hansen, Sheila Harsdorf, Jim Holperin, Luther Olsen and Robert Wirch survived attempted recalls, while Senators Randy Hopper and Dan Kapanke were recalled.

2011: Arizona Senate President Russell Pearce was recalled on November 8.

2011: Michigan state representative Paul Scott was recalled on November 8.

2012: Wisconsin state senator Van Wanggaard was recalled. Senate Republican leader Scott Fitzgerald and Senator Terry Moulton survived recall elections. Senator Pam Galloway resigned earlier in the year when sufficient signatures were gathered to trigger a recall election. Even though her name wasn't on the ballot, a recall election was still held for her seat. All four senate seats in the recall election were held by Republicans; after the recall, three remain in Republican hands and one switched to the Democrats, giving control of the Senate to the Democratic Party.

2013: Colorado Senate President John Morse and Senator

Angela Giron were recall on September 10, 2013 because of their support for very strict anti-Second Amendment gun control laws in Colorado.

If you plan to recall any official you will need to check with you local or state elections office to see what the law is in your state or county.

Closing Statement and some patriotic doctrine

I hear people say that the government would never attack the citizens, because if they did they would lose because the people would rise up against the government and we out number them. BULL, I say! If you really believe that, you are in for a rude awakening! First off the government would have 30% or more willing to fight at their command, because they'd be paid off to do so. Couple that with all the troops that would gladly join in the slaughter from the UN Forces and all that military equipment just waiting for a fight, and the fact that the US has won wars against better armed countries than we citizens have... and add into all of that, the 70 or so percent left will be women, children and elderly folks which will stay out of the fight, and guess what? You Lose! Not hard math to do. Unless we can win over the military and get most of the citizens on board, it don't look too good for a winnable revolution. So we better hope we can educate the dumbed-down masses to freedom again, because if we can't the game in over and freedom loses once again, as history has proven.

It may be that mankind really wants to be enslaved and really doesn't want to be free, because freedom takes work and freedom also can mean failure if you make the wrong decisions. A content slave likes the thought they will be fed and taken care of if they can't take care of themselves. A content slave never questions the master and never gets involved in the master's business. A content slave always obeys!

I will leave you with this Statement by Patrick Henry. If you take out all of the reference to the British and the King and replace it with the American Government and President, it fits perfectly today. I just wish that people today would take a stand, as our forefathers did when they stood up against the tyranny and created this nation.

March 23, 1775.

By Patrick Henry

"No man thinks more highly than I do of the patriotism, as well as abilities, of the very worthy gentlemen who have just addressed the house. But different men often see the same subject in different lights; and, therefore, I hope it will not be thought disrespectful to those gentlemen if, entertaining as I do opinions of a character very opposite to theirs, I shall speak forth my sentiments freely and without reserve. This is no time for ceremony. The question before the house is one of awful moment to this country. For my own part, I consider it as nothing less than a question of freedom or slavery; and in proportion to the magnitude of the subject ought to be the freedom of the debate. It is only in this way that we can hope to arrive at the truth, and fulfill the great responsibility which we hold to God and our country. Should I keep back my opinions at such a time, through fear of giving offense, I should consider myself as guilty of treason towards my country, and of an act of disloyalty toward the Majesty of Heaven, which I revere above all earthly kings.

Mr. President, it is natural to man to indulge in the illusions of hope. We are apt to shut our eyes against a painful truth, and listen to the song of that siren till she transforms us into beasts. Is this the part of wise men, engaged in a great and arduous struggle for liberty? Are we disposed to be of the numbers of those who, having eyes, see not, and, having ears, hear not, the things which so nearly concern their temporal salvation? For my part, whatever anguish of spirit it may cost, I am willing to know the whole truth, to know the worst, and to provide for it.

I have but one lamp by which my feet are guided, and that is the lamp of experience. I know of no way of judging of the future but by the past. And judging by the past, I wish to know what there has been in the conduct of the British ministry for the last ten years to justify those hopes with which gentlemen have been pleased to solace themselves and the House. Is it that insidious smile with which our petition has been lately received?

Trust it not, sir; it will prove a snare to your feet. Suffer not yourselves to be betrayed with a kiss. Ask yourselves how this gracious reception of our petition comports with those warlike preparations which cover our waters and darken our land. Are fleets and armies necessary to a work of love and reconciliation? Have we shown ourselves so unwilling to be reconciled that force must be called in to win back our love? Let us not deceive ourselves, sir. These are the implements of war and subjugation; the last arguments to which Kings resort. I ask gentlemen, sir, what means this martial array, if its purpose be not to force us to submission? Can gentlemen assign any other possible motive for it? Has Great Britain any enemy, in this quarter of the world, to call for all this accumulation of navies and armies? No, sir, she has none. They are meant for us: they can be meant for no other. They are sent over to bind and rivet upon us those chains which the British Ministry have been so long forging. And what have we to oppose to them? Shall we try argument? Sir, we have been trying that for the last ten years. Have we anything new to offer upon the subject? Nothing! We have held the subject up in every light of which it is capable; but it has been all in vain. Shall we resort to entreaty and humble supplication? What terms shall we find which have not been already exhausted? Let us not, I beseech you, sir, deceive ourselves. Sir, we have done everything that could be done to avert the storm which is now coming on. We have petitioned; we have remonstrated; we have supplicated; we have prostrated ourselves before the throne, and have implored its interposition to arrest the tyrannical hands of the ministry and Parliament. Our petitions have been slighted; our remonstrance's have produced additional violence and insult; our supplications have been disregarded; and we have been spurned, with contempt, from the foot of the throne! In vain, after these things, may we indulge the fond hope of peace and reconciliation.

There is no longer any room for hope. If we wish to be free--if we mean to preserve inviolate those inestimable privileges for which we have been so long contending--if we mean not basely to abandon the noble struggle in which we have been so long engaged, and which we have pledged ourselves never to abandon until the glorious object of our contest shall be obtained--we must fight! I repeat it, sir, we must fight! An appeal to arms and to the God of hosts is all that is left us! They tell us, sir, that we are weak; unable to cope with so formidable an adversary. But when shall we be stronger? Will it be the next week, or the next year? Will it be when we are totally disarmed, and when a British guard shall be stationed in every house? Shall we gather strength by irresolution and inaction? Shall we acquire the means of effectual resistance by lying supinely on our backs and hugging the delusive phantom of hope, until our enemies shall have bound us hand and foot? Sir, we are not weak if we make a proper use of those means which the God of nature hath placed in our power. The millions of people, armed in the holy cause of liberty, and in such a country as that which we possess, are invincible by any force which our enemy can send against us. Besides, sir, we shall not fight our battles alone.

There is a just God who presides over the destinies of nations, and who will raise up friends to fight our battles for us. The battle, sir, is not to the strong alone; it is to the vigilant, the active, the brave. Besides, sir, we have no election. If we were base enough to desire it, it is now too late to retire from the contest. There is no retreat but in submission and slavery! Our chains are forged! Their clanking may be heard on the plains of Boston! The war is inevitable--and let it come! I repeat it, sir, let it come.

It is in vain, sir, to extenuate the matter. Gentlemen may cry, Peace, Peace--but there is no peace. The war is actually begun! The next gale that sweeps from the north will bring to our ears the clash of resounding arms! Our brethren are already in the field! Why stand we here idle? What is it that gentlemen wish? What would they have? Is life so dear, or peace so sweet, as to be purchased at the price of chains and slavery? Forbid it, Almighty God! I know not what course others may take; but as for me, give me liberty or give me death!"

American's Dependence on Government has destroyed the very document that gave us Independence from Government enslavement; The Declaration of Independence. – RW GLESS

The Declaration of Independence

When, in the course of human events, it becomes necessary for one people to dissolve the political bonds which have connected them with another, and to assume among the powers of the earth, the separate and equal station to which the laws of nature and of nature's God entitle them, a decent respect to the opinions of mankind requires that they should declare the causes which impel them to the separation.

We hold these truths to be self-evident, that all men are created equal, that they are endowed by their Creator with certain unalienable rights, that among these are life, liberty and the pursuit of happiness. That to secure these rights, governments are instituted among men, deriving their just powers from the consent of the governed. That whenever any form of government becomes destructive to these ends, it is the right of the people to alter or to abolish it, and to institute new government, laying its foundation on such principles and organizing its powers in such form, as to them shall seem most likely to effect their safety and happiness. Prudence, indeed, will dictate that governments long established should not be changed for light and transient causes; and accordingly all experience hath shown that mankind are more disposed to suffer, while evils are sufferable, than to right themselves by abolishing the forms to which they are accustomed. But when a long train of abuses and usurpations, pursuing invariably the same object evinces a design to reduce them under absolute despotism, it is their right, it is their duty, to throw off such government, and to provide new guards for their future security.

Such has been the patient sufferance of these colonies; and such is now the necessity which constrains them to alter their former systems of government. The history of the present King of Great Britain is a history of repeated injuries and usurpations, all having in direct object the establishment of an absolute tyranny over these states. To prove this, let facts be submitted to a candid world.

He has refused his assent to laws, the most wholesome and necessary for the public good.

He has forbidden his governors to pass laws of immediate and pressing importance, unless suspended in their operation till his assent should be obtained; and when so suspended, he has utterly neglected to attend to them.

He has refused to pass other laws for the accommodation of large districts of people, unless those people would relinquish the right of representation in the legislature, a right inestimable to them and formidable to tyrants only.

He has called together legislative bodies at places unusual, uncomfortable, and distant from the depository of their public records, for the sole purpose of fatiguing them into compliance with his measures.

He has dissolved representative houses repeatedly, for opposing with manly firmness his invasions on the rights of the people.

He has refused for a long time, after such dissolutions, to cause others to be elected; whereby the legislative powers, incapable of annihilation, have returned to the people at large for their exercise; the state remaining in the meantime exposed to all the dangers of invasion from without, and convulsions within.

He has endeavored to prevent the population of these states; for that purpose obstructing the laws for naturalization of foreigners; refusing to pass others to encourage their migration hither, and raising the conditions of new appropriations of lands.

He has obstructed the administration of justice, by refusing his assent to laws for establishing judiciary powers.

He has made judges dependent on his will alone, for the tenure of their offices, and the amount and payment of their salaries.

He has erected a multitude of new offices, and sent hither swarms of officers to harass our people, and eat out their substance.

He has kept among us, in times of peace, standing armies without the consent of our legislature.

He has affected to render the military independent of and superior to civil power.

He has combined with others to subject us to a jurisdiction foreign to our constitution, and unacknowledged by our laws; giving his assent to their acts of pretended legislation:

For quartering large bodies of armed troops among us:

For protecting them, by mock trial, from punishment for any murders which they should commit on the inhabitants of these states:

For cutting off our trade with all parts of the world:

For imposing taxes on us without our consent:

For depriving us in many cases, of the benefits of trial by jury:

For transporting us beyond seas to be tried for pretended offenses:

For abolishing the free system of English laws in a neighboring province, establishing therein an arbitrary government, and enlarging its boundaries so as to render it at once an example and fit instrument for introducing the same absolute rule in these colonies:

For taking away our charters, abolishing our most valuable laws, and altering fundamentally the forms of our governments:

For suspending our own legislatures, and declaring themselves invested with power to legislate for us in all cases whatsoever.

He has abdicated government here, by declaring us out of his protection and waging war against us.

He has plundered our seas, ravaged our coasts, burned our towns, and destroyed the lives of our people.

He is at this time transporting large armies of foreign mercenaries to complete the works of death, desolation and tyranny, already begun with circumstances of cruelty and perfidy scarcely paralleled in the most barbarous ages, and totally unworthy the head of a civilized nation.

He has constrained our fellow citizens taken captive on the high seas to bear arms against their country, to become the executioners of their friends and brethren, or to fall themselves by their hands.

He has excited domestic insurrections amongst us, and has endeavored to bring on the inhabitants of our frontiers, the merciless Indian savages, whose known rule of warfare, is undistinguished destruction of all ages, sexes and conditions.

In every stage of these oppressions we have petitioned for redress in the most humble terms: our repeated petitions have been answered only by repeated injury. A prince, whose character is thus marked by every act which may define a tyrant, is unfit to be the ruler of a free people.

Nor have we been wanting in attention to our British brethren. We have warned them from time to time of attempts by their legislature to extend an unwarrantable jurisdiction over us. We have reminded them of the circumstances of our emigration and settlement here. We have appealed to their native justice and magnanimity, and we have conjured them by the ties of our common kindred to disavow these usurpations, which, would inevitably interrupt our connections and correspondence. We must, therefore, acquiesce in the necessity, which denounces our separation, and hold them, as we hold the rest of mankind, enemies in war, in peace friends.

We, therefore, the representatives of the United States of America, in General Congress, assembled, appealing to the Supreme Judge of the world for the rectitude of our intentions, do, in the name, and by the authority of the good people of these colonies, solemnly publish and declare, that these united colonies are, and of right ought to be free and independent states; that they are absolved from all allegiance to the British Crown, and that all political connection between them and the state of Great Britain, is and ought to be totally dissolved; and that as free and independent states, they have full power to levy war, conclude peace, contract alliances, establish commerce, and to do all other acts and things which independent states may of right do. And for the support of this declaration, with a firm reliance on the protection of Divine Providence, we mutually pledge to each other our lives, our fortunes and our sacred honor.

JOHN HANCOCK, President

Attested, CHARLES THOMSON, Secretary

New Hampshire

JOSIAH BARTLETT

WILLIAM WHIPPLE

MATTHEW THORNTON

Massachusetts-Bay

SAMUEL ADAMS

JOHN ADAMS

ROBERT TREAT PAINE

ELBRIDGE GERRY

Rhode Island

STEPHEN HOPKINS

WILLIAM ELLERY

Connecticut

ROGER SHERMAN

SAMUEL HUNTINGTON

WILLIAM WILLIAMS

OLIVER WOLCOTT

Georgia

BUTTON GWINNETT

LYMAN HALL

GEO. WALTON

Maryland

SAMUEL CHASE

WILLIAM PACA

THOMAS STONE

CHARLES CARROLL OF CARROLLTON

Virginia

GEORGE WYTHE

RICHARD HENRY LEE

THOMAS JEFFERSON

BENJAMIN HARRISON

THOMAS NELSON, JR.

FRANCIS LIGHTFOOT LEE

CARTER BRAXTON.

New York

WILLIAM FLOYD

PHILIP LIVINGSTON

FRANCIS LEWIS

LEWIS MORRIS

Pennsylvania

ROBERT MORRIS

BENJAMIN RUSH

BENJAMIN FRANKLIN

JOHN MORTON

GEORGE CLYMER

JAMES SMITH

GEORGE TAYLOR

JAMES WILSON

GEORGE ROSS

Delaware

CAESAR RODNEY

GEORGE READ

THOMAS M'KEAN

North Carolina

WILLIAM HOOPER

JOSEPH HEWES

JOHN PENN

South Carolina

EDWARD RUTLEDGE

THOMAS HEYWARD, JR.

THOMAS LYNCH, JR.

ARTHUR MIDDLETON

New Jersey

RICHARD STOCKTON

JOHN WITHERSPOON

FRANCIS HOPKINS

JOHN HART

ABRAHAM CLARK

Notes: After Our Founding Fathers Wrote The Declaration of Independence the British Law Enforcers demanded they turn over all weapons… Do you know what our Founding Fathers did when the Law Enforcers Demanded they give up their arms? Our Founding Fathers Shot the Law Enforcers and that was a shot heard around the world!

I hope that now you have finished reading this book it has given you some knowledge and encouragement to become more politically involved! The choice is up to you. Will it be: Freedom or Enslavement? America is running out of time and our freedom depends on each and everyone of you to help us survive!

Credits

Some of the information in this book was gathered from: The Early Years of American Law - Colonial Freedom, Britain's Push For Greater Control, A New Start, A New Criminal Court System - JRank Articles http://law.jrank.org/pages/11900/Early-Years-American-Law.html#ixzz2bgK18tXY. Wikipedia.org, and the Internet. Some Pictures taken by RW Gless

ABOUT THE AUTHOR

RW GLESS was a former elected official in Marysville, California, 1993 through 1996, and a former Radio Talk Show Host as well he is the Owner Publisher of The Nor-Cal Paper which was a weekly political newspaper in the Northern California Area from 1997 to 2005. The Nor-Cal Paper is now online only.

He is also an electronic and HVAC technician and commercial truck driver and heavy equipment operator and former wild-land fire fighter.